THE NEW CAMBRIDGE HISTORY
OF INDIA

Ideologies of the Raj

THE NEW CAMBRIDGE HISTORY OF INDIA

General editor GORDON JOHNSON

President of Wolfson College, and Director, Centre of South Asian Studies,
University of Cambridge

Associate editors C. A. BAYLY

Vere Harmsworth Professor of Imperial and Naval History, University of Cambridge,
and Fellow of St Catharine's College

and JOHN F. RICHARDS

Professor of History, Duke University

Although the original *Cambridge History of India*, published between 1922 and 1937, did much to formulate a chronology for Indian history and describe the administrative structures of government in India, it has inevitably been overtaken by the mass of new research over the past fifty years.

Designed to take full account of recent scholarship and changing conceptions of South Asia's historical development, *The New Cambridge History of India* will be published as a series of short, self-contained volumes, each dealing with a separate theme and written by a single person. Within an overall four-part structure, thirty-one complementary volumes in uniform format will be published. As before, each will conclude with a substantial bibliographical essay designed to lead non-specialists further into the literature.

The four parts planned are as follows:

I The Mughals and their contemporaries

II Indian states and the transition to colonialism

III The Indian empire and the beginnings of modern society

IV The evolution of contemporary South Asia

A list of individual titles in preparation will be found at the end of the volume.

THE NEW CAMBRIDGE HISTORY OF INDIA

III.4

Ideologies of the Raj

THOMAS R. METCALF

UNIVERSITY OF CALIFORNIA
BERKELEY

CAMBRIDGE
UNIVERSITY PRESS

CAMBRIDGE UNIVERSITY PRESS
Cambridge, New York, Melbourne, Madrid, Cape Town, Singapore, São Paulo,
Delhi, Dubai, Tokyo

Cambridge University Press
The Edinburgh Building, Cambridge CB2 8RU, UK

Published in the United States of America by Cambridge University Press, New York

www.cambridge.org
Information on this title: www.cambridge.org/9780521589376

First published 1995
Reprinted 1997
First paperback edition published 1997
Eighth printing 2010

Printed in the United Kingdom at the University Press, Cambridge

A catalogue record for this publication is available from the British Library

Library of Congress Cataloguing in Publication data
Metcalf, Thomas R., 1934–
Ideologies of the Raj / Thomas R. Metcalf.
p.   cm. – (The New Cambridge History of India: III.4)
ISBN 0 521 39547 X
1. India – History – British occupation, 1765–1947.   I. Series.
DS346.N47   1987 pt. 3, vol. 4
[DS463]
954.03 – dc20   94-6117   CIP

ISBN 978-0-521-39547-2 hardback
ISBN 978-0-521-58937-6 paperback

CONTENTS

ILLUSTRATIONS

Figures 1, 4, 6, 10, 11, and 13 are reproduced by permission of The British Library. Figure 12 is reproduced courtesy of the British Architectural Library, Royal Institute of British Architects. Figures 2, 3, and 8 are reproduced courtesy of Barbara Groseclose.

PREFACE

This volume examines the ways in which the British sought to justify, and thus legitimate, their rule over India. The Indian Empire, as it was put together by the conquests of the East India Company during the late eighteenth and early nineteenth centuries, was for the British unprecedented in its extent and character. As Thomas Macaulay exclaimed in wonder in his speech on the renewal of the Company's charter in 1833, the Indian Empire, 'the strangest of all political anomalies', was a state that 'resembled no other in history'. To be sure, precedents could be found. The Spanish Empire in Latin America could have provided a model. But Spain had been Britain's enemy since the sixteenth century, and it was always in British eyes associated with the vices of popery and tyranny. The British had, of course, conquered Ireland, and this conquest, in Tudor times, had helped shape the British image of themselves as an 'imperial' people. Yet, especially after the Union of 1800, the British chose not to avow the colonial nature of their dominion over Ireland. Then too, they had colonized the eastern coast of North America. But this, the so-called First British Empire, had involved driving the original inhabitants of America into the wilderness and replacing them with settlers of British stock. From the outset these settlers had been awarded a large measure of self-government, and until the crises of the 1770s they proudly proclaimed themselves to be British.

Hence, as the British set out to make space for themselves as the rulers of India, they had to devise novel, and exceptional, theories of governance. This task was made more difficult by the evolving British definition of their own society through the discourse of nationalism. In contrast to most continental European states, for which conquest simply involved extension of the sway of a ruling dynasty over additional peoples, the 'United Kingdom' of Great Britain, though it might accommodate within itself the peoples of Wales and Scotland, and, uneasily, those of Ireland, by its very nature could not incorporate into its 'imagined community' the peoples of a distant India. Indeed, if anything, the notion of a 'British' national community implied that the people of India were equally entitled to form their own national identity. Furthermore, as Britain became, during the course of the nineteenth century, a society shaped by the ideals of liberalism, and, in time, of democracy, the existence of an autocratic rule over India stood in sharp contrast with the presumption, ever more deeply embedded in the British constitution, that the people, through election and representation, possessed the right to choose those who were to rule over them. By what right, the Victorian British had to ask themselves, could a liberal democracy assert a claim to imperial dominion based on conquest?

At the heart of this volume is the contention that there existed, as the British contemplated India, an enduring tension between two ideals, one of similarity and the other of difference, which in turn shaped differing strategies of governance for the Raj. At no time was the British vision of India ever informed by a single coherent set of ideas. To the contrary, the ideals sustaining the imperial enterprise in India were always shot through with contradiction and inconsistency. At some times, and for some purposes, the British conceived of the Indians as people like themselves, or as people who could be transformed into something resembling a facsimile of themselves; while at other times they emphasized what they believed to be enduring qualities of Indian difference. Sometimes, indeed, they simultaneously accommodated both views in their thinking, making it perilously difficult to discern any larger system at all. This book argues that, throughout the Raj, and especially during the years of uncontested British supremacy from 1858 to 1918, the ideas that most powerfully informed British conceptions of India and its people were those of India's 'difference'.

Despite an enduring commitment to the production of knowledge about India, the British made little effort at any time explicitly to construct an ordering system of ideology for their imperial enterprise. As a people, after all, the British had always eschewed grand political theories in favour of ones presumed to be derived from empirical observation, and, from John Locke onward, they insisted upon the value of experiential modes of understanding. As one seeks the sustaining ideologies of the Raj, therefore, much has to be inferred from theories devised to serve other purposes, as, for instance, in John Stuart Mill's *Considerations on Representative Government*. Much, too, that one might regard as theory was elaborated only to meet the needs of particular occasions, or in response to particular challenges, such as the 1857 revolt or the Ilbert Bill controversy of 1883. And much remained always embedded in practice. Assumptions about gender, and even those concerning race, although centrally important to British conceptions of India's people, were rarely the subject of systematic inquiry.

As a result, much in this book involves an attempt to tease out larger implications from an array of decisions, policies, and activities on the part of the British in India. These range from the construction of administrative categories in the census to the layout of British Indian residential areas, from the strategies of archaeological preservation to the diagnoses of disease. In addition to the works of established political theorists – James Mill, Henry Maine, and J. F. Stephen, among others – the sources consulted include works of imaginative literature, among them the writings of Rudyard Kipling and Flora Annie Steel; the memoirs of Indian civil servants, like Alfred Lyall and W. W. Hunter, who reflect upon their careers in Indian service; and, of course, the important recent writings of the growing numbers of scholars of Indian history. I have endeavoured to give credit to these secondary works, ever more stimulating and suggestive, on the many occasions where they have helped shape my own thinking. In addition, I have consulted government records in the National Archives of India on some subjects, and for others I have drawn upon the research materials which I have collected during more than thirty years study of the Raj.

It is important to emphasize that this book does not attempt to examine the character of the Indian response to the ideologies imposed upon them by the British, nor does it make any claim to be a general history of India during the British era. Although I have attempted to make clear that much in the elaboration of these systems of knowledge was a collaborative enterprise, above all in the British reliance on Brahmin pandits for information about the nature of Indian society and religion, the British presented these ideologies as their own and for the most part used them to convince themselves of their right to govern India. The Indian response to, and, as the years went on, their interaction with, the various British descriptions of their land was complex and multi-faceted. It involved simultaneous processes of acceptance, accommodation, adaptation, and rejection. I have tried to hint at some of the ways Indians endeavoured to come to terms with the ideas that defined their status as colonial subjects, but this is a vast topic, currently an exciting area of new research, and one that would require a volume of its own. I have furthermore, so far as possible, avoided analysing or pronouncing general opinions upon the nature and overall development of India's social, cultural, or political institutions. This work seeks only to understand the ways in which the British endeavoured to create a system of knowledge, about India and themselves, which would sustain that 'strange anomaly', the British Indian Empire.

I am deeply indebted to the director, Robert Connor, and the staff of the National Humanities Center (North Carolina) for a fellowship during the academic year 1989–90. Their help and encouragement, and the extraordinarily congenial environment of the Center, made possible a year of uninterrupted work on this project. I especially wish to thank Kent Mullikin, associate director, and the Center librarians, Alan Tuttle and Rebecca Vargas, for their unstinting assistance throughout the year. I appreciate too the lively and supportive criticism I received from the other fellows in residence, especially Suzanne Graver and Melvin Richter. For supporting a summer's research in India in 1990 I am indebted to the American Institute of Indian Studies and its ever-helpful director in New Delhi, Pradeep Mehendiratta.

I am grateful to several institutions who invited me to share my ideas with them during the writing of the manuscript. Among them are the Nehru Memorial Museum and Library, New Delhi, and especially its director, Ravinder Kumar; the Shelby Cullom Davis Center in the Department of History at Princeton University, and its then director, Natalie Davis; the Berkeley–Paris exchange lectureship programme, organized by Lucette Valensi at the Ecole des Hautes Etudes en Sciences Sociales in Paris; and the University of Cincinnati, for an invitation to participate in the conference on feminism and imperialism organized by Barbara Ramusack. Many friends, among them the members of the Triangle South Asia Group in North Carolina, and in Berkeley, Sandria Freitag, Stephen Greenblatt, David Keightley, with the other Yuppie Bikers, and especially Thomas Laqueur, have offered informed and helpful suggestions for the improvement of early drafts of the manuscript. Kevin Grant and Nasser Hussain, together with the other members of various graduate seminars over the past several years, provided ideas and stimulus, as well as bibliographical and research assistance, for which I am most grateful. As always, Barbara Metcalf has encouraged me throughout with her support and example.

CHAPTER 1

INTRODUCTION: BRITAIN AND INDIA IN THE EIGHTEENTH CENTURY

As they extended their rule across the face of India during the late eighteenth and early nineteenth centuries, the British had to confront the problem of how to govern this far-flung dependency, and, more importantly, how to justify this governance to themselves. How could the British, as a members of a society who adopted as their own the ideals of nationalism, in good conscience extend their authority over this distant and densely peopled land? There was, to be sure, agreement, after the rapacious years of conquest following Plassey, that, as Edmund Burke reiterated, Britain must secure the 'prosperity' of India's people before seeking any gain itself. Britain's right to rule India, so its leaders argued, could be made legitimate, but only through just governance. Yet such a principle by itself gave little guidance for a fledgling empire. How was such a governance to be secured, and what principles might give the English a claim upon such legitimacy?

This introductory chapter examines the intellectual foundations upon which, during the eighteenth century, the British constructed their rule in India. Of necessity, as they sought to come to terms with the existence of their new dominion, the British drew upon a range of ideas that had for a long time shaped their views of themselves and, more generally, of the world outside their island home. As products at once of Britain's own history of overseas expansion and its participation in the larger intellectual currents of Europe, these ideas included settled expectations of how a 'proper' society ought to be organized, and the values, above all those of the right to property and the rule of law, that for the English defined a 'civilized' people. As they extended their conquests to India, the British had always to determine the extent to which that land was a fundamentally different, 'Oriental' society, and to what extent it possessed institutions similar to those of Europe; how far its peoples ought to be transformed in Europe's image, and how they should be expected to live according to the standards of their own culture. Under the leadership of men like Warren Hastings and Lord Cornwallis, Edmund Burke and Thomas Munro, the British had begun by 1800 to lay out ordering principles for what was to become the most extensive empire since that of Rome.

BRITAIN AND THE WORLD OUTSIDE

The British idea of themselves as an imperial people, charged with the governance of others, had its origin in the discoveries and conquests of the Tudor state in the sixteenth century. As Elizabeth's lieutenants set out in the 1560s and 1570s to subdue Ireland and establish there 'plantations' of their followers, they endeavoured to devise explanations, satisfactory to their own consciences, which would justify these expeditions. Although a simple 'right of conquest' provided some measure of legitimation, the English conquerors sought further justification for practices that often involved massacre and expropriation by asserting that the Irish, especially the Gaelic-speakers beyond the Pale surrounding Dublin, were, despite their professed Christianity, no more than pagans, or even barbarians. As evidence, the English cited their wandering pastoralism, so unlike the settled agriculture of England, and their unorthodox belief. 'They are all', so Edmund Spenser wrote, 'Papists by their profession, but in the same so blindly and brutishly informed for the most part as that you would rather think them atheists or infidels.' The Irish, as another put it, living like 'beastes, void of lawe and all good order', were 'more uncivill, more uncleanly, more barbarous and more brutish in their customs and demeanures, then in any other part of the world that is known'.

Consequently the English had no difficulty convincing themselves that the imposition of their rule would benefit the Irish. As Sir Thomas Smith argued, God had given the English responsibility to 'inhabite and reform' this 'barbarous' nation. It was their task, he said, to educate the Irish 'in vertuous labour and in justice, and to teach them our English lawes and civilitie and leave robbyng and stealing and killyng one of another'. In so doing the English saw themselves acting as the Romans had done in England itself. 'Ones as uncivill as Ireland now is,' so Smith insisted, 'this contrey of England was by colonies of the Romaynes brought to understand the lawes and orders of thanncient orders whereof there hath no nacion more streightly and truly kept the mouldes even to this day than we, yea more than thitalians and Romaynes themselves.' With the conquest of Ireland the English thus made of themselves for the first time – but not the last – new Romans, charged with civilizing backward peoples. Conquest henceforth found justification not, as in the Crusades, in the punishment of heretics and infidels, though the Irish were of course degraded by their Catholicism, nor as the outcome of dynastic rivalry, but as the product of a conception of civilization whose differing levels secured a place for the English at its apex. The English took this rationale for the subjugation of foreign peoples from Ireland to America, and thence to India and to Africa.[1]

During the early eighteenth century, united into a single state, the peoples of Great Britain began to construct a view of themselves as an integral nation, joining English, Scots, and Welsh into one community set apart, as 'British', from others. Much in the creation of this 'British' national identity was, as Linda Colley argues, a product of a shared Protestantism, especially as the three peoples together confronted Catholic France in a succession of major wars lasting throughout the eighteenth century. The 'British' patriotism evoked by these recurrent wars, however, gained further strength from the extension of British power across the seas. Shared participation in the imperial enterprise, from which the Scots, the Scots-Irish and Anglo-Irish benefited disproportionately, as it forged a new 'British' identity, not only obscured the differences between the three peoples, but encouraged the British at the same time to see themselves as distinct, special, and superior. Whatever their internal differences, Colley writes, 'Britons could feel united in dominion over, and in distinction from, the millions of colonial subjects beyond their own boundaries.' The growth of empire, and a conviction of 'Britishness', went hand in hand.[2]

In the mid-eighteenth century this sense of imperial patriotism found expression pre-eminently in a populist politics. While the Hanoverian dynasty fought on the continent to shape the fortunes of Europe, enthusiasm for empire defined an arena of dissent, set apart from the narrow struggles of court and ministers, in which Britain's

---

[1] Nicholas Canny, 'The Ideology of English Colonization: From Ireland to America', *William and Mary Quarterly*, 3rd series, vol. 30 (1973), pp. 575–98.
[2] Linda Colley, 'Britishness and Otherness: An Argument', *Journal of British Studies*, vol. 31 (1992), pp. 309–29.

merchants and artisans, with the residents of its provincial towns, gloried in the country's overseas triumphs. In 1739 Admiral Vernon was made a popular hero for his victories in the West Indies.[3] The following year 'God Save the King' was first sung in Britain, and the same year brought the first publication of 'Rule Britannia'. This empire was, however, for the most part a maritime empire, an oceanic empire of trade and settlement, not an empire of conquest; an empire defended by ships, not troops. Indeed, the British people, while proud of their navy, were fearful of a standing army, and apprehensive of too deep an involvement on the continent of Europe, for they saw a powerful army under royal control as a threat to their liberties. The simultaneous conquest of India and loss of America, from the late 1770s, gave this imperial patriotism a new character. Henceforth, 'Britishness', as Colley argues, manifested itself not through an inclusive sense of community shared with the American colonists, but by the demarcation of 'an essential quality of difference'. Foreshadowed in Tudor Ireland, Britain's empire was now to be like that of Rome, defined by ideals of law and order flung across a subcontinent, united by roads and by rulers. Its heroes were not admirals, but generals, like Clive and Wellesley, brother of the Duke of Wellington; its military, quartered abroad and so no threat to its masters, was a mercenary army comprised of its conquered subjects.

As the British defined their own identity as a nation in opposition to the world outside, so too, more generally, did they as Europeans, under the influence of the ideals of the Enlightenment, announce their own pre-eminence as a 'modern' and 'civilized' people. The medieval Christian world view envisaged the 'East' as a fabulous land of miracles and monsters, of gold and heroism. For many it was the location of paradise; for others the abode of the terrible Gog and Magog, perhaps even of the anti-christ himself. Despite this often fearsome vision of a land utterly different from the known world of Christendom, the 'East' was, paradoxically, part of that known world. Bound into a unified cosmology with the European centre, Hell and Paradise, the anti-christ and the devil, were all integral, even necessary, elements of the medieval world order. Familiar, even if frightening, the 'East' was always described through the forms of Western iconography. Partha Mitter has shown how Hindu gods, conceived as

---

[3] Kathleen Wilson, 'Empire, Trade and Popular Politics in Mid-Hanoverian Britain: The Case of Admiral Vernon', *Past & Present*, no. 121 (1988), pp. 74–109.

inventions of the devil, took shape in Western painting as monsters and demons. Similarly, though more sympathetically, in a famous fourteenth-century painting, the *devadasis*, or women consecrated to a temple, described in Marco Polo's travel account, were represented in such a way that, did the caption not state the subject of the picture, it would be impossible to recognize it as Indian, for the *devadasis* were transformed into blonde nuns attired in flowing habits![4]

From the seventeenth century scientific study of comparative religion, with greater knowledge of India, dissolved the old 'monster' image of a frightening 'East'. Under the influence of Enlightenment rationalism and secularism, distant lands lost their cosmological significance for Europeans, and were described instead through the taxonomic structure of eighteenth-century natural science. Much of this description was sympathetic, and informed by a search for the underlying unities that bound together the family of 'Man'. Nevertheless, it decisively set the non-European world apart as an 'Other'. Several elements in Enlightenment thinking together produced this result. One was the use of such societies as platforms from which to criticize the governmental structures and social conventions of Europe itself. From Montesquieu's 'Persian Letters' to the invocation of the 'noble savage', the philosophes of the Enlightenment drained non-European societies of all content. Imagined places, they served only, through the device of irony, to reflect Europe's gaze back upon itself.

Furthermore, and more importantly, the taxonomies of natural history, by constructing secularized notions of the 'modern', and the 'civilized', inevitably emphasized at once the difference, and the inferiority, of non-European societies. No longer occupying broadly 'sacralized' roles of symbolic inversion, as monsters and devils, distant lands either marked out, as in America and the Pacific, early 'natural' stages of human social organization, or, like Egypt, whose antique greatness caught Europe's attention during these years, societies forever in decline. However described, such societies, though comprehended within a universalistic framework, and no longer stigmatized for their religious beliefs, still, so Europeans insisted, were excluded by their cultural backwardness from the 'progressive' world order defined by a newly 'modern' Europe.

One might argue further that, as Europeans constructed a sense of self for themselves apart from the old order of Christendom, they had

[4] Partha Mitter, *Much Maligned Monsters* (Oxford, 1977), chapter 1, especially pp. 1–31.

of necessity to create a notion of an 'other' beyond the seas. To describe oneself as 'enlightened' meant that someone else had to be shown as 'savage' or 'vicious'. To describe oneself as 'modern', or as 'progressive', meant that those who were not included in that definition had to be described as 'primitive' or 'backward'. Such alterity, what one might call the creation of doubleness, was an integral part of the Enlightenment project. As the British endeavoured to define themselves as 'British', and thus as 'not Indian', they had to make of the Indian whatever they chose *not* to make of themselves. This process, as we shall see in the following chapters, had as its outcome the creation of an array of polarities that shaped much of the ideology of the Raj. These oppositions ranged from, among others, those of 'masculinity' and 'femininity' to those of 'honesty' and 'deceit'. In the end, such contrasts encompassed anything that would serve to reassure the British of their own distinctive character and keep the Indian 'Other' in its proper place.

INDIA AND 'ORIENTAL DESPOTISM'

As they began to put together their Raj in the latter half of the eighteenth century, the British had to devise a vision at once of India's past and of its future. Without such a vision there was no way they could justify their rule to themselves, much less shape a coherent administrative system. This section examines some of the ways the British conceived of India, and with it their role in India, in the early years of their rule. In particular it examines the tension between the notion of India as a society stamped by despotism, and that which saw it as an ancient land with its own enduring laws and customs.

Among the central categories the British employed as they sought to comprehend India was the notion of 'Oriental despotism'. From the time of Aristotle 'despotism' had existed as a description of a style of governance in which legitimate royal power was nearly the same as that of a master over a slave. For the ancient Greeks, the home of despotism was, not surprisingly, the land of their antagonists, the Persians. In the process this concept became a way of setting off people like themselves, conceived of as 'Europeans', from those, conceived of as 'Asians', who, in their view, willingly submitted to 'absolutism'. Although the notion of despotism later fell into disuse, the concept enjoyed a renewed currency in the eighteenth century, as

Europeans, under the influence of the Enlightenment, began systematically to regard themselves, and Europe, as distinct from Asia, and Asians. Despotism described the way 'Oriental' states were organized.[5]

At the same time, however, as critics, above all of the French monarchy, men such as Montesquieu and Voltaire, sought ways of challenging the growth of royal absolutism, 'despotism' became not only something to be found in the Orient, but a form of government to be feared, and fought, in Europe. The 'tyranny of the Turk', as in Montesquieu's 'Persian Letters', was a foil for that of Louis XIV. The model of 'despotism' thus helped Europeans define themselves in European terms by making clear what they were not, or rather were not *meant* to be. Europeans, one might say, projected onto the 'Turk' the elements of unrestrained violence and sexual licentiousness they endeavoured to suppress within themselves. Part of the cost of European liberty was to be a distorted imagining of the nature of non-European societies.

Although 'despotism' faded from European concerns after 1789, with the ending of French absolutism, the notion of 'Oriental despotism' had enduring implications for the emerging Raj in India, for it carried with it the connotation that Asian countries had no laws or property, and hence its peoples no rights. Everything, in this view, derived solely from the will of the despotic ruler, who could take back what he had granted. Asia was at once, as Alexander Dow wrote in his *History of Hindostan* (1770), 'the seat of the greatest empires', and 'the nurse of the most abject slaves'. As the British, India's new rulers, began, from Dow's time onward, to write the history of India, the concept of 'despotism' took on fresh life. It was now a way of contrasting India's earlier history with the law and order that the British conceived they were bringing. Henceforward 'despotism' was in India a thing of the past, but at the same time the 'idea' of despotism had to inform the whole of that past.[6]

Yet, ironically, as the British were the inheritors of India's past, many of the assumptions about India's peoples that shaped their view of that past found a place in their own government. Dow himself

---

[5] Richard Koebner, 'Despot and Despotism: Vicissitudes of a Political Term', *Journal of Warburg and Courtauld Institute*, vol. 14 (1951), pp. 275–302.

[6] Alexander Dow, *History of Hindostan*, vol. 3, *Dissertation on Despotism* (London, 1770), pp. vii-xxii.

found implicit justification for Britain's own authoritarian rule over the subcontinent when he wrote, 'When a people have long been subjected to arbitrary power, their return to liberty is arduous and almost impossible. Slavery, by the strength of custom, is blended with human nature; and that undefined something, called Public Virtue, exists no more.' The British, as India's rulers, not only sought to create 'Public Virtue' in their subjects, but willingly accepted the responsibilities its supposed non-existence imposed upon them. As the eighteenth century's 'enlightened' despotism in Europe had drawn admirers as well as critics, so too did its nineteenth-century variant flourish, as we shall see, in the paternalism of the Raj. In so doing, it drew as well, looking back to Hobbes, on a tradition that insisted on the enduring power of the royal prerogative. As such eighteenth-century jurists as Lord Mansfield repeatedly affirmed, the exercise of rule could not, in overseas territories, always be contained within the bounds of 'law'.

The tropical climate of India powerfully reinforced European ideas of it as a land fitted for 'despotism'. For the inhabitants of India the 'labour of being free', as Alexander Dow put it, simply could not surmount the 'languor' occasioned by the heat and humidity the English saw as the characteristic features of the country's climate. With 'tranquillity' and 'ease' the chief objects of their desire, Indians let themselves be subjected 'without murmuring' to the 'arbitrary sway' of despotic rulers. The 'enervating character' of India's climate was complemented by the subjection of the land for six centuries to rulers who accepted the 'faith of Mahommed'. The perception of Islam as a religion, in Dow's words, 'peculiarly calculated for despotism', was of course deeply rooted in the European consciousness. Its origins go back at least to the medieval and early modern perceptions of Islamic states, above all the Ottoman Empire, as at once infidel and menacing. What Europeans feared most they not surprisingly associated with the most vicious of governmental forms.

Dow laid out in careful detail the ways Islam encouraged the growth of despotism. In so doing he took for granted that India was a land inhabited by 'Mahommedans' and by 'Hindoos'. Muslim rulers, he argued, derived their position from the sword, whose 'abrupt argument' enslaved the mind as well as the body; Muslim law gave every male unlimited power over his family in a 'private species of despotism' that reproduced in miniature that of the state, and so 'habituated mankind to slavery'; polygamy, the immurement of women, the absence of primogeniture, with a host of other customs, all contributed to a state of society in which cunning and passion, jealousy and intrigue, flourished. Freedom and independence, by contrast, and with them justice and security for property, withered and died. In India, furthermore, Islamic despotism found its perfect foil. There climate and faith alike contributed to produce in the native Hindu a being so ineffectual and submissive, the 'most effeminate inhabitant of the globe', as Robert Orme described him, that he was an ideal subject for the 'fierce' and 'hardy' Muslim invaders from the north.[7]

Emphasis on the formative influence of the environment in making India a land so well suited for despotism reflected of course the enduring influence of Montesquieu. Yet such explanations raised awkward difficulties. In Orme's view, for instance, the 'climate and habits of Indostan' had even 'enervated the strong fibres with which the Tartars conquered it'. As Europeans, following the conquests of Clive, began to contemplate extended years of residence in India, climatic explanations for India's degeneracy had of necessity largely to be set aside. Europeans sought, on the one hand, as we shall see in a subsequent section, to protect themselves physically from India's threatening climate by erecting walls of distance marked out by distinctive styles of residence and behaviour. At the same time, as they undertook from the 1770s a more detailed study of India, the British turned their attention increasingly from climatic determinism to what they saw as the enduring cultural and racial characteristics of its peoples.

In this extended process of study the British endeavoured to secure at once understanding of India's uncharted civilization and a sense of mastery over it. Both the interpretations such study yielded, and the self-assured mastery it produced, became lasting foundations for British claims to rule India. In the process some ancient notions came into question. Among these was the idea of a pervasive 'Oriental despotism'. This concept necessarily implied that no will, and hence no law, existed apart from that of the despot himself. During the 1770s, however, just after Dow had completed his history, the Governor-General Warren Hastings began elaborating a view of the Hindus as a people who 'had been in possession of laws which

---

[7] Dow, *Dissertation*, pp. xiii-xx; Robert Orme, *Government and People of Indostan*, part 1 (London, 1753; reprinted Lucknow, 1971), especially Book 4, pp. 38–48.

continued unchanged from remotest antiquity'. The country's 'ancient constitution', he insisted, was very much intact. What the British must do, in his view, if they were successfully to govern India, was to master these laws and the Sanskrit language in which they were contained, and, more generally, to respect the customs of their new subjects. As he told the company directors in 1772, 'We have endeavoured to adapt our Regulations to the Manners and Understandings of the People, and the Exigencies of the Country, adhering as closely as we are able to their ancient uses and Institutions.'[8]

Both practical and scholarly concerns fuelled Hastings's commitment to the study of ancient Indian learning. Shaped by the Enlightenment ideal of understanding all cultures, he saw in the 'cultivation of language and science' in India a way to secure the 'gain of humanity'. Yet such learning would also be 'useful to the state', as it would 'lessen the weight of the chain by which the natives are held in subjection' and at the same time 'imprint on the hearts of our own countrymen the sense and obligation of benevolence'. This mixture of scholarly curiosity and administrative convenience, neither purely disinterested nor purely manipulative, was by no means unique to Hastings. Rather it informed the scholarly activity of such organizations as, above all others, the Asiatic Society of Bengal. Founded in 1784, under the patronage of Hastings, and with William Jones as its first president, the Asiatic Society was for some fifty years a centre of learning that took the shape of a host of translations of texts and other scholarly endeavours, and the publication of a uniquely influential journal, *Asiatick Researches*.[9]

The scholarship of the Hastings era was informed by assumptions whose consequences were to shape all subsequent British understanding of India. The first was the belief that there was something which could be identified as a separate religion called 'Hinduism'. Europeans were from the beginning determined to make of Indian devotional practice a coherent religious system possessing such established markers as sacred texts and priests. This process of definition gained momentum during the later eighteenth century as the British secured greater knowledge of India and its languages. It can be seen in the

---

[8] Cited in Bernard Cohn, 'The Command of Language and the Language of Command', in Ranajit Guha (ed.), *Subaltern Studies IV* (Delhi, 1985), p. 289.

[9] P.J. Marshall (ed.), *The British Discovery of Hinduism in the Eighteenth Century* (Cambridge, 1970), p. 189; O.P. Kejariwal, *The Asiatic Society of Bengal and the Discovery of India's Past, 1784–1838* (Delhi, 1988).

supersession of such discursive, and often credulous, accounts as J. Z. Holwell's *Religious Tenets of the Gentoos* (1767) by Sir William Jones's and H. T. Colebrooke's detailed descriptions of Indian belief published in the volumes of *Asiatick Researches*. No longer simply the congeries of practices of the 'Gentoos', by 1800 Hinduism was, in the British view, beginning to resemble a 'proper' religion.

The coherence of the Hindu religion, so these early scholars insisted, was, like that of Christianity itself, to be found in its sacred texts. In their view, the ancient Sanskrit texts would reveal the doctrinal core of the Hindu faith, and they turned for advice in the interpretation of those texts to those whom they saw as the 'priests' of the religion, the Brahmin pandits. These texts were seen as embodying not only moral injunctions but precise legal prescriptions. The first fruits of this enterprise can be seen as early as 1776, when N. B. Halhed published *A Code of Gentoo Laws*. Subtitled *The Ordination of the Pundits*, this work involved a collaboration between Halhed and eleven 'professors' of Sanskrit, who created a text 'picked out sentence by sentence from various originals in the Shanscrit language'. The articles thus collected 'were next translated literally into Persian ... and from that translation were rendered into English'. From this laboriously contrived text, Halhed conceived, could be formed a 'precise idea of the customs and manners of these people', as well as making available materials for the 'legal accomplishment of a new system of government in Bengal'.[10]

A view of Indian society derived from the study of texts and cooperation with pandits inevitably encouraged the British to view Brahmins as the predominant group in Indian society, and to adopt their perspectives on it. To justify his reliance on Brahmin collaborators, Halhed insisted that the people paid his eleven pandits a 'degree of personal respect little short of idolatry in return for the advantages supposed to be derived from their studies'. A Brahminical Hinduism was of course not only the result of conversations with pandits, for such an orientation was embedded in the texts themselves. Almost all were written by Brahmins and incorporated mythic accounts such as that, faithfully reported by British writers from Dow to Colebrooke, which saw the Brahmins 'proceeding, with the Veda, from the mouth of Brahma', while the three lower orders sprang from his arms, thighs, and feet. Though themselves occasionally sceptical of Brahminical

[10] Marshall, *Hinduism*, p. 143.

claims, these scholars nevertheless insisted that this ordering of society was accepted by all. If, as Halhed remarked, the ordinary people 'blame any thing it is the original turn of chance which gave them rather to spring from the belly or the feet of Brihma, than from his arms or head'. In the end, indeed, one can only see the 'constructed' Hinduism of the early colonial era as a joint product of British scholars and Brahmin pandits. Yet, ironically, though the Brahmins were the chief beneficiaries of this collaboration, still for them the Hindu religion was a living system, not a mere collection of texts. Hence they were sometimes reluctant participants, occasionally even protesting the British denial of authenticity to medieval, and vernacular, materials.[11]

The discovery of ancient Indian legal texts inevitably undercut the notion that India was a land subject to an 'Oriental' despotism. As Halhed proudly proclaimed, his 'Code of Gentoo Laws' offered a 'complete confutation of the belief too common in Europe, that the Hindoos have no written laws whatever'. Yet the amassing of Sanskrit texts did not put an end to the notion that India was a distinctively 'Oriental' land. Men like Jones saw themselves not only as rescuing India's ancient laws, but as ordering these 'original texts' in a 'scientific method'. This 'method' involved the assumption, foreign to indigenous Indian scholarship, that somewhere there existed fixed bodies of prescriptive knowledge in India – one for Hindus and one for Muslims – and that the closest approach to certainty was to be gained by establishing the oldest texts. These alone were authoritative; all subsequent versions were invariably corrupted by the accretions and commentaries of later ages. To be sure, during the Renaissance Europeans had themselves looked to the classical past for 'authentic' knowledge. But after the seventeenth-century 'battle of the ancients and moderns', and the subsequent adoption of the idea of 'progress', such notions had fallen out of favour. By Jones's time, though the British steeped themselves in the classics of Greece and Rome, they took pride in the Europe of their own time as 'modern' and 'progressive'. Asia alone was a land where all greatness was to be found in antiquity.

The outcome of British study of the ancient texts, in Jones's view, was to be a 'complete digest' of Hindu and Muslim law, which could be enforced in the Company's courts, and would preserve 'inviolate' the rights of the Indian people. As Jones proudly told Lord Corn-

[11] Ibid., pp. 114–15, 165, 169.

wallis, the governor-general, with such a code the British government could give to the people of India 'security for the due administration of justice among them, similar to that which Justinian gave to his Greek and Roman subjects'. Cornwallis, Jones's patron, would thus become the 'Justinian of India'. Nor was Jones the first to conceive of Britain's role in India in these terms. Halhed had already in 1776 held up the model of the Romans, who 'not only allowed to their foreign subjects the free exercise of their own religion, and the administration of their own civil jurisdiction, but ... even naturalized such parts of the mythology of the conquered, as were in any respect compatible with their own system'. Parallels between Britain's empire and that of Rome, as we shall see, were to be drawn ever more insistently as time went on.

The notion that there existed 'original texts', and that these could be taken as representing an enduring Indian reality, inevitably meant that any code based on these texts would devalue India's historic experience. The contrast with the British conception of their own law was striking. The common law, which formed the basis of jurisprudence in England, was, to be sure, based upon a presumption of antiquity and stability in legal culture. Precedent was honoured, and the origins of the law were sought in the forests of Saxon times. In England too, as in India, the law was meant to fit the 'disposition' and 'habits' of the people whose lives it shaped. Yet the common law, as a succession of precedents derived from individual cases, flexible in accommodating multiple interpretations, embodied in its very nature the history of England. In it could be seen, so English jurisprudence believed, the changing 'habits' and 'usages' of the English people. There was no sense that Hindu 'usages' were similarly responsive to historical change. To the contrary, Jones's conception of Hindu law implied that Indians lived a timeless existence. In practice, the British courts in India, as at home, developed their own case law, including such distinctive forms as 'Anglo-Muhammadan law', so that by the later nineteenth century most pleading in the courts was conducted on the basis of prior judicial decisions. The idea of India as a country somehow lost in time nevertheless remained, and was to have profound effects not only on the working of the British Indian judicial system, but on the fundamental structures of the Raj itself.[12]

[12] Bernard Cohn, 'The Command of Language', p. 295; Marshall, *Hinduism*, p. 147. See also Bernard Cohn, 'Law and the Colonial State in India', in J. Starr and J. Collier (eds.), *History and Power in the Study of Law* (Ithaca, 1989), pp. 131–52.

The late-eighteenth-century Oriental scholars further sought ways of locating India's civilization in the larger world of European classical antiquity. This activity took several forms. One was the search, almost obsessive in character, for shared origins and 'resemblances'. Jones, for instance, arduously contrived equivalences between Hindu and classical gods – between Ganesh and Janus, Krishna and Apollo, and many others; and he sought as well to link the Hindu chronology of *kalpas* and *yugas* with the established signposts of the Deluge, the dispersion from Babel, and the Mosaic revelation. The structure of the Hindu religion too, as he wrote in an extended essay on 'The Gods of Greece, Italy, and India', shared a fundamental resemblance with that of the classical world. Jones's greatest triumph was of course his discovery, on the basis of linguistic affinities, of an origin shared by Sanskrit with the other languages that subsequently came to be known as 'Indo-European'. Of the ties of Sanskrit to Greek and Latin, he stated simply that, 'No philologer could examine them all three without believing them to have sprung from some common source, which, perhaps, no longer exists.' Whether far-fetched or full of insight, these parallels, by giving the country a shared classical past with Europe, brought India into a familiar framework, and so made the strange and exotic comprehensible in European terms for a European audience.[13]

This scholarly enterprise reflected at all times an exuberant overflowing alike of wonder and of curiosity. Some of the earliest expressions of Romantic sentiment can be found in the writings of such men as Jones. Above all, attracted by the 'glories' of ancient India's civilization, Jones and his fellow scholars sought to convince their fellow countrymen of what they perceived as the 'fertile and inventive genius' of the Hindus. Jones, for instance, described their poetry as 'lively and elegant', their epics as 'magnificent and sublime', and the Upanishads as 'noble speculations'. Above all, he spoke of the Sanskrit language as a 'wonderful structure, more perfect than the Greek, more copious than the Latin, and more exquisitely refined than either'.[14]

Yet the Orientalist project as it emerged was clearly fitted to the needs of Europe. Classification always carried with it a presumption of hierarchy. Jones, perhaps more than most, was drawn to a sympathetic understanding of Hinduism, yet even his enthusiasm for things Indian excluded the most recent centuries of its history, perhaps, one might

---

[13] Marshall, *Hinduism*, pp. 196–245, 252, 259, 262–89.   [14] Ibid., pp. 252, 259.

even say, the thousand and more years that had elapsed since antiquity. At best, in his view, contemporary Indians might be living relics of pagan antiquity, 'adorers of those very deities who were worshipped under different names in old Greece and Italy'. The glories of the 'golden age' had of necessity to be located in the most distant past. Such ideas were not wholly a European invention, for Indian cosmology itself was built upon a conception of decline, albeit cyclical in character, to a contemporary *kaliyuga*. But India was for Jones always, despite his appreciation of its 'many beauties', the 'handmaid' of a 'transcendently majestick' Europe. Asian learning, he insisted, could supply many 'valuable hints' for 'our own improvement and advantage'. Europe's 'superior advancement in all kinds of useful knowledge' nevertheless remained unquestioned.[15]

In the last decades of the eighteenth century, then, shaped by notions of 'Oriental despotism', together with belief in an India once 'magnificent' but now fallen, the British began to put together what was to be an enduring vision of this land. Fundamental categories of analysis were set in place, a comparative philology was constructed, and the enduring structures of what were to be 'Hindu' and 'Muslim' law were established. Yet the British still worked only with fragments imperfectly understood, and they framed them in an idealized conception of India which made its present another's past. Only in the nineteenth century, with the conquest of the subcontinent, and the creation of the 'scientific' apparatus of the Victorian era, were the scattered insights of the era of Hastings and Jones to be welded together into an ideology that endeavoured to explain at once India's enduring 'difference' and its relationship to Europe.

LAW, PROPERTY, AND 'IMPROVEMENT'

The British attempt to reach some understanding of the nature of Indian society and religion was inseparable from the parallel effort, during the last quarter of the eighteenth century, to devise an ideology that would sustain their rule, initially over Bengal and subsequently over the entire Indian subcontinent. This process involved several elements. The British had, first of all, to decide how far, and in what ways, the East India Company should be involved in governance as

---

[15] William Jones, 'The Second Anniversary Discourse' (1785), in *Asiatic Researches*, vol. 1 (5th edn, London, 1806), pp. 405–14.

1 *The East Offering its Riches to Britannia*, by Spiridion Roma (1778). This painting, originally set in the ceiling of the East India House, shows Britannia, seated on a rock, guarding the East India Company, represented as children behind her and shadowed by her veil. At the lower left the genius of the Ganges is shown pouring out a stream on Britannia's footstool. To the right, under Mercury's supervision, various Asian provinces present produce before the throne. At the centre is Calcutta, presenting a basket of jewels and pearls; China is shown with jars of porcelain and a chest of tea; Madras and Bombay present corded bales of textiles. In the distance an Indiaman bearing these treasures sets sail.

well as, or in place of, trade. They had to set in place principles that would enable them to justify to themselves their rule over India. And they had further to establish enduring structures to order that governance. By the end of Lord Cornwallis's years as governor-general (1786–93), the British had put together a fundamental set of governing principles. For the most part these were drawn from their own society, and included the security of private property, the rule of law, and the idea of 'improvement'. By the coming of the new century, though their meaning in India was often substantially different than it was at home, these principles had become so deeply embedded in the shaping ideology of the Raj that to question them would have been to challenge the very purpose of the Raj itself.

Clive's conquests, beginning at Plassey in 1757, with those of his successors, undertaken on the initiative of the East India Company, forced Britain to face the question of whether this mercantile body should play a role in India apart from that of making money. (See fig. 1.) By the 1780s, following the passing in 1784 of Pitt's India Act, the Company, though for some years still retaining its trading privileges, had been largely transformed into a governing body, its servants no longer traders but magistrates and judges. This was by no means an inevitable transformation. As it existed in 1770 the Company was rather a barrier than an asset to an effective government of India. A logical strategy might then have been to abolish this commercial body and subject India to direct Crown rule. Though such an outcome was proposed on several occasions, most notably in Fox's 1783 India Bill, mutual mistrust on the part of Crown, Company, and parliament doomed such proposals until the vastly altered circumstances of the mid-nineteenth century. As a result, in the settlement of 1784, the Company's directors retained control of patronage and day-to-day administration in India, but a Board of Control subordinate to parliament was created in London. This Board, whose president was effectively an Indian Secretary, supervised all activities of the Company and had to approve in advance all dispatches sent to India. The Indian governor-general similarly was appointed by the Company but subject to recall by the Crown.

This so-called 'double government', which also found expression within Cornwallis's India in the separation of the powers of district judge and collector, embodied many of the central elements of eighteenth-century Whig political philosophy. In the Whig view, going back to John Locke, the main organs of government, executive, legislative, and judicial, ought to exercise separate powers; each would then check and counterbalance the others, and so together they would secure the liberties of the individual. This division of power was not introduced into the Indian government as part of a self-confident assertion of the superiority of English institutions. To the contrary it testified to a Whig belief that power was always liable to abuse. The British imagined – and not without reason – Crown, parliament, and Company as alike all corrupt, and so unworthy of being entrusted with so important a task as the governance of Britain's new Indian dependency. Only a complex set of institutional checks could contain the venality of those who sought profits and places in India for themselves and their friends. Indeed the entire structure of the rule of law established by Hastings and Cornwallis can be seen in large measure as a way of containing British fear of their own complicity in Asian despotism.

Fears of such complicity also informed the unrelenting attacks on the Company's government of two of late-eighteenth-century England's most eminent political thinkers – Philip Francis and Edmund Burke. Though each had personal interests at stake, for Francis especially sought to make his reputation by venomous attacks on the Company, nevertheless by bringing before the English public what they saw as the misdeeds of their countrymen in the East, they helped shape a new sense of purpose and a new strategy for the governance of India. As Burke argued, in the memorable phrases of his speech on Fox's India Bill, the English conquerors were worse even than their 'Tartar' predecessors. 'Animated with all the avarice of age and all the impetuosity of youth', he said, they 'roll in one after another, wave after wave; and there is nothing before the eyes of the natives but an endless, hopeless prospect of new flights of birds of prey and passage.' This rhetorical vision informed Burke's tenacious pursuit of Warren Hastings in the latter's impeachment trial. In this trial, begun in theatrical fashion in 1787 only to end inconclusively with Hastings's acquittal seven years later, Burke sought to make of Hastings a symbol of the rapacity with which the East India Company had exercised 'arbitrary power' in India. Rejecting Hastings's contention that his position as in some measure an 'Asian' ruler necessitated the exercise of a discretionary authority, Burke charged his opponent not simply with specific acts ranging from the misuse of the revenues of Bengal to the extortion of funds by force from the rulers of Benares and Avadh, but, more generally, with 'cruelties unheard-of, and devastations almost without a name!'[16]

In creating what Sara Suleri calls a 'litany of such uncontainable evil', the managers of Hastings's trial inevitably wove together not merely a catalogue of one man's misdeeds, which were no worse than those of many others at the time, but a 'fabric of colonial anxiety' that caught up everyone in a guilty sense of recognition. In its larger meaning, as Suleri argues, the event was less the trial of an individual than 'a documentation of the anxieties of oppression, where both the prisoner and the prosecutors are equally implicated in the inascribability of colonial guilt'. If Burke's rhetoric were followed to its logical conclusion, the trial would have had to end not with the impeachment of Hastings alone, but with the overturning of the Company's rule in India. This neither Burke nor Hastings, nor the English public – now with the growth of the press for the first time an active participant in politics – was prepared to contemplate. Hence the trial became theatre, a spectacle for an applauding English public to observe, and the stage upon which Burke, and the English Whigs, struggled to erect barriers against arbitrary rule, alike in India and in England. Far from being an exotic land that could easily be known and controlled, Burke's India was a place of English wrong-doing that could easily recoil on England itself. 'I am certain', he said in 1783, 'that every means effectual to preserve India from oppression is a guard to preserve the British Constitution from its worst corruption'.[17]

To legitimate the conquest of India it was necessary, so Burke argued, not only to discipline Britain's agents in that country, but to reorder their activities. England, he insisted, could right the wrongs of the past, and so contain the guilt implicit in the colonial enterprise, by constructing a government that would rule India in the interests of the Indian people. Time and again throughout a period of some twenty years beginning in the late 1770s, Burke insisted that 'the prosperity of the natives must be previously secured, before any profit from them whatsoever is attempted'. He further argued that the interests of the Indian people and those of Britain were, 'in effect, one and the same'. There is nothing, he continued, 'which can strengthen the just auth-

[16] P.J. Marshall (ed.), *The Writings and Speeches of Edmund Burke*, vol. 5, *India: 1774–1785* (Oxford, 1987), p. 402.
[17] Sara Suleri, *The Rhetoric of English India* (Chicago, 1992), chapters 2 and 3.

ority of Great Britain in India, which does not nearly, if not altogether, in the same proportion, tend to the relief of the People'. Imperialism, in other words, could be made moral by a just governance that would reconcile the Indians to their subject status. Such views, as we will see, were to echo down the years to 1947.[18]

The exercise of this trust required, in Burke's view, that the British refrain from 'shaking ancient Establishments' and 'lightly adopting new Projects'. Such views were of course part of Burke's larger conservative conception of human nature and his veneration of the past. For Burke, as for most Englishmen, private property in land lay at the heart of an enduring social order. Hence, to bring about a justly ruled India, property, above all else, had to be made secure. Philip Francis, a friend of Burke's and a member of the Supreme Council in Calcutta in the 1770s, drew up in 1776 the first comprehensive plan for a 'rule of property' for Bengal. Its basic elements subsequently informed Cornwallis's 1793 Settlement, which ordered Bengal rural society until the end of British rule. The Bengal land system, Francis insisted, resembled neither the Oriental 'despotism' of an all-powerful monarch who could dispose of his subjects' property at will, nor the feudal order of the European Middle Ages. Rather, he conceived that India possessed an ancient aristocracy, whose title to their estates had always been recognized as hereditary until it was subverted by Bengal's British rulers. The landholder, in his view, was a proprietor, and hence entitled to the security of knowing 'once and for all how much he is to pay to Government' with the assurance that 'the remainder will be his own'.[19]

Francis's imagined Bengal bore only a faint resemblance to the functioning society of the Indian countryside as contemporary scholarship now sees it. The zamindar, as the landholder was known, performed a variety of tasks. Among them were collecting tax revenue from the peasantry who tilled the soil, regulating the holding of land, maintaining order, and dispensing justice. At least in principle, the zamindar paid over to the nawab, or other superior government official, nine-tenths of the revenue he collected, retaining for his own use as compensation the remaining one-tenth. During the eighteenth century, as the power of the Mughal central government waned, the zamindars enlarged their estates and acquired ever greater power over

[18] Marshall, *Writings of Burke*, vol. 5, pp. 179, 221.
[19] Ranajit Guha, *A Rule of Property for Bengal* (Paris, 1963), especially chapter 4.

them. Still, though they possessed by custom a hereditary right to their dues, zamindars never held title to the land comprising their estates. Technically they remained no more than revenue collecting intermediaries placed between the villager and the government.

Hence the idea of restoring the 'ancient institutions of the country' by the award of proprietary rights to the zamindars concealed a commitment to a European, and Whig, conception of the proper ordering of society. A physiocrat, Francis saw in landed property, and the figure of the gentleman-entrepreneur, the source of England's prosperity; and he consequently cast the Bengal zamindar in this same image. Cornwallis too sought to 'restore' the 'principal landholders' to what he conceived of as their previous position of prosperity and influence. But underpinning this vision was a firm belief in a 'regular gradation of ranks . . . nowhere more necessary than in this country for preserving order in civil society'. The 1793 settlement therefore had as its objective, not the reconstruction of some timeless rural India, but the conversion of the zamindar into an 'improving' landlord on the model of 'Turnip' Townshend. Under a permanent settlement, Cornwallis wrote, 'Landed property will acquire a value hitherto unknown in Hindoostan', with the result that 'the large capitals possessed by the natives', now employed in usury, will be applied to the 'more useful purposes of purchasing and improving lands'.[20]

Guided by the ideal of 'improvement', Cornwallis thus set on foot what was meant to be an agrarian revolution in Bengal. In the end, however, the permanent settlement proved to have been misconceived to achieve its ends. The zamindars, their taxes fixed in perpetuity, and their lands held by peasants engaged in subsistence agriculture, had no incentive to undertake productive investment. A rentier class, often residing in Calcutta, they sought instead to take advantage of their new legal position by extracting ever greater rents from a tenantry left bereft of the protection of custom. Already by the early 1800s doubt about the wisdom of the settlement had hardened into disillusionment. Yet the permanent settlement was not repudiated, and the ideas of private property and 'improvement' which defined it remained central to the Raj of the nineteenth century.

By 1793, when he left India, Cornwallis had set in place the institutional structure of the Whig vision. The Company's servants were no longer allowed to engage in private trade or to amass large

[20] Ibid., chapter 5, especially pp. 167–73.

2   A Brahmin, on the Monument to Warren Hastings, by Richard Westmacott (1830). This tall, classically proportioned figure, with shaved head and
topknot, represents the heroic image of the Brahmin, as Oriental scholar and
Hindu priest, prevalent among the British in the early years of their rule. (See
also figure 8.)

incomes by extortion; instead they were paid high, but fixed, salaries. The district collector was strictly restricted to the task of collecting the public dues; he was, as Cornwallis's Code of Regulations described it, 'amenable for them to the courts of judicature', and subject to personal prosecution for 'every exaction' exceeding the amount he was authorized to collect. The district judge, given magisterial authority and control of the police, embodied the Whig ideal of a government whose primary task was the impartial administration of laws that secured property and order. The era of 'flights of birds of prey and passage' had come to an end, and with it British fear of their own complicity in the practices of 'Oriental' despotism.

Despite these Whig reforms the British remained dependent on an array of Indian intermediaries. Brahmins especially, in the courts and countryside alike, played an indispensable role both in the collection of revenue and the administration of justice. (See fig. 2.) This dependence at once angered and frustrated their British superiors. As William Jones wrote Hastings in 1784, soon after his arrival, 'I can no longer bear to be at the mercy of our Pundits, who deal out Hindu law as they please.' If, he later told Cornwallis, 'we give judgment only from the opinions of native lawyers and scholars, we can never be sure that we have not been deceived by them'. In the countryside too, as Cornwallis wrote of Madras, the Company's servants 'are obliged, both from habit and necessity, to allow the management of their official, as well as their private business, to fall into the hands of dubashes [Indian intermediaries]'. These men, 'cruel instruments of rapine and extortion', were capable of rendering even 'the most upright and humane intentions ... perfectly useless to the interests of the company, and to the unfortunate natives who happen to be within reach of their power and influence'.[21]

Jones's remedy for this 'evil' was to learn Sanskrit himself and then to compile a complete digest of Indian laws. With such a digest, he said, 'we should never perhaps be led astray by Pandits or Maulavis who would hardly venture to impose on us, when their impositions might be so easily detected'. Knowledge, that is, could effectively subordinate and contain the Company's Indian underlings. Yet,

---

[21] S.N. Mukherjee, *Sir William Jones: A Study in Eighteenth-Century British Attitudes to India* (Cambridge, 1968), p. 118; Carol Breckenridge and Peter van der Veer (eds.), *Orientalism and the Postcolonial Predicament* (Philadelphia, 1993), chapters 7 and 8 especially pp. 234–40; Burton Stein, *Thomas Munro* (Delhi, 1989), p. 38.

despite the publication of Jones's 'Digest' in 1798, Hindu and Muslim legal advisers remained attached to the British Indian courts until the 1860s, while on the executive side Indian revenue officials and collectorate clerks, as Robert Frykenberg has vividly demonstrated in his account of Guntur district, could easily subvert the intentions of government and divert substantial funds from its coffers to their own pockets.[22]

Hence British frustration did not abate with the growth of knowledge. Rather, as the British became ever more convinced of their own 'upright and humane intentions', they sought to make of the Indians a people uniquely predisposed to corruption, extortion, and mendacity. A once shared sense of complicity in the practices of despotism had now to be borne by the Indians alone. As Cornwallis boldly announced, 'Every native of Hindustan, I verily believe, is corrupt.' In this way, with chicanery and lying established as the norm of Indian behaviour, the British could at once reaffirm their own moral superiority, and quell the anxiety generated by their uneasy control of a colonial order they did not fully comprehend. If Indians were people without moral principles, then inevitably they lied in court, pocketed bribes, and wilfully rejected the benefits of British justice. Throughout the nineteenth century, alike in James Mill's strictures on the Hindu habit of 'deceit and perfidy' and in such satirical accounts of life under the Raj as I. T. Pritchard's *The Chronicles of Budgepore*, the Indians were in their character decisively set apart from the British. This stereotyped sense of Indian 'difference', as we shall see, was to loom ever larger in the British imagination, and helped shape an enduring ideology that marked out Indians as fit only to be colonial subjects.

The notion of despotism as an appropriate mode of governance for India did not wholly disappear with the Cornwallis reforms. Rather, the growth of Romanticism in Europe in the first years of the nineteenth century brought to India a new kind of sensibility that enhanced the appeal of a more personal style of rule. With its concern for individual introspection, its focus on the emotions and the glories of the past, its distrust of artifice, uniformity, and abstract learning, Romanticism necessarily challenged much in the Cornwallis system, with its faith in impersonal laws and limited government. Men who

---

[22] Garland Cannon, *Letters of Sir William Jones*, vol. 2 (Oxford, 1970), pp. 643, 720–21, 794–95; Robert Frykenberg, *Gunter District, 1788–1848* (Oxford, 1965).

came of age during the Napoleonic era, as the Raj spread itself across the face of the subcontinent, the Romantics in India included such figures as Thomas Munro, John Malcolm, Mountstuart Elphinstone, and Charles Metcalfe. Sensitive to history as an organic expression of a society's character, anxious to conserve the enduring institutions, as they saw them, of India's past, these men endeavoured to rehabilitate, and reclaim for the Raj, what they conceived of as the Indian tradition of personal government. Their aim, as Eric Stokes has written, was 'to take the peasant in all his simplicity, to secure him in the possession of his land, to rule him with a paternal and simple government, and so avoid all the artificialities of a sophisticated European form of rule'. The romantic temperament in similar fashion reaffirmed notions of Indian 'difference'. As childlike peasants, Indians stood in sharp contrast with the Britons who were then fighting for their liberties against the tyranny of Napoleon.[23]

The Romantics in India necessarily believed in an active government, and they sought to make the district collector, in place of Cornwallis's judge, the central figure of the British administration. In their view, the collector was to be the *ma-bap,* or compassionate father and mother, of the peasantry. This ideal inevitably involved a rejection of the idea of ruling through landed intermediaries of any sort. Although some, like Malcolm, sensitive to fallen greatness, endeavoured to cushion the blow, and sought to sustain an array of princely states, for the most part the men of this generation placed their faith in the British officer. As Burton Stein has written of Munro, 'the play of Indian traditional forms had to be directed by men like himself, knowledgeable and sympathetic, with great and concentrated authority'. From 1800 onward, idealized as a kind of miniature, if benevolent, despot, the collector came to embody the British vision of proper Indian governance.[24]

A government committed to a sympathetic understanding of India and its people required more intimate knowledge of the country than was the case under the more distant Cornwallis regime. Hence the years after 1800 saw the first of many detailed surveys that were to define the subsequent British comprehension of India's lands and peoples. Pre-eminent among them were those of Francis Buchanan, who surveyed Mysore and then eastern India for the East India

[23] Eric Stokes, *The English Utilitarians and India* (Oxford, 1959), pp. 9–22.
[24] Stein, *Munro,* pp. 352–53.

Company, and Colin Mackenzie, cartographer and indefatigable traveller throughout southern India who became India's first surveyor general. The work of both men testifies to the relentless quest of the colonial state for detailed information, above all that which could be collected in lists or reported in numerical fashion. By 1820 the Raj was already based far more on direct observation and measurement in the Indian countryside than on the citation of Sanskrit texts. As we shall see, the production of such knowledge continued to flourish as part of a larger positivist enterprise that sought empirically verifiable information about all societies everywhere.

Munro's vision informed directly the *ryotwari*, or peasant, settlement in the South, and inspired the work of Elphinstone, Malcolm, and Metcalfe in the Bombay Deccan and the North. Assessment in each area was based upon a detailed survey of rural life and local tenures. Nevertheless, local knowledge did not invariably carry with it comprehensive understanding of India's past or the structure of its society. Munro, for instance, endeavoured to make of ryotwari, a style of landholding he had discovered as a young officer in the Baramahal, a procrustean bed to which all of rural India was meant to conform. He had little patience with the superior rights even of the lowly village headman. At the same time in the area around Delhi, as Metcalfe sought to preserve the distinctive features of the village community, his vision of India drained its past of all content. Unlike the Romantics in Europe, for whom the past provided a rich texture of meaning, Metcalfe cast India in the timeless mould of the Sanskrit scholars. In a famous passage he insisted that the village communities were 'little republics, having nearly everything that they can want within themselves, and almost independent of any foreign relations'. They seem to last, he continued, 'where nothing else lasts. Dynasty after dynasty tumbles down; revolution succeeds to revolution; Hindoo, Patan, Mogul, Mahratta, Sikh, English, are all masters in turn; but the village community remains the same.' The village, like so much else in India, became in British hands a living fossil.[25]

The officials of the Romantic generation in India shared a great deal with those of the Cornwallis era. To be sure, as Munro wrote with exasperation, 'It is too much regulation that ruins everything.' Yet these men were in fact themselves committed to the fundamental

[25] Clive Dewey, 'Images of the Village Community: A Study in Anglo-Indian Ideology', *Modern Asian Studies*, vol. 6 (1972), pp. 296–97. See also chapter 3 below.

values of the rule of law, of property, and of 'improvement'. In similar fashion, though they might accuse Cornwallis of 'rash innovation', neither they nor their Whig predecessors were prepared to restore the India that existed before Plassey. Their ideas shaped as youths in eighteenth-century England, the officials of the Munro era had no more conception than Cornwallis of the currents of change that were to sweep over India after 1830. None imagined the Raj driven by the forces of liberalism, evangelicalism, and capitalism. Munro's vision of empire, as Burton Stein has observed, like that of Warren Hastings, 'contemplated an India so distant from Britain, and so different, that it must have its own future, one that built upon a foundation of Indian institutions, cultures and peoples under the watchful hand of architects like himself'.[26]

By 1820 much that was to endure in the framework of the Raj had been set firmly in place. The British had convinced themselves of the righteousness of their conquest of India, and, after the agonies of the Hastings trial, of their own moral superiority over their Indian subjects. This assured sense of superiority further informed the adoption by the Indian government of institutions and values – above all those of law and property – that lay at the heart of the English national consensus. Together these were to provide a bed-rock for the years that were to follow. The years from 1780 to 1820 also foreshadowed tensions between competing visions of the Raj. Some portion of the tension is revealed perhaps in the contrast between Cornwallis's elevation of the district judge and Munro's preference for the district collector. For the one the rule of law, though built on English ideas, was presumed to embody universal principles of justice, and assumed as well that men everywhere would, unless checked, abuse power to their own advantage. For the other, India was a different kind of place from England, so much so that even despotism, so long as it was exercised by enlightened rulers, might properly flourish. Such contradictions grew ever more intense as the Victorian era brought new ideas, and new enthusiasms, to British India. At no time, however, did these internal tensions ever call into question the fundamental British vision of India as a land lost in the past, whose people were shaped by the heat of their climate, the distinctive character of their religion, and the immemorial antiquity of their social institutions.

[26] Stein, *Munro*, p. 358.

27

CHAPTER 2

LIBERALISM AND EMPIRE

THE AGE OF REFORM

With the coming of Lord William Bentinck as Governor-General in 1828, the British avowedly embarked upon a thorough-going programme of reform. Building upon what had previously been little more than a vague expectation that somehow British rule ought to bring 'improvement' to India, free traders, utilitarians, and evangelicals created a distinctive ideology of imperial governance shaped by the ideals of liberalism. From Bentinck's time to that of Lord Dalhousie (1848–56) this reformist sentiment gained a near universal ascendancy among the British in India.

A product of the industrial revolution and the growth of a new morality, as well as of Britain's worldwide predominance after the Napoleonic wars, liberalism was in no way simply a vision of how empire ought to be organized. Informed by the thought of Adam Smith and Jeremy Bentham, it provided a strategy for the remaking of Britain itself. A host of legislative enactments, from the Reform Bill of 1832 through the New Poor Law, the repeal of the Corn Laws and the creation of the administrative state, mark out its progress through British society. Liberalism was, to be sure, in no sense a coherent doctrine. Indeed, as Richard Bellamy has pointed out, it is a 'notoriously elusive notion', extremely difficult to circumscribe and to define accurately. It incorporated a variety of heterogeneous views and evolved piecemeal over a long period of social upheaval. As a result, within early Victorian England there existed liberals of many kinds. One can identify as liberals, among others, men of such diverse political views as aristocratic Whigs, classical political economists, Tory Peelites committed to economic reform, radicals, and Benthamite utilitarians. The distance separating, say, the radical John Bright from the Whig Lord Palmerston was immense. And there was, of course, no organized Liberal Party until the rise of William Gladstone in the 1860s.[1]

[1] Richard Bellamy (ed.), *Victorian Liberalism* (London, 1990), chapter 1, especially pp. 1–3.

Those who may be considered liberals shared, nevertheless, a set of fundamental assumptions which set them off sharply from Burke's oligarchic Whigs, or, subsequently, from Disraeli's Tory conservatives. Above all, liberals conceived that human nature was intrinsically the same everywhere, and that it could be totally and completely transformed, if not by sudden revelation as the evangelicals envisaged, then by the workings of law, education, and free trade. Liberals differed over the urgency of reform and the relative importance of particular measures of reform, say of law or education. But invariably they sought to free individuals from their age-old bondage to priests, despots, and feudal aristocrats so that they could become autonomous, rational beings, leading a life of conscious deliberation and choice. Liberals had for the most part little sympathy with established institutions that were sustained by simple antiquity alone. What shaped a proper society was individual self-reliance, character, and merit, not a hierarchy that rewarded individuals on the basis of patronage and status. Necessarily optimistic, liberals never doubted that the wholesale transformation of society was not only possible but certain. Nor were the values they cherished relevant only to the reform of their own society. Universally valid, they belonged to all peoples throughout the world.

In Britain, despite the new order inaugurated by the 1832 Reform Act, liberals often found themselves tightly constrained. Local bodies, backed by riotous urban workers, opposed sanitary legislation; landed gentry frequently contested the reorganization of local government as well as repeal of the Corn Laws; aristocrats sought to retain the right to duel and to purchase army commissions. Though far from a democracy in the 1830s and 1840s, England still possessed vocal constituencies who could not be brushed aside. In India, by contrast, a conquered people could not as easily protest measures introduced for their presumed benefit. Hence, India could become something of a laboratory for the creation of the liberal administrative state, and from there its elements – whether a state sponsored education, the codification of law, or a competitively chosen bureaucracy – could make their way back to England itself. Furthermore, in India, as we shall see, the conflicts within liberalism became muted. Away from the contentious political environment of England, liberalism, as a programme for reform, developed a coherence it rarely possessed at home. For the most part evangelicals, free traders, law reformers, educational

29

reformers, and utilitarian theorists worked amicably side by side in India.

The liberal view of Indian society found its fullest expression in James Mill's classic *History of British India,* first published in 1818. A man who prided himself on his philosophic disinterestedness, Mill himself served the East India Company for some seventeen years, from 1819 until his death in 1836, and rose to the post of examiner, the highest position in the Company's home government. Informed with the historicist ideals of the Scottish Enlightenment, which laid out a series of stages by which the degree of 'civilization' of any society could be measured with 'scientific' precision, Mill set himself the task of ascertaining India's 'true state' in the 'scale of civilization'. For Mill, following Bentham, the criterion of utility was the measure of social progress. 'Exactly in proportion as Utility is the object of every pursuit', he wrote, 'may we regard a nation as civilized.' After scrutinizing India's arts, manufactures, literature, religion, and laws, he concluded, vigorously disputing Sir William Jones's claims, that the Hindus did not possess, and never had possessed, 'a high state of civilization'. They were rather a 'rude' people who had made 'but a few of the earliest steps in the progress to civilization'. There existed in India, he wrote, a 'hideous state of society', inferior even to that of the European feudal age. Bound down to despotism and to 'a system of priestcraft, built upon the most enormous and tormenting superstition that ever harassed and degraded any portion of mankind', the Hindus had become 'the most enslaved portion of the human race'. Moreover – and here Mill agreed with Jones – Hindu society had been stationary for so long that 'in beholding the Hindus of the present day, we are beholding the Hindus of many ages past; and are carried back, as it were, into the deepest recesses of antiquity'.[2]

To free India from stagnation and set it on the road to progress, James Mill proposed a remedy which was at once, as he saw it, simple and obvious. All that was required was a code of laws that would release individual energy by protecting the products of its efforts. 'Light taxes and good laws', he insisted, in good Benthamite fashion, 'nothing more is wanting for national and individual prosperity all over the globe.' In fact, of course, the simplicity was deceptive, for Mill's scheme, with its creation of individual property rights enforced

---

[2] James Mill, *The History of British India* (reprinted Chicago, 1975), pp. 226–27, 236–37, 246–48.

by 'scientific' codes of law, involved a wholesale revolution in Indian society. Nor did it matter to him that India's government remained unrepresentative. For James Mill, as for his mentor Bentham, happiness and not liberty was the end of government, and happiness was promoted solely through the protection of the individual in his person and property. Once secure in their property, the Indians could find in their own 'industry' the means for their 'elevation'. In England, Mill supported representative government as the only way to keep power-hungry elites in check. But he insistently denied that participation in government was a key to moral improvement. So long as the business of India's government was 'well and cheaply performed', it was, he argued, 'of little or no consequence who are the people that perform it'. From these views came an enduring British belief in the value of good government provided by British experts.[3]

John Stuart Mill inherited from his father both the mantle of liberal leadership and the family tie with India. First employed in 1823 to assist his father in the office, he remained with the East India Company until its dissolution in 1858, and he too rose in time to the post of examiner. The younger Mill's diagnosis of India's ills differed but little from that of his father. He elaborated more carefully, however, the rungs on the 'ladder of civilization', and prescribed a somewhat different plan for ascending them. J.S. Mill is best known for his *On Liberty*, in which he argued, against his father, that liberty possesses an intrinsic value of its own beyond mere happiness. In his *Representative Government*, however, he made clear his view that this 'ideally best polity', as he called it, was not suited to all peoples. Only those capable of fulfilling its 'conditions', he argued, were entitled to enjoy the benefits of representative government. For the rest, subjection to 'foreign force', and a government 'in a considerable degree despotic', was appropriate, and even necessary.

Behind Mill's views lay a hierarchical classification of all societies. 'The state of different communities, in point of culture and development', Mill wrote, 'ranges downwards to a condition very little above the highest of the beasts.' At its lowest point were those who lived in 'savage independence', and so required an 'absolute ruler' who would teach them to obey. Just above them were slave societies, where the people were being taught the need for 'continuous labour of an unexciting kind'. The next step upward was that of a 'paternal despo-

3 Stokes, *Utilitarians*, pp. 64–70.

tism', where the government exercised a general superintendence over society but left individuals to do much for themselves. The Inca state of Peru was of that sort, together with the societies of Egypt, India, and China, which had reached that point in ancient times. But these 'Oriental' societies were then 'brought to a permanent halt for want of mental liberty and individuality; requisites of improvement which the institutions that had carried them thus far entirely incapacitated them from acquiring'.

Among the 'Oriental races', in Mill's view, only the Jews escaped this enduring stagnation, and they only because the existence of a line of 'Prophets' kept alive among them 'the antagonism of influences which is the only real security for continued progress'. Elsewhere, since improvement could not come from within, it had to be 'superinduced from without', by a 'government of leading strings' that could break down old institutions. Yet the peoples of Europe, who alone could provide a government of this sort, were not themselves uniformly advanced. The southern Europeans, with the Latin Americans, fell short of the topmost rungs, for they shared with the Orientals a debilitating passivity which left them prey to corrupt, if not despotic, rule. The French too were 'essentially a southern people' who, if they possessed 'great individual energy', still could not match the 'self-helping and struggling Anglo-Saxons'.[4]

A cynic might contend that the rungs on this ladder marked out not stages of civilization but the relative distance of these societies from England, or more precisely, from the values cherished by John Stuart Mill. Yet Mill's object in constructing this scale was not to condemn those whom he saw as less advanced, but rather to make clear what had to be done to propel them forward. Above all, Mill insisted that neither race nor environment dictated whether a people could enjoy the benefits of representative government. To be sure, there was some ambivalence. Britain's settlement colonies, he argued, were entitled to immediate self-government, but whether because they shared with the 'ruling country' a 'similar civilization' or because they were 'of European race', was not wholly clear. Similarly, his references to the 'indolence' and 'envy' of southern peoples implied a measure of environmental determinism. Still, for Mill civilization alone truly mattered, and that was not unalterably fixed either by a people's

---

[4] John Stuart Mill, *Utilitarianism, Liberty, Representative Government* (London, 1957), pp. 197–201, 213–14, 218–27.

biological nature, or, challenging Montesquieu, by the climatic zone in which they lived.

Mill was adamant in his insistence that 'leading strings' were 'only admissible as a means of gradually training the people to walk alone'. The great advantage of 'the dominion of foreigners', like that of Britain in India, was that it could, more rapidly than any but the most exceptional indigenous ruler, carry a people 'through several stages of progress', and 'clear away obstacles to improvement'. For Mill this 'training' in self-government involved much more than simple codification of the laws. Unlike his father, the younger Mill did not see men as inherently selfish, moulded only by the external sanctions of law. They could be taught to pursue the public good, and to develop the 'active self-helping' character that self-government required. Together, he argued, good government and education could so transform India's peoples that in the end their claim to freedom would be irresistible.

John Stuart Mill was not alone in repudiating the rigors of Benthamite utilitarianism in favour of a more eclectic liberalism. Even in the 1830s, at the height of utilitarian influence, few reformers were strict Benthamites. Distinguished less by sectarian zeal than by a belief in the limitless malleability of human character, most combined an interest in legal reform with evangelical Christianity and a commitment to free trade, education and moral improvement. The young and ardent Charles Trevelyan, who served under Metcalfe at Delhi and then in the Calcutta secretariat under Bentinck, can be taken as representative. As Macaulay wrote of him in 1834:

He is quite at the head of that active party among the younger servants of the Company who take the side of improvement ... He has no small talk. His mind is full of schemes of moral and political improvement, and his zeal boils over in his talk. His topics, even in courtship, are steam navigation, the education of the natives, the equalisation of the sugar duties, the substitution of the Roman for the Arabic alphabet in the Oriental languages.[5]

Nor was John Stuart Mill alone in looking forward without hesitation to the eventual end of British rule. 'Trained by us to happiness and independence, and endowed with our learning and political institutions', as Trevelyan put it, 'India will remain the proudest

---

[5] Macaulay to his sister, Margaret, 7 December 1834, in G.O. Trevelyan, *The Life and Letters of Lord Macaulay*, vol. 1 (London, 1876), p. 385

monument of British benevolence.' Most stirring perhaps was Macaulay's peroration in his speech on the 1833 renewal of the Company's Charter.

It may be [he said], that the public mind of India may expand under our system till it has outgrown that system; that by good government we may educate our subjects into a capacity for better government; that, having become instructed in European knowledge, they may, in some future age, demand European institutions. Whether such a day will ever come I know not. But never will I attempt to avert or retard it. Whenever it comes, it will be the proudest day in English history.

At its heart, therefore, liberalism can be seen as informed by a radical universalism. Contemporary European, especially British, culture alone represented civilization. No other cultures had any intrinsic validity. There was no such thing as 'Western' civilization; there existed only 'civilization'. Hence the liberal set out, on the basis of this shared humanity, to turn the Indian into an Englishman; or, as Macaulay described it in his 1835 Minute on Education, to create not just a class of Indians educated in the English language, who might assist the British in ruling India, but one 'English in taste, in opinions, in morals and in intellect'. The fulfillment of the British connection with India involved, then, nothing less than the complete transformation of India's culture and society. Its outcome would be the creation of an India politically independent, but one that embodied an 'imperishable empire of our arts and our morals, our literature and our laws'.

This liberal idealism was inevitably fraught with troubling implications. With neither racial nor environmental theories to sustain it, culture alone remained to distinguish Europeans from those overseas. As a result, the more fully non-European peoples were accorded the prospect of future equality, the more necessary it became to devalue and depreciate their contemporary cultures. The hierarchical ordering of societies on a 'scale of civilization' reflected not just the classifying enthusiasms of the Enlightenment, but was a way to reassure the British that they themselves occupied a secure position, as the arbiter of its values, on the topmost rung. It was not some chance prejudice, but the liberal project itself, that led Macaulay in 1835 to scorn the 'entire native literature of India and Arabia' as not worth 'a single shelf of a good European library'. Similarly, in looking forward to the eventual freedom of India, he had of necessity to insist that the Indians of the present day were 'sunk in the lowest depths of slavery and superstition'. The future triumphs of 'reason' demanded as their counterpart the present existence of 'barbarism'. Such an insistence was especially necessary in the case of India, where the existence of an ancient civilization could not be denied. Unlike Africa, whose 'savagery' could be taken for granted, in India the notion of its 'barbarism' required a defiantly assertive rhetorical exercise.

By its very nature the liberal transformation of India meant the flowering on Indian soil of those institutions which defined Britain's own society and civilization. Among the most important of these, as we have seen, were private property, the rule of law, the liberty of the individual, and education in Western knowledge. The triumph of liberalism was not, however, to be simple or straightforward. Invariably, contestation with other more conservative visions of empire, as well as the day-to-day exigencies of colonial rule, shaped the final outcome of the reform enterprise. The stirring rhetoric of Mill and Macaulay should not be allowed to obscure the transformations that did not, as well as those that did, take place.

Central to an understanding of both the contradictions and the transforming power of British reform in India was the notion of the 'rule of law'. In nineteenth-century England the legal order was meant above all to guarantee the rights of property, conceived of as vested in individuals and secure from arbitrary confiscation. In India too, from Cornwallis's permanent settlement of 1793 onward, private landed property was made the cornerstone of Britain's commitment to an India transformed. In the hands of James Mill and his utilitarian disciples, as Eric Stokes has pointed out, this ideal carried with it radical implications. Some few theorists, among them James Mill himself, committed to Ricardian theory, argued that the entire rental of land, conceived of as an unearned surplus, rightfully belonged to the government. For the most part, however, men like Holt Mackenzie and R. M. Bird in the North-Western Provinces instead used utilitarian theory to advocate what Stokes called 'an agrarian revolution' that, ousting 'parasitic' intermediaries, would vest all property rights in the actual cultivators of the soil.[6]

In keeping with this ideal, during the settlements of the 1820s and 1830s in the upper Gangetic plain, the revenue-collecting *taluqdars* and zamindars were largely set aside, and ownership rights were

[6] Stokes, *Utilitarians*, chapter 2, especially pp. 110–16.

awarded to the villagers. Yet property relations in the north Indian countryside were for the most part not transformed. Theory meant little to many settlement officers as they struggled to make sense of the complex patterns of landholding they encountered, nor for their part did the courts vigorously promote the rights of individuals as a way of ushering in a new liberal order. To the contrary, much of Anglo-Indian law enshrined a conception of Indian society that in fact placed the family and community above the individual, and enforced values seen as embedded in religion from antiquity. The purpose of these laws was, as David Washbrook has written, 'to keep society in the structure of relations in which the colonial authority had found it and to construe the moral problems of the present against standards taken directly from the past'. This conception of India first took shape in Sir William Jones's time in the enforcement of 'Hindu' and 'Muslim' personal law. From there it found its way into British Indian property law. Despite Cornwallis's permanent settlement, and subsequent declarations of private property rights, the Hindu joint family, many Brahmin communities, and cosharing village brotherhoods, among others, secured rights which sharply restricted the working of the market in land, and with it prevented any far-reaching transformation of society or the widespread diffusion of capitalist agriculture. The more closely, Washbrook concludes, 'is the Anglo-Indian law's "freedom" of property scrutinized, the more limited does it seem to become'.[7]

At the same time the British sharply distinguished the 'religious' from the 'secular'. They sought to confine the activities of the state to what they considered 'secular' affairs, and, consequently, to withdraw it from such activities as the management of Hindu temples and Muslim shrines. Such a distinction contrasted sharply with practice in England, where an 'established' church drew support from a state whose monarch was also the head of that church. In India as well pre-colonial states traditionally had secured much of their legitimacy from association with the institutions of religious faith. Raja and priest always depended on, and sustained, each other. Yet the British in India, anxious to distance themselves from any appearance of supporting 'heathen' faiths, insisted that the spheres of the 'religious' and the 'secular' should be identified and kept separate. Such views were not

[7] David Washbrook, 'Law, State and Society in Colonial India', *Modern Asian Studies*, vol. 15 (1981), pp. 649–60.

easily implemented. The disassociation of the Company's government from Hindu and Muslim religious institutions, a long and arduous process involving the establishment of local managing committees, still left the government with the task of mediating disputes over succession and the control of property held by temples and shrines. Despite the colonial state's hostility to religions whose beliefs it did not share, it remained locked in an uneasy embrace with them.

In addition to the foot-dragging of those committed to a more conservative ideology, liberal reform was further thwarted by the fiscal and military requirements of a government only recently, and still insecurely, established in power. The East India Company, whose rule was in some ways little more than that of a 'garrison state' in the early nineteenth century, simply dared not risk antagonizing its subjects by disturbing the bases of religious authority or interfering too openly with their intimate personal relations. Even the disassociation of the government from Hindu temples was undertaken with reluctance, and then largely in response to unremitting pressure from outraged evangelicals. Beyond this, until 1850 the Company was caught up in ceaseless military campaigning with a large and expensive sepoy army. This placed an enormous drain on state finances, and, together with economic depression throughout the 1830s, forced the government always to concern itself with the size and security of its revenue collections. In such circumstances the British had but little space, or leisure, in which to experiment with measures that might unsettle society. Of necessity they kept up much of the extractive mechanism they had inherited from their eighteenth-century predecessors.

Yet the vision of the transforming power of the 'rule of law' was never abandoned. It triumphed above all in the codes of civil and criminal procedure, proposed by Macaulay's Law Commission and finally enacted in the 1860s. The process of codification marked an end to an India seen as a land of 'Oriental despotism'. By their very nature, codes of procedure introduced into the law predictable rules and regulations for the adjudication of disputes, and so did away with the wilfulness, and by extension the immorality, that marked despotism. Further, codified law created a public sphere – a place where equity and justice were seen to be meted out – in place of what was imagined as the despot's 'dark and solemn' justice executed in private, and often at midnight. Codifying procedural, rather than substantive, law had the additional, great advantage that such codes could incorporate the Benthamite, and utilitarian, desire for unity, precision, and simplicity in the law; yet they could do so without challenging Hastings's and Jones's decision to utilize the ancient Sanskrit texts as the basis of the Hindu civil law. The legal system of colonial India thus accommodated both the assimilative ideals of liberalism, which found a home in the codes of procedure, and the insistence upon Indian difference in a personal law defined by membership in a religious community.

To be sure, the codifying enterprise was never wholly compelling. Many continued to see India as a land suited for despotism, only now that of enlightened British officers. In part a nostalgia nourished by early nineteenth-century Romanticism, this dissident ideal flourished principally among officials in newly conquered territories, before the courts had been established, in what were called non-regulation provinces. It reached its ultimate flowering in the Punjab during the decade after its conquest in 1849, when the province was ruled by the brothers John and Henry Lawrence. For the officers of this 'Punjab School', the ideal, as John Beames described it, was that of 'personal government', in which the magistrate would 'decide cases either sitting on horseback in the village gateway, or under a tree outside the village walls, and write his decision on his knee ... and be off to repeat the process in the next village'. Not all officers, as the dissident Beames reported, liked being turned into 'homeless vagrant governing-machines', and in any case regulation and the rule of law could not forever be kept at bay even in the Punjab.[8] Still, throughout the later nineteenth century, the self-assurance fostered by the Punjab ideal permitted officers in that province a wider range of discretionary authority than was customary elsewhere in India.

This belief in a legitimate concentration of authority drew sustenance from a conviction that in the colonies a resort to vigorous executive action, including even the abrogation of habeas corpus, in England seen as the guarantor of the subject's liberties, could not wholly be avoided. Such acts found justification in the Crown's prerogative to secure order, and generated frequent tension between the courts and the executive government. At times of perceived crisis officials unashamedly resorted to exemplary measures of punishment. To crush an uprising among the Kukas of the Punjab in 1872, for instance, a local official summarily shot seventy protestors who had

[8] John Beames, *Memoirs of a Bengal Civilian* (London, 1961), pp. 101–3.

been rounded up by the police, and had forty-nine blown from guns, while his superior, the divisional commissioner, hastening to the scene, himself hanged another sixteen. Though these two officers were censured, their vigorous defence of their actions marked out a path that was to lead in 1919 to the infamous Amritsar massacre.

The British were nevertheless determined always to mark out the Raj as a moral, 'civilized', and 'civilizing', regime. For this purpose a 'rule of law', conceived of as the use of standardized impartial procedures for the settlement of disputes, was in their view essential. The British could not give to India their own, English, law; that was impractical. But they could give India codes of legal procedure. In this fashion, even though they could not introduce into India the substance of their law, the British could, or so they thought, bring its *spirit*. In so doing they could fulfil, to their satisfaction, their avowed 'civilizing' mission. In place of a religious faith shared with its subjects, the British colonial state thus found its legitimacy in a moralization of 'law'. No one stated this more vigorously than James Fitzjames Stephen, legal member of the viceroy's Council from 1869 to 1872. As he wrote:

The establishment of a system of law which regulates the most important parts of the daily life of the people constitutes in itself a moral conquest more striking, more durable, and far more solid, than the physical conquest which rendered it possible. It exercises an influence over the minds of the people in many ways comparable to that of a new religion. . . . Our law is in fact the sum and substance of what we have to teach them. It is, so to speak, a compulsory gospel which admits of no dissent and no disobedience.[9]

In the reformers' programme, next only in importance to law, stood education in Western learning. By education alone, as Macaulay made abundantly clear in his Minute on Education, could India truly be reshaped in England's image. Yet the educational enterprise was beset by many of the same difficulties and contradictions as that of law reform. Altogether apart from enduring fiscal constraints, which meant that the government never founded more than a very few schools, a further fundamental problem stood in the way of using English education to transform Indian society. In England in the early Victorian period all schooling was religious in nature. Although the government eventually awarded them grants-in-aid, the schools were

[9] J.F. Stephen, 'Legislation under Lord Mayo', in W.W. Hunter, *Life of Mayo*, vol. 2 (London, 1875), pp. 168–69.

run by various Christian sects, and they taught Christianity as an integral part of their mission. Indeed, intellectual training was not conceived of as existing apart from the moral training of Christianity. The mission societies, as they set up their schools in India, followed the same pattern, for they conceived of them as elements in a strategy of religious conversion. The British government, however, dared not introduce the teaching of Christianity into the schools it sponsored in India, for its officials, even those who looked forward eagerly to the Christianization of India, realized any such patronage of religion might well provoke intense hostility. In the end, although men such as Trevelyan and Macaulay solaced themselves with a vision of Hinduism as 'identified with so many gross immoralities and physical absurdities that it gives way at once before the light of European science', the British of necessity made of religious neutrality, like the notion of the state as 'secular', a liberal virtue of its own. A symbol of free intellectual inquiry, religious non-interference generated an image of the Englishman as benign, disinterested, and impartial. Assertion of the ideals of neutrality and secularism should not, however, be allowed to obscure the highly interventionist role the colonial state played as it set out to remake Indian society.

The tension between an increasing involvement in Indian education and an enforced non-interference in religion, as Gauri Viswanathan has shown, was resolved through the introduction of English literature as the central element of the school curriculum. Although education in India was to be secular, moral training was to be supplied by study of the great works of England's historic literature. No such schools existed in England, nor was English literature seen there as a substitute for Christian training. The guiding ideal was that of 'godliness and good learning', enunciated by the educator Thomas Arnold. Indeed, humanistic study in English schools in the early Victorian period centred around classical literatures, Greek and Latin, not English at all. Professorships of English literature did not even exist in Oxford and Cambridge until the 1870s. In India, by contrast, eighteenth-century neo-classical literature, along with Shakespeare, formed the core of the curriculum in the government schools. Despite the fierce criticism of such missionaries as Alexander Duff that education without Christian training would produce converts only to 'atheism' and 'rebellion', the government had no choice. As reformed codes of procedure had in India to stand for, or one might say represent, a commitment to the 'rule of law', so too in similar fashion did a secular and literary education represent the larger transformation of character and morality envisaged by Macaulay and Mill. In British India cultural value, as Viswanathan has described it, was relocated 'from belief and dogma to language, experience, and history'.[10]

Though dedicated to rooting out the evils of Indian 'barbarism', the liberal enterprise had itself the effect of disseminating more widely than ever before notions of Indian difference. Indeed, somewhat paradoxically, the attack on 'difference' served often to embed in the popular imagination persisting images of Indian exoticism, linked to a fascinated horror at practices that involved death or the mutilation of the body. The campaign against *sati*, or widow burning, for instance, as we shall see later, reinforced notions of Indian women as helpless victims of religion, while lurid tales of the doings of the *thags* powerfully reinforced the idea of Indians as treacherous and unreliable. Stranglers in the service of the goddess Kali, thags were perceived as roving bands of men, linked by hereditary ties, who preyed upon travellers along the roads, luring them into their company and then ritually murdering them. The discovery of *thagi* afforded the British once again an opportunity to take pride in their commitment to reforming a depraved Indian society. Yet thagi was never a coherent set of practices, nor could thags easily be differentiated from other armed robbers, who were known more generally as *dacoits*. What gave thagi its distinctive appeal was rather the way it enabled the British to give voice to their own enduring fears and anxieties. Uneasily dependent upon native intermediaries, whom they could not bring themselves to trust, but without whose collaboration the Raj could not function, the British saw deception and deceit everywhere in India. Thagi thus became a metaphor for the representation of what they feared most in India, the inability to know and control their colonial subjects. By projecting these fears outward onto thags, and then destroying this threatening conspiracy, the British could in some degree contain what they could not openly avow and hence reassure themselves of their mastery of India. Despite W. H. Sleeman's acclaimed extirpation of thagi, this successful campaign did not put an end to a fear of 'criminal communities', nor did it eradicate apprehension of Indian duplicity and dishonesty. On the contrary, the fascination with thagi, and with

[10] Gauri Viswanathan, *Masks of Conquest: Literary Study and British Rule in India* (New York, 1989), chapter 4, especially p. 117.

it the idea that there existed 'deceivers' who lived at the heart of Indian society, lived on, and found a place in novels, films, and the English language itself, where 'thug' came to mean a particularly nasty kind of ruffian or tough.[11]

The liberal remaking of India never involved, then, the simple transplantation of English values and institutions onto Indian soil. The vision of Indian 'difference', first articulated by Dow, Halhed and Jones, continued always to make its presence felt, and itself shaped much of the programme of reform. Nor could the exuberant optimism of the reformers of the 1830s be indefinitely sustained. By mid-century, in India and England alike, powerful currents of disillusionment had set in. Mid-Victorian British liberalism defined a consensus among a people buoyed up by pride and prosperity, and often brought Whigs, Peelites, and Radicals together in broad based coalition governments. It did so, however, at the cost of papering over latent contradictions and circumscribing the objectives of the liberal programme. Following Anthony Trollope and Walter Bagehot, who may be seen as representative figures of the age, mid-century liberals clung to the semi-reformed constitution, with its aristocratic bias, and embraced ideas of deference and dignity as appropriate safeguards against the feared tumults of mass rule. Even while elaborating the machinery of the modern state, they sought to avoid what Bagehot called 'sweeping innovation' as much as the 'old tory way' of keeping 'everything which is because it is'.

Nevertheless, liberal ideals, although less apocalyptic in their expectations, continued into the 1850s to shape British perceptions of their imperial mission in India. Dalhousie's years as governor-general can even be seen as constituting a 'second age of Indian reform'; for Dalhousie at once consolidated British dominion over the subcontinent by his policy of annexation and set firmly in place the structures of the modern administrative state. To him India owes its railways and telegraphs, its central Public Works Department, its Legislative Council, and a commitment, confirmed by Sir Charles Wood's education despatch of 1854, to a broader vernacular education. The confidence that India could somehow be made over in the image of Britain was never in subsequent years wholly to disappear.

[11] See Radhika Singha, 'Providential Circumstances: The Thuggee Campaign of the 1830s and Legal Innovation', *Modern Asian Studies*, vol. 27 (1993), pp. 83–146.

But after 1857 such ideals had to contend with newly powerful, alternative visions of empire.

1857: THE CRISIS OF THE RAJ

On 10 May 1857 the sepoys of the Bengal Army, refusing to accept cartridges greased with pork and beef fat, rose in revolt throughout northern India. Within weeks the mutinous soldiery, who had seized Delhi and raised anew the standard of the Mughal Empire, were joined by disaffected groups in the countryside. Landlords and peasants, princes and merchants, Hindus and Muslims, each for their own reasons threw off the British yoke and sought their own independence. Large reaches of the country, above all in the Gangetic plain from Bihar to the Punjab, remained out of British control for a year and more. In the recently annexed province of Oudh, where opposition to British rule was nearly universal, as all classes fought on behalf of their sepoy brethren and recently deposed king, desperate fighting continued until the very end of 1858.

For the British the searing trauma of this revolt was but the first of a series of checks to the expectation of a slow but steady march of progress whose end point would be the triumph of liberal principles throughout the world. Eight years later, in 1865, a rising of former slaves took place at Morant Bay in Jamaica. Together these two uprisings raised troubling questions about how far the 'blessings' of British rule, and liberal reform with it, were appreciated by those upon whom they were conferred. Two years after the Jamaican rising, in 1867, Benjamin Disraeli led Britain's 'leap in the dark' to vastly extended male suffrage, and thus transformed British politics forever. The remaining sections of this chapter examine, firstly, the crisis of the Raj which the Indian revolt precipitated, and, secondly, the subsequent crisis of liberalism in Britain itself. The outcome was to be a conception of empire grounded ever more firmly in notions of Indian 'difference', and a revitalized conservatism that gave that empire a central place in Britain's vision of itself.

As the victorious British armies moved on the rebel strongholds, the 1857 revolt was ruthlessly suppressed. Sepoys, even if only suspected of mutiny, were blown from cannon; villagers were, on occasion, indiscriminately shot; while the erstwhile Mughal capital of Delhi was sacked, and its major monuments saved from destruction only by the intervention of John Lawrence. The intensity of the punishment meted out reflected the vulnerability of the British in India, precariously set over a vast land they barely comprehended. Desperate and fearful, they sought to quell by a vengeful terror the harrowing vision of the loyal sepoy or faithful bearer as a treacherous murderer. The rebel leaders, above all, were never conceived of simply as honourable opponents. To the contrary, men such as Nana Saheb, responsible for the massacre at Kanpur, were made into fiends and monsters. Above all, the murder of English women at his hands stirred a fierce hatred of those who seemed to put at risk the 'purity' of English womanhood, and left as an enduring legacy lurid tales of rape and molestation.

Such a demonization of course made it easier for the British to obscure their own responsibility for the events of 1857, and thus to justify the continuance of the Raj. But it opened up as well a gulf between Briton and Indian that could not easily be closed again after the restoration of order. As G. O. Trevelyan noted in *The Competition Wallah*, 'Men cannot at will cast aside the recollection of those times when all was doubt and confusion and dismay; when a great fear was their companion, day and night ... The distrust and dislike engendered by such an experience are too deeply rooted to be plucked up by an act of volition.' From the rage, and fear, of 1857 emerged a new and enduring sense of the importance of the bonds of race, in contrast to those of culture.[12]

Despite the widespread expression of Indian hostility revealed by the events of 1857, Britain's right to rule India went unexamined. Unlike the divisive debates over the future of South Africa that accompanied the Boer War a half-century later, at the time of the Indian Mutiny no one in Britain, or among the British in India, ever considered leaving India. To the contrary, with its fierce retribution against those who had had the temerity to rebel, the 1857 revolt evoked a cleansing sense of heroism and self-assertion. As Trevelyan wrote, the struggle 'irresistibly reminded us that we were an imperial race, holding our own on a conquered soil by dint of valour and foresight'. Many officials, above all those whose reputations were at stake, sought by an exercise of denial to exculpate the Raj, and with it the work of the reformers, from complicity in the revolt. Dalhousie's disciples, especially, insisted, with John Lawrence, that the cause of

---

[12] G.O. Trevelyan, *The Competition Wallah* (London, 1864), pp. 283–304; Thomas Metcalf, *The Aftermath of Revolt: India, 1857–1870* (Princeton, 1964), chapter 8.

the Mutiny was to be found in the 'cartridge affair and nothing else'; that the people had been 'for the most part in our favour'; and that the revolt was consequently nothing more than an irrational panic on the subject of caste among credulous and superstitious sepoys. The enduring representation of the events of 1857 in British historiography as a 'sepoy mutiny' reflected too this determination to preserve Britain's reputation as an imperial power.

Conservative critics like Disraeli, never an admirer of Dalhousie or of liberal reform, described the mutinous sepoys as 'not so much the avengers of professional grievances as the exponents of general discontent', and insisted that the events of 1857 were 'occasioned by adequate causes'. Among these Disraeli included the 'destruction of Native authority', the 'disturbance' of property rights, and the 'tampering with religion' of a government bent on reform of Indian society. Yet he never called into question the legitimacy of that government. He urged only a return to what he saw as the path of conciliation followed in the pre-reform era. In this recommendation, most liberals, despite their endeavour to deflect blame for the revolt from the government, joined with Disraeli. Even for the most enthusiastic reformer the Mutiny was a sobering experience. As Charles Raikes, an officer in the North-Western Provinces, wrote in his *Notes on the Revolt*, 'The fatal error of attempting to force the policy of Europe on the people of Asia ... must be corrected for the future, as it has been atoned for in the past.' In similar fashion, Sir Charles Wood, President of the Board of Control for much of Dalhousie's governor-generalship, although he denied that the Mutiny had revealed the existence of any widespread popular hostility to British rule, nevertheless, when again placed in charge of the India Office after 1859, acknowledged that the 'mistake we fell into, under the influence of the most benevolent feelings, and according to our notion of what was right and just, was that of introducing a system foreign to the habits and wishes of the people'. Henceforth, he said, 'we ought to adopt and improve what we find in existence and avail ourselves as far as possible of the existing institutions of the country'. Indians, in other words, were not like Englishmen, and it was fatal to treat them as though they were.[13]

As they assessed the character of the revolt, no one among the

[13] Metcalf, *Aftermath of Revolt*, chapter 2, especially pp. 72–79; Rudrangshu Mukherjee, *Awadh in Revolt, 1857–58* (Delhi, 1984).

British took seriously, or even tried to comprehend, the complex forces that moved Indians to act. All behaviour during the rebellion was viewed through the lens of 'loyalty' and 'rebellion', and evaluated according to notions of how Indians *ought* to respond. In particular, the British endeavoured to ascertain the extent of 'gratitude' for benefits conferred. From this perspective the behaviour of the Oudh peasantry, above all, came as a rude shock. In keeping with the principles of liberal reform, the village communities of this mid-Gangetic state had been made the beneficiaries of its 1856 annexation, when both the nawab and the aristocratic taluqdars were set aside. Consequently the British had expected that these men would come forward in support of the government in its hour of need. Instead, the peasantry joined the rebellion, and even subjected themselves to their former taluqdari masters. As a result, frustrated and angry, the British considered themselves betrayed. As Lord Canning, looking back on the course of the revolt in Oudh, wrote in October 1858:

Our endeavour to better, as we thought, the village occupants in Oudh has not been appreciated by them ... It can hardly be doubted that if they had valued their restored rights, they would have shown some signs of a willingness to support a Government which had revived those rights. But they have done nothing of the kind. The Governor General is therefore of opinion that these village occupants deserve little consideration from us.

The behaviour of the Oudh peasantry during the uprising, and indeed that of their taluqdari superiors as well, cannot, of course, be so easily explained. Loyalty to the Oudh king and sympathy with the sepoys, many of whom came from Oudh, as well as a host of particular interests, not least a desire to secure themselves from plunder in a time of anarchy, impelled villagers to join the taluqdars. The British, however, saw none of this. As they had failed to live up to the expectations imposed upon them, the villagers had become, by definition, rebels. Hence they deserved to be punished. As an embittered Lord Canning wrote, 'Their conduct amounts almost to the admission that their own rights, whatever these may be, are subordinate to those of the talookdar; that they do not value the recognition of these rights by the ruling authority; and that the Talookdaree system is the ancient, indigenous, and cherished system of the country.' In no way could the British accept any responsibility for the hostility of men upon whom they had themselves lavished benefits. That the annexation itself, or the subsequent level of revenue assessment, might have had something to do with the behaviour of the villagers in 1857, was simply dismissed.[14]

As the participation of the taluqdars gave the revolt roots in the Oudh countryside, and indeed kept the rebellion alive for a full six months after the fall of the capital city of Lucknow in March 1858, it was not surprising that, as the British set out to restore their authority, they endeavoured to secure the cooperation of men whose power had been so visibly manifested. Yet the reinstatement of the taluqdars in their former estates found justification not only as an act of political expediency, but as the restoration of a legitimate authority. Canning had spoken of the taluqdari system as 'ancient, indigenous, and cherished'; the Oudh chief commissioner in 1858, Robert Montgomery, for his part described the 'superiority and influence of these talookdars' as 'a necessary element in the social constitution of the province'. With Oudh rural society conceived of in such a fashion, the British obviously had no need for an uneasy conscience as they abandoned the villagers to their fate.

Yet the use of such explanations inevitably called into question the underlying assumptions of the liberal enterprise. If the Oudh villagers did not, in the British view, pursue their own best interest, but obstinately clung to their traditional ways, then the liberal presumption that all men were inherently rational and educable fell to the ground, and with it the expectation that India could be transformed on an English model. In similar fashion, after the Mutiny, the conversion of India to Christianity ceased to evoke much enthusiasm. For evangelicals the Mutiny was a blow sent by God to humble Britain for its remissness in Christianizing India; and the evangelical party in Britain, together with a group of Punjab officials who saw God's providence in the escape of their province from the uprising, urged renewed efforts at conversion by such measures as Bible classes in the government schools. But missionary zeal was fast waning in mid-Victorian Britain. Lord Derby in December 1857 even spoke of 'what I own seems to be the somewhat hopeless task of Christianizing India'. In India, talk of conversion evoked a uniformly hostile response among the senior offficals of the government. In a phrase expressive of the growing British distaste for 'fanaticism' of all sorts Lord Canning

---

[14] Thomas R. Metcalf, *Land, Landlords, and the British Raj: Northern India in the Nineteenth Century* (Berkeley, 1979), chapter 7.

dismissed the ardent Herbert Edwardes, commissioner of Peshawar, as 'exactly what Mahomet would have been if born at Clapham instead of Mecca'.

By the 1850s and 1860s Christianity was for most Englishmen increasingly a mark of their own difference from, and superiority to, their Indian subjects. The government's expensive ecclesiastical establishment, with its English bishops and 'station' churches, had nothing to do with conversion and meant little for the struggling community of Indian Christians. Tellingly, perhaps, when the Society for the Propagation of the Gospel in London proposed, as a memorial for the Kanpur massacre of 1857, that a church be erected for the use of the Indian residents of the city, with a missionary clergyman and prayers 'perpetually made for their conversion', the local English community rebelled. 'Feeling is unanimous', wrote the commanding general of the garrison, that the memorial should take the form of a church 'for the use of the soldiers and residents of the cantonment', with tablets and windows on which would be inscribed the names of all those who had lost their lives in the tragedy. While acknowledging that Kanpur required no additional church accommodation, the Government of India still underwrote the construction costs for this 'Memorial' church. Despite the presence of dedicated missionaries throughout India, Christianity had become, as the Secretary of State Lord Stanley put it in 1858, to the consternation of his evangelical countrymen, 'the religion of Europe'.[15]

Although abandonment of the hoped-for conversion of India undercut much of the logic that sustained liberal reform, still the new policy had room for other enduring liberal ideals. One was religious toleration, elevated after the Mutiny to a new place of pride. This was, above all, the message of the Queen's Proclamation on the abolition of the East India Company. Although the Queen added to the draft proclamation drawn up by the Prime Minister Lord Derby the phrase 'firmly relying ourselves on the truth of Christianity', the document made no reference to conversion. Rather it repudiated any 'desire to impose our convictions on any of our subjects', and enjoined abstinence from interference with the customs or beliefs of the Indian people.

---

[15] Metcalf, *Aftermath of Revolt*, pp. 92–97; for Kanpur Memorial Church, see NAI Home Public Dept., 18 November 1859, No. 20–22; Home Ecclesiastical Dept., 4 December 1863, no. 1–4.

In similar fashion the value of education remained unquestioned despite the trauma of the Mutiny. In part, of course, this was because the Western educated had remained loyal during the uprising. As the young Indian official George Campbell had appreciated as early as 1853, 'The classes most advanced in English education, and who talk like newspapers, are not yet those from whom we have anything to fear; but on the contrary they are those who have gained everything by our rule, and whom neither interest nor inclination leads to deeds of daring involving any personal risk.' The challenge which the educated would pose to the Raj still lay in the future.[16]

Yet the effort to preserve elements of an ongoing liberalism within a conception of Indian 'difference' further accentuated the contradictions which had marked the course of reform since the 1830s. Although it was unthinkable to contemplate ending, or even curtailing, government support for an ever wider network of schools, an educational policy which embodied the Macaulayesque vision of an India transformed on a Western model consorted awkwardly with the vision of an India presided over by princely and aristocratic elites seen as 'natural' leaders of the people. The British were likewise unwilling to abandon altogether their perceived sense of responsibility for the well-being of the tenants and subjects of these newly favoured intermediaries. The result was the enactment of tenancy legislation, especially in Bengal and Oudh, that endeavoured to succour the peasantry, but without unduly antagonizing their landlord superiors. Not surprisingly, such measures satisfied neither party, while making ever more unlikely the capitalist transformation of India envisaged, though only half-heartedly encouraged, since Cornwallis's time. The British in similar fashion paired the award of *sanads*, or patents, guaranteeing all India's princes the right to adopt heirs, and so save their states from extinction, with a closer scrutiny of their succession, education, and rule.

At the same time the Mutiny forced Britain to consider afresh the way it represented itself as an imperial power. Although the East India Company was not charged with responsibility for the uprising, the British government nonetheless took advantage of the occasion, twenty-five years after the Company had lost all commercial functions, but only five years after its charter had last been renewed, to bring this ancient corporation to an end. Even in its death throes, the

[16] George Campbell, *India as It May Be* (London, 1853), p. 410.

Company was not without supporters. John Stuart Mill, as examiner, fought tenaciously on its behalf, and he subsequently devoted a chapter of his *Representative Government* to arguing that a free people could best rule a 'semi-barbarous' one by delegating their authority to an 'intermediate' body composed of trained administrators devoted to the land which formed their 'special trust'.

Even though the Company could in this fashion be incorporated into the liberal scheme of empire, the continuing existence of this once commercial body as the governing power in India, together with the perpetuation of the Mughal emperor on his throne in Delhi, made it difficult for the British effectively to mark out their sovereignty over the subcontinent. Since Clive's treaty of 1765, when the British secured the *diwani* [revenue management] of Bengal, the East India Company had acknowledged a ritual subordination to the king in Delhi. Its coins, for instance, continued to bear the Mughal emperor's name until 1835, while the Company stopped the payment of an annual *nazr*, visibly denoting its tributary status, only in 1843. As the Mughal's vassal, lacking a clear-cut sovereignty of his own, the governor-general could only with difficulty award honours or devise rituals of hierarchy and subordination. Before 1858 there existed, as Bernard Cohn, following F. W. Buckler, has argued, 'an incompleteness and contradiction in the cultural-symbolic constitution of India'. The abolition of the Company ended this ambiguity, for the British Crown was now the uncontested centre of authority, ordering into a single hierarchy all its subjects, Indian and British alike.[17]

Complementing the abolition of the East India Company was the trial for treason of the king of Delhi, Bahadur Shah. Confined to his palace, the king had long ceased to exercise any effective power, yet his name kept alive the memory of the empire the British had pushed aside. For half a century the British had themselves endeavoured to use the power of that name to secure their own position, while in 1857 the rebel soldiery, in turn, forced their way into his fort in order to command that legitimate authority. Although the British could not legally try the king for treason, inasmuch as he was the king and they his vassals, nevertheless the trial, and Bahadur Shah's subsequent

---

[17] Bernard Cohn, 'Representing Authority in Victorian India', in Eric Hobsbawm and Terence Ranger (eds.), *The Invention of Tradition* (Cambridge, 1983), pp. 165–79; F.W. Buckler, 'The Political Theory of the Indian Mutiny' (1922), in M.N. Pearson (ed.), *Legitimacy and Symbols: The South Asian Writings of F. W. Buckler* (Ann Arbor, Michigan, 1985).

banishment to Burma, enabled the British at last to represent themselves as the unquestioned rulers of India. A new order had begun.

With the end of the East India Company, Lord Canning adopted
the new title of viceroy, and toured India in the years after 1858 to
make manifest the new relationship proclaimed by the queen. In a
series of durbars, or assemblies, he distributed Indian titles, such as
those of Raja, Nawab, and Rai Bahadur, as well as lands and money, to
a number of loyal princes, notables, and officials. Yet uncertainty, and
even contradiction, remained. In addition to the award of Indian titles,
for instance, the government at the same time, in 1861, created a
special English order of knighthood. Called the Star of India, it was
restricted to the most influential princes and senior officials, and it at
once became the most coveted of all the distinctions at the disposal of
the viceroy. In similar fashion British building in India in the years
immediately following the Mutiny remained wedded to classical and
Gothic forms. From the early days of their rule the British had erected
neo-classical buildings across the face of India. These, above all the
imposing baroque Government Houses in Calcutta and Madras,
expressed not only contemporary British taste, but the ideals of
empire, for the 'ordered beauty' of classical architecture had long best
fitted the European conception of how a worldwide empire ought to
be represented in stone. As such, these buildings inevitably linked
Britain's empire not to India but to the world of ancient Greece and
Rome. As William Hodges had written of Madras as early as 1781, its
'long colonnades, with open porticoes and flat roofs' offered to the eye
'an appearance similar to that what we conceive of a Grecian city in the
age of Alexander'. Britain's celebratory construction of the early 1860s
– from the Mutiny Memorial Hall in Madras to the Lawrence and
Montgomery halls in Lahore – similarly evoked the conquests of
Alexander and of Caesar, not those of Akbar.

Such architecture, furthermore, by setting Europe's building styles
on Indian soil, at the same time held out to the Indian people the image
of a modern world they might themselves aspire to join. A building
such as Pachaiyappa's Hall in Madras, modelled on the Athenian
Temple of Theseus, announced, much as did the English style education that took place within its walls, the transformation of India's
society on a European model. Hence, despite the coming of Crown
rule, the British had not yet by 1860 decided how far, and in what
ways, their liberal ideals would accommodate the more forthright

assertion of empire, and the vision of an India seen as enduringly different, portended by the events of 1857. The late Victorian ideology of empire had still to be hammered out.

THE CRISIS OF LIBERALISM

Eight years after the Indian Mutiny, in 1865, on the opposite side of the globe, at Morant Bay on the West Indian island of Jamaica, a group of freed slaves, who had become peasant cultivators, rose in protest against their desperate economic condition. Though the rebels were few in number and possessed no armed force, the rising was ruthlessly suppressed by the governor of Jamaica, Edward Eyre, who instituted martial law, had hundreds of blacks killed, and executed a mulatto leader who had challenged his authority in the assembly. To be sure, the scale of these reprisals was far less than the indiscriminate murder of Indians undertaken by the British troops as they marched on the rebel strongholds during 1857 and 1858. But the justification too was far less, for the rebellion posed but little threat to British rule in Jamaica. Hence the outbreak, and the manner of its suppression, provoked an immense outcry in Britain. In the ensuing debate, although the enduring liberal ideals of Victorian Britain found champions, the breadth and intensity of support for Eyre portended a shift in the conception of what empire meant, and how colonized peoples were to be governed.

Among Governor Eyre's critics, perhaps the most outspoken and influential was John Stuart Mill. Denouncing Eyre's actions as the abandonment of the 'rule of law' for that of 'arbitrary power', Mill insisted that no one could be allowed to stand above the law. In so doing, Mill spoke for the enduring liberal tradition, in which the procedural guarantees of the law alone secured the legitimacy of the imperial enterprise. Mill was joined by a number of other mainly middle-class professional men, from John Bright and T.H. Green to Charles Lyell and T.H. Huxley, who together made up the Jamaica Committee, and who sought to prosecute Eyre for murder. Eyre, by contrast, argued that in a country occupied by a 'mere handful of troops amidst a numerous and disaffected peasantry' prompt and decisive measures alone could preserve order. Only the 'dread of immediate and severe retribution', he insisted, prevented the rebellion from extending itself throughout the island, and so vastly increasing the amount of suffering and misery. Such rhetoric, with its appeal to colonial order, echoed throughout the empire as the British over the years sought justification for exemplary acts of punishment.[18]

As the prosecution marshalled evidence against Eyre, British opinion increasingly rallied not to Mill's, but to his opponent's side. Some of Eyre's supporters, like Thomas Carlyle, had long distrusted what they saw as a 'sentimental' liberalism driven by a desire to 'make the niggers happy' even at the expense of Britain's imperial responsibilities. For him Britain, and its empire, could only be saved by fashioning 'heroes' left free to act on its behalf. In similar fashion England's Poet Laureate, Alfred Tennyson, harking back to 1857, argued that, 'The outbreak of our Indian Mutiny remains as a warning to all but mad men against want of vigour and swift decisiveness.' John Ruskin and Charles Dickens too, less concerned about the fate of Jamaican blacks than that of 'white slaves' in Britain's factories, added their voices to the campaign on Eyre's behalf.

Common to all the arguments in support of Eyre was a sense of disillusionment with the results of slave emancipation. Jamaica's black population, in this view, had repaid trust with hostility, and so deserved the treatment meted out to it by Governor Eyre. As The Times explained it, though a 'fleabite compared with the Indian mutiny', the Jamican uprising 'is more in the nature of a disappointment'. It had previously appeared, they said, 'to be proved in Jamaica that the negro could become fit for self-government ... Alas for grand triumphs of humanity, and the improvement of races, and the removal of primeval curses ...'[19] Carlyle, of course, since the writing of his provocative Occasional Discourse Upon the Nigger Question in 1849, had insisted that, without strong white supervision, blacks would revert to indolence, if not to savagery. The Morant Bay rising, following so closely after the 1857 revolt, appeared to vindicate Carlyle's argument. Reform was pointless as well as dangerous. In the West as in the East Indies, so it appeared, colonized peoples, perverse and unreasoning, did not appreciate the benefits Britain chose to confer upon them. Whether black or brown, they were of necessity fundamentally different from Europeans.

One immediate consequence of the 1865 uprising was the disso-

---

[18] Bernard Semmel, The Governor Eyre Controversy (London, 1962), especially pp. 90–91, 102–18.
[19] Cited in Christine Bolt, Victorian Attitudes to Race (London, 1971), p. 71.

lution of the white-dominated Jamaican Assembly, and the reversion of the island to Crown Colony governance. Far from opposing this action, the colony's planter elite, fearful of black majority rule, had themselves initiated it. The result of this change was, however, to sharpen the distinction, growing ever more visible during the 1860s, between the constitutional position of colonies of predominantly white, and those of non-white, populations. The process had begun in the 1840s with the publication of the Durham Report, which awarded responsible government to Britain's Canadian colonies. By 1867 Canada had been confederated and responsible government extended to Australia, New Zealand, and the Cape. Such a process of encouragement to colonial self-government was of course implicit in the liberal ideal. By mid-century, following such notions to their logical conclusion, some had even begun to contemplate the eventual separation of these colonies from the imperial system altogether. For the most part, however, rigorous 'Little Englandism' of this sort was rare and confined to the radicals of the Manchester School. Most liberals, while encouraging settlers to govern themselves, sought continued ties of association with these colonies. The ideal was that of ancient Greek colonization, defined by Gladstone as the creation of 'so many happy Englands' united by bonds of 'perfect freedom and perfect self-government'. The model for colonies of non-white settlement, by contrast, whether in Jamaica or India, was the empire of Rome. In these territories Britain, like its Roman predecessor, had imposed upon it the 'duty and task and high privilege' of extending the rule of law and 'the great and glorious fabric of truly civilized society' around the globe.[20]

At home, while the Jamaica Committee was trying to rally support for the prosecution of Eyre, working-class discontent erupted in the famous Hyde Park riots of July 1866. Although hardly revolutionary in its objectives, this demonstration exposed the vulnerability of England's 'respectable' classes, and so, by extension, helped to increase sympathy for Eyre as he too, as they saw it, had endeavoured to control an unruly 'rabble'. Whether the English working classes, Irish Fenians, or Jamaica's blacks, all such labouring classes were inherently lazy, undisciplined, and potentially violent in their chal-

---

[20] C.C. Eldridge, *England's Mission: The Imperial Idea in the Age of Gladstone and Disraeli, 1868–1880* (Chapel Hill, 1973), chapter 2; Gladstone speech cited in Paul Knaplund, *Gladstone and Britain's Imperial Policy* (London, 1927), pp. 202–6, 224–26.

lenge to established property relations; hence '*all* rioting', as Matthew Arnold put it, had to be 'put down with a strong hand, or [the state] is sure to drift into troubles'.[21]

But in 1866 in England, unlike Jamaica, it was no longer practical politics, as it had been even a quarter century before during the Chartist agitation, vigorously to suppress working-class ambitions. To the contrary, schemes of partial enfranchisement had been floated even before the Hyde Park riots. In mid-1866, following the death of Lord Palmerston, the Tory Party came into office under Lord Derby. Disraeli, as leader in the Commons, resolved that the Tories should themselves settle the franchise question by a comprehensive measure of reform. The outcome, following a series of complex parliamentary manoeuvres in which each party outbid the other, was the famed 'leap in the dark' which extended the franchise to all urban working men.

This radical extension of the franchise carried with it the presumption that the English working classes had become sufficiently disciplined and law abiding – had acquired, as it were, a sufficient stake in the constitution – to be safely trusted to share in the working of the country's institutions. But the inclusion of the English working classes in the constitution inevitably altered the way the British perceived of themselves in relation to the world outside. No longer was it possible, as had been the case before, for Englishmen to conceive of the lower classes at home as in some measure equivalent to colonized peoples overseas: each subject to a state whose institutions ordered their lives, but allowed them no place in its deliberations. After 1867, apart from some feared 'dangerous' classes, isolated for the most part in such places as the East End of London, all English men (though not women) necessarily had to be considered as possessed of a 'sound sense', as Derby said in justification of the reform; and hence as participants together in the larger national enterprise. In so doing, however, the extension of the franchise, like the award of responsible government to the settlement colonies, further sharpened the distinction between white and non-white, between those who were deemed fit for freedom and those who must remain subjects. The existence of such a dichotomy in turn provided what might be called a 'common sense' justification for the growing racial ideology of late Victorian Britain. So long as there was no visible evidence of non-white inclusion in a free political system, or of white exclusion (apart from the

[21] Cited in Semmel, *Govenor Eyre Controversy*, p. 134.

ambiguous case of Ireland, at once part of Britain and separate from it), a racial theory of politics was at once logical and appropriate.

If the 1867 reform encouraged racial thinking, so too did this 'leap in the dark' strengthen an explicitly authoritarian strand within liberalism. The intellectual elite, especially, were fearful of the consequences as Gladstone, the 'People's William', set out to reconstitute the Liberal Party on the basis of a mass franchise. For such critics, of whom the first was Robert Lowe, leader of the small band of liberal 'Adullamites' contesting the reform bill in parliament, nothing could be further from true liberalism than the rule of an uneducated majority, manipulated by wire-pullers and demagogues, and with no object in view apart from the satisfaction of its baser instincts. As Lowe put it during the debates:

Because I am a Liberal and know that by pure and clear intelligence alone can the cause of true progress be promoted, I regard as one of the greatest dangers with which this country can be threatened a proposal to subvert the existing order of things, and to transfer power from the hands of property and intelligence to the hands of men whose whole life is necessarily occupied in daily struggles for existence.[22]

This opposition to franchise reform drew upon a set of principles whose intellectual roots could be traced back to Hobbes and Bentham. Its flowering, however, was a response to the crises of the critics' own day as they perceived them – alike on the plains of northern India, the shores of Morant Bay, and before the gates of Hyde Park. The result was to call into question as never before the reformist ideology associated with men like Macaulay and J.S. Mill. In its place was set a darker and more pessimistic view of human nature, and with it different ideals of governance. The empire provided at once cautionary lessons, and hope for the future. Lowe had lived in Australia for some eight years, and he saw its populist democracy as a political system to be avoided, while the India of the Raj now stood forth as a model not only for the empire but for Britain itself.

The most outspoken exponent of this authoritarian liberalism was James Fitzjames Stephen, who on his return from his service as legal member of the viceroy's Council published the manifesto of the new school, *Liberty, Equality, Fraternity* (1873). At the heart of Stephen's

---

[22] Speech of 3 May 1865, *Hansard's Parliamentary Debates*, cols. 1439–40; see also John Roach, 'Liberalism and the Victorian Intelligentsia', *Cambridge Historical Journal*, vol. 13 (1957), pp. 58–81.

philosophy lay the Benthamite, and ultimately Hobbesian, conviction that the aim of government was to secure, not liberty, as J. S. Mill proclaimed, but the greatest happiness of the greatest number. Stephen further insisted that most men cared only for their own immediate interests; hence the state of nature was one of perpetual conflict and warfare. The judicious application of force, wielded by a powerful legislator, was thus in a fundamental sense its own justification. As expressed in the coercive sanctions of law, force was not an evil, Stephen maintained, but a necessary element in the creation of a civilized social order. This insistence upon the civilizing power of law, sustained by the coercive power of the state, Stephen shared of course with liberal reformers from Bentham onward. Like them too he saw the British as the representatives of a 'belligerent civilization', whose rule over India found its justification in the 'superiority of the conquering race'. As he wrote, with an almost evangelical fervour, British power in India was 'like a vast bridge' over which an enormous multitude of human beings were passing from a 'dreary' land of 'cruel wars, ghastly superstitions, wasting plague and famine', on their way to a country 'orderly, peaceful, and industrious', and which might be the cradle of changes comparable to those 'which have formed the imperishable legacy to mankind of the Roman Empire'.

Where Stephen parted company with the liberal idealism of men such as J. S. Mill was in his assertion that the propensity to seek one's own selfish advantage was not curbed with the advance of civilization. Human nature was such, he insisted, his Benthamite views reaffirmed by the disillusioning experience of the crises of mid-century, that the bulk of the people would forever remain under the sway of passion, beyond the reach of rational discussion or improvement. Even in the modern parliamentary state, where compulsion was mild and disguised, the power of the sword still underlay the whole social fabric. To base any society on the ideals of liberty, or the presumption that men were other than 'fundamentally unequal', was a mirage. The common people required not universal suffrage but the disinterested rule of a gifted elite, able to command obedience and operate an efficient economical government.

Never an apologist for the old social order, with its hereditary aristocracy, Stephen found his ideal ruler in the trained bureaucrat of the Indian civil service. The 'best corrective in existence to the fundamental fallacies of liberalism', the Indian government, in his view, was 'the only government under English control still worth caring about'. John Stuart Mill, as we have seen, had himself shrunk from a too ready application of the principles of *On Liberty* outside the British Isles, and had praised the East India Company's government. But an imperial dominion, that for Mill was justified only by the larger transformation that was inevitably to follow, Stephen exalted as one the British need never be ashamed of. To the contrary, he urged the British not to shrink from the 'open, uncompromising, straight-forward assertion' of their own superiority over the people of India. As Stephen's disciple John Strachey put it, 'the only hope for India' was 'the long continuance of the benevolent but strong government of Englishmen'.[23]

Stephen called *Liberty, Equality, Fraternity* 'little more than the turning of an Indian lantern on European problems'. His enduring objective was not to praise empire, but to remake England in the image of the Raj. In this endeavour, as democracy took hold in Britain, Stephen was bound to fail. Ever less comfortable in the Liberal Party, Stephen and his disciples deserted the Liberal banner in the mid-1880s to protest Gladstone's attempt to extend the ideals of self-government to Ireland. Nevertheless, allied with a revived Tory Party, these Liberal Unionists, as they called themselves, secured for themselves an influential place in late Victorian political life.

More importantly, through the rigour of his advocacy, Stephen forced the British to confront the fundamental contradiction, long evaded, that lay at the heart of the liberal conception of empire. As early as September 1857, during the height of the revolt, the *Economist* had told the British people that they had now to choose

whether in future India is to be governed *as a Colony or as a Conquest*; whether we are to rule our Asiatic subjects with strict and generous justice, wisely and beneficently, as their natural and indefeasible superiors, by virtue of our higher civilization, our purer religion, our sterner energies ... or whether we are to regard the Hindoos and Mahomedans as our equal fellow citizens, fit to be entrusted with the functions of self-government, ripe (or to be ripened) for British institutions, likely to appreciate the blessings of our rule, and, therefore, to be gradually prepared, as our own working classes are preparing, for a full participation in the privileges of representative assemblies, trial by jury, and all the other palladia of English liberty.[24]

---

[23] Stokes, *Utilitarians*, especially pp. 287–309; John Strachey, *India* (London, 1888), p. 360.
[24] *The Economist*, vol. 15 (26 September 1857), p. 1062.

Increasingly, as the 1860s and 1870s went by, although it could not secure much support at home, Stephen's authoritarian liberalism, linked with parallel theories of scientific racism and historical jurisprudence, powerfully reshaped Britain's imperial ideology. Under the influence of these ideas, buffeted by the crises of mid-century, John Stuart Mill's vision of an emergent 'similarity' of Indian and Briton gave way to an insistence on India's enduring 'difference'.

CROWN AND EMPIRE: THE REVIVAL OF TORYISM

On 24 June 1872, speaking at the Crystal Palace, Benjamin Disraeli challenged the English people to choose between a 'comfortable England, modelled and moulded upon continental principles', and 'a great country – an Imperial country', able to 'command the respect of the world'. As he sought to find a place for the Conservative Party in the new democratic era he had himself set in motion, Disraeli with this speech brought the empire for the first time into the heart of British politics. The invocation of empire was part of a larger redefinition of tory principles. In the new tory strategy, empire was to be set alongside the 'maintenance of the institutions of the country', which for Disraeli included, above all, the monarchy, the established church, and the House of Lords. Further, and central to Disraeli's scheme, the Tory party would devote itself to the 'improvement of the condition' of the working classes. With the support of the workers, who were, Disraeli insisted, 'conservative – proud of belonging to an Imperial country', the Tories could put an end to the fear of 'the caprice and passion of multitudes' that so obsessed men like Stephen. By weaving together this alliance of Crown, empire, and working classes, Disraeli put not only the Conservative Party but the discourse on empire in British politics on a new footing.

During his years in power, from 1874 to 1880, Disraeli did not embark on any plan of imperial conquest, though he was prepared to sanction campaigns in Afghanistan and South Africa; and these helped precipitate his downfall. Disraeli's contribution to imperial ideology was rather to shift the focus of attention from the settlement colonies to India, from colonial self-government to the empire as a source of national pride, from a Grecian, as one might say, to a Roman imperial vision. In the process the ideals of mid-Victorian individualism, and of the liberal industrial order, were challenged for almost the first time since their inception.

The shift toward the 'Eastern Empire' was first revealed in Disraeli's 1875 purchase of the Suez Canal shares belonging to the bankrupt Egyptian Khedive. Altogether apart from any financial or commercial advantage, the purchase was, Disraeli told the House of Commons, 'necessary to maintain the empire'. From the control of this waterway it was but a short step, first to the annexation of the Mediterranean island of Cyprus in 1878, and then, by an anguished Gladstone in 1882, to the occupation of Egypt itself. Disraeli's imperial vision revealed itself most clearly, however, with the enactment in 1876 of the Royal Titles Bill, which secured for Queen Victoria the title of Empress of India.

Making the monarch 'Empress' can be seen to some degree as the logical conclusion of the process, begun in 1858, of resolving India's anomalous status within the empire. With the simultaneous abolition of the East India Company and the Mughal dynasty at Delhi, the British Crown had then become the country's unquestioned sovereign, so that the new title simply marked out visibly the new order. Further, Queen Victoria was anxious to have this additional title for herself; and Disraeli, ever anxious to please his sovereign, happily acquiesced. Far more was at stake, however, than the whim of the monarch, as the intense Liberal opposition to the bill soon made clear. Liberals feared that the change of title implied a more active role for the monarch in British politics – and the queen herself was not averse to being styled 'Empress of Great Britain, Ireland, and India' – but what roused the strongest hostility was the apparent identification of the British Crown in this fashion with the hated imperialisms of Napoleon III and the new German Empire. Though the British were proud of their own empire, as Robert Lowe reminded the House of Commons, 'sentiment clothes the title of emperor with bad associations'. The imperial ideal, in the liberal view, was that of the union of Britain with its own kin, and their descendants around the globe; it connoted loyalty and liberty, the 'happy Englands' of Britain's settler colonies, not the despotisms of continental states.

For the Liberal opposition neither the empire of Rome nor that of the Mughals offered attractive precedents for Britain's imperialism. Both empires, Lowe pointed out, had frequently had as their sovereigns men at once raised to the throne by military violence and sunk in debauchery. Lowe admitted, to be sure, that Britain had won India 'by the sword', and intended to retain it. But with Gladstone he insisted that it would not be desirable to advertise the fact of conquest by giving the queen an imperial title. 'Would it be wise or prudent in us', he asked, 'to confound our wise and beneficent government with that of the rulers who preceded us? Would it not be better for us to teach the Natives of India that those men reigned for their own pleasure and gratification . . . and that our object, on the contrary, is simply to do as much good as possible?'[25]

As Disraeli sought to justify the new title, the larger implications of the change came into view. One was a determination to assert Britain's equivalence as a major power with her European rivals. 'Do not let Europe', he said in closing the debate, 'suppose for a moment that there are any in this House who are not deeply conscious of the importance of our Indian Empire.' The enforced restriction of the title to India alone further enhanced the growing dichotomy, increasingly conceived of in racial as well as cultural terms, between India and the white settler colonies. Although Disraeli insisted that the 'amplification of titles' was a universal way to 'touch and satisfy the imagination of nations', still, as the change applied only to India, it inevitably furthered the notion that as 'Orientals', Indians were a different kind of people, who attached 'enormous value to very slight distinctions'. 'What to us', as Stafford Northcote explained it to the Commons, 'may appear exceedingly trumpery and trivial distinctions, are in their eyes of the greatest importance.' The titles act debate thus forced the British to consider directly what it meant to be an imperial state and helped bring about a reversal, from negative to positive, of the value attached to the term 'imperialism'.

Furthermore, the new title made legitimate, and so reinforced, the idea of India as a land 'of many nations', and of 'various and varying races', as Disraeli described its peoples. It was a land also of princes and of an unchanging past. Many of India's princes, Disraeli announced with hyperbole, 'occupy thrones which were filled by their ancestors when England was a Roman Province'. These varied 'princes and nations', he assured his countrymen, would welcome a great imperial sovereign who could properly regulate their position as feudatories in a hierarchic order. In addition, Disraeli and the Conservatives sought to exonerate both the Roman and the Mughal empires from charges of debauchery. The 'happiness of mankind',

[25] *Hansard's Parliamentary Debates*, 17 February 1876, cols. 413–18, and 3 September 1876, cols. 1719–37.

Disraeli insisted, was never so completely assured as in the age of the Antonines, while the retired Sir George Campbell rose to the defence of the Mughal Empire. It was, he said, though not perfect, still 'very great and glorious, and in many respects an excellent and good Empire'. Praise of the Mughal Empire was essential for the success of the new title, for its supporters imagined Victoria as empress assuming 'in name as in effect, the position hitherto occupied by the Great Mogul in India', and so standing in a direct line of descent from these predecessors. As Disraeli's Viceroy Lord Lytton exulted in writing to the Queen, the new title would 'place her authority upon the ancient throne of the Moguls, with which the imagination and tradition of [our] Indian subjects associate the splendour of supreme power'. The larger implications of the endeavour to define the Raj as 'Mughal', India's princes as 'feudal' rulers, and its society as 'medieval', will be examined in subsequent chapters.

In England too the change of title marked out a new vision of the monarch. It is perhaps not wholly a coincidence that Victoria, for the first time since the death some fifteen years before of her husband Prince Albert, opened parliament in person to announce the change in the royal title. In the early years of her reign Victoria, like monarchs before her, had actively intervened in British politics, and reaped the hostility such partisanship carried with it. Her lengthy seclusion, combined with her piety and the probity of her personal life, made possible the transformation of the monarchy that took place from the 1870s onwards. In an arena dominated by mass politics and rival parties, the monarch could in any case no longer exercise effective political power. But the upheavals of the era at the same time made ever more urgent the creation of a symbolic figure at the head of the nation as a whole. Indeed, in such an age, the 'preservation of anachronism', as David Cannadine has argued, the deliberate, ceremonial presentation of an impotent but venerated monarch as a unifying symbol of permanence and unity became both possible and essential. Such a transformation gained legitimacy at the time from the writings of Walter Bagehot, who described the monarch as the 'dignified' element of a government whose 'efficient' elements lay elsewhere, with the Prime Minister and parliament. Once available to represent the nation, the monarch could by extension easily be conceived of as the embodiment of empire as well. From 1877 onward, every great royal occasion, culminating in the Diamond Jubilee of 1897, was also an imperial occasion. In this fashion, by associating it with a cherished monarchy, the novelty of the new 'imperialism' could be to some degree concealed, and the empire given a place, as never before, at the heart of the national consensus.[26]

Formally of course the rehabilitation of the monarch as a ceremonial figurehead transcended party. Nevertheless, it is not surprising that Disraeli inaugurated the new regime, for the Conservatives stood to benefit the most from the 'invention' of a tradition that emphasized consensus, continuity, and deference. The ideology of the new conservatism further tapped a growing distaste in the later Victorian era for the liberal industrial order, its individualism and spirit of competition, with the ugliness of design that it was seen as having spawned. In its place there sprang up a powerful nostalgia for a pre-industrial arcadia. A vision of India as a land of abiding traditions and enduring artisanal crafts at once sustained, and itself gained strength from, this conservative revival.

Disraeli's final contribution to the creation of a new 'imperialism' was to inform British foreign policy with its spirit. In 1877, as Russo-Turkish animosity flared into war in the Balkans, Disraeli devised a new strategy for the defence of Britain's interests in the eastern Mediterranean. For decades Britain had sought to deter Russia by alliance with Ottoman Turkey, even to the extent of going to war in the Crimea. Now, however, with Turkey discredited among large sections of British opinion for its massacre of Bulgarian Christians, Disraeli sought to justify continued support of Turkey by a direct appeal to Britain's own 'imperial interests'. The British Empire, he argued, formed by the 'enterprise and energy of our ancestors', had given millions 'justice and order'. As the defence of 'provinces in every zone' had been entrusted to Great Britain, so the foreign policy 'of these islands' had of necessity to be imperial in character; hence Britain had to be ready itself to counter such threats to the lifeline of empire as Russian expansion into the Mediterranean. To make visible this new determination Disraeli in 1878 dispatched 7,000 Indian troops to Malta and occupied Cyprus.

Though the crisis of 1877–78 was ultimately resolved peaceably at the Congress of Berlin, by linking England's honour and its interests

---

[26] David Cannadine, 'The Context, Performance and Meaning of Ritual: The British Monarchy and the "Invention of Tradition", c. 1820–1977', in Hobsbawm and Ranger, *Invention of Tradition*, pp. 108–32.

with the defence of the empire, Disraeli further enhanced the political importance of the empire and of India. To be sure, the new imperialism aroused intense hostility. In his famous Midlothian campaign Gladstone passionately condemned an empire based on force and splendour, and his moral ardour helped bring about the Conservative defeat of 1880. Nevertheless, British patriotism was now inextricably bound up with the empire. By itself, one might argue, imperialism as an ideology never commanded more than limited support among the British populace. Those committed to the idea of 'empire' comprised powerful voices, including much of the intellectual elite, above all the Liberal Unionists, who thought of themselves as a 'great governing race'. But beyond this narrow class it was not easy, as one student of British conservatism has written, 'to wean people away from the specifically English patriotism of landscape and culture'. Still, as the British from Disraeli's time onward defined their national interests ever more explicitly in imperial terms, the values of 'patriotism' came to encompass those of imperialism. Imagining in retrospect the words and associations that 'marched in a grand chain, hand to hand' through the heads of those attending George V's 1910 coronation, Vita Sackville-West listed: 'England, Shakespeare, Elizabeth, London; Westminster, the docks, India, the Cutty Sark, England; England, Gloucestershire, John of Gaunt; Magna Carta, Cromwell, England.' The Raj, and the overseas trade that secured such dominion, had clearly found a secure place in England's vision of itself.[27]

'Jingoism' also emerged from the upheavals of the Balkan crisis. A song sung in the music halls during 1878 celebrated British truculence with the chorus: 'We don't want to fight/Yet by jingo if we do/We've got the ships/We've got the men/And got the money too.' During the subsequent decades of British imperial expansion, the term 'jingoism' was used to denote a blustering chauvinism which gloried in conquest. Jingoism did not imply any particular stance towards the empire, nor did it ever command a universal assent. At its core it was patriotic, not imperial, in its content, expressive of an exuberant sense of nationalism. Nevertheless, by placing that patriotism at the service of empire, jingoism, like the more sedate patriotism of such events as the royal coronation, deepened the hold of empire over the British people.

British patriotism, then, especially as it was mediated through the

---

[27] Hugh Cunningham, 'The Conservative Party and Patriotism', in Robert Colls and Philip Dodd (eds.), *Englishness: Politics and Culture, 1880–1920* (London, 1986), pp. 292–301.

Crown, provided a reservoir of sentiment that undergirded what A. P. Thornton has called the 'imperial idea'. The content of that imperial patriotism could of course be contested; it was not at the disposal of the Conservatives, or anyone else, to do with what they pleased, as the intense struggles at the end of the century over the Boer War and Chamberlain's imperial preference scheme visibly revealed. It is not by chance, however, that the era of greatest imperial enthusiasm, from 1885 to 1905, was also a period of Conservative predominance in British politics. By the last decades of the nineteenth century, a new imperialism sustained a new vision of India. No longer a land to be remade in Britain's image, it was now the cherished 'jewel in the crown' of the queen-empress.

CHAPTER 3

THE CREATION OF DIFFERENCE

For the Rede Lecture at the University of Cambridge in 1875, after his return from seven years as law member of the Viceroy's Council in India, Henry Maine set out to explain 'The Effects of Observation of India on Modern European Thought'. India shared with Europe, he said, as Sanskrit scholarship since the time of William Jones had revealed, a 'whole world' of Aryan institutions, customs, laws and beliefs. India was thus part of that 'very family of mankind to which we belong'. Yet, he went on, those Aryan institutions had 'been arrested in India at an early stage of development'. The country was, as a result, 'a barbarism', but it remained one which 'contains a great part of our own civilisation, with its elements as yet inseparate and not yet unfolded'. India was implicated with Britain, somewhat paradoxically, in a common origin, and yet was fundamentally different. In much the same way, the British were, in Maine's view, at once agents of 'progress', charged with setting India on the road to modernity, and at the same time custodians of an enduring India formed forever in antiquity. As Maine put it in the conclusion to his Rede lecture, India's rulers had to keep their watches set simultaneously to two longitudes. Throughout the later nineteenth century, as they constructed their 'India', the British had always to negotiate this disjuncture: between an acknowledgement of similarity, and an insistence upon difference. The task was never to be easy, nor was the result to be a coherent ideology of rule.[1]

For men like Maine, India was Europe's past, or rather its various pasts. In India Europe could find, alive in the present day, its entire history. India was at once a land of Teutonic village 'republics'; it was 'the old heathen world' of classical antiquity; it was a set of medieval feudal kingdoms; in the coastal cities 'something like a likeness of our own civilisation' could even be discerned; and India was, of course, also an 'oriental' land forged by despotism. In the later nineteenth

[1] Henry Maine, *The Effects of Observation of India on Modern European Thought* (London, 1875. Reprinted, Folcroft, Pa., 1974); and Henry Maine, *Village Communities in the East and West* (London, 1871).

66

century all of these various conceptions of India existed side-by-side with little sense of incongruity. Each, in its own context, represented the 'real' India; and each, as we shall see, served the needs of the Raj.

The creation of varied pasts was not confined to India alone. For the Victorians, and indeed for Europeans more generally, history played a critical role in organizing the world around them. They used it, in particular, to create for themselves a national identity, even if often troubled and fractured, that brought together English, Scots, and (with difficulty) Irish in a 'United' Kingdom; and to constitute sets of relationships with the world outside that would position their own 'progressive' society at the leading edge of the development of civilization. Though the varied British 'histories' of India might be inconsistent with each other, they were united by this nineteenth-century 'historicism'. Together they shaped the way the British constructed the difference they ascribed to India. Above all, through a theory of 'decline' that complemented Britain's own 'progress', the history of India was made to accommodate not just the existence of the Raj, but a course of historical development that made the imposition of British rule its necessary culmination.

The Victorians set out, in addition, to order and classify India's 'difference' in accordance with scientific systems of 'knowing'. British progress could not be simply a matter of cultural pride. The study of India was thus made part of a larger scholarly enterprise in which the Victorians, as children of the Enlightenment, sought rational principles that would provide a comprehensive, and comprehensible, way of fitting everything they saw in the world around them into ordered hierarchies. The existence of empire, by imparting a sense of urgency to the process, spurred on this creation of knowledge, and at the same time the unequal power relationships of imperialism helped shape the categories within which that knowledge was constructed. No longer a product of mere assertion, in the manner of James Mill, Western pre-eminence was now demonstrated, or, more properly, assumed, as it underlay the scientific structures that grew up around it. Victorian science, like its historicism, thus necessarily if not always consciously, fitted India into a hierarchical relationship with Europe and provided the firm footing of legitimacy which the British sought for their Raj.

This chapter will examine the persisting tensions between the claims of similarity and those of difference as they informed the ideology of the late Victorian Raj in the arenas of history, race, and gender.

67

Chapter 4 will assess how, in the light of their understanding of India's past – and its present – the British devised structures for ordering its society.

INDIA'S PRESENT AND BRITAIN'S PAST

Maine is most widely remembered for his striking, aphoristic statement in *Ancient Law* (1861) that 'the movement of progressive societies has hitherto been a movement from Status to Contract'. In his Rede lecture he reiterated his conviction that civilization was 'nothing more than a name for the old order of the Aryan world' reconstituted around 'several property' in place of an earlier collective ownership. Indeed, he insisted fiercely, 'Nobody is at liberty to attack several property and to say at the same time that he values civilisation.' Such views expressed a concept of social progress whose roots went back to the eighteenth-century Scottish Enlightenment. But Maine, with the other evolutionary theorists of his time, repudiated the utilitarian vision of an infinitely malleable human nature. Societies were different, and history had shaped the path each had followed. As John Burrow has written, in this view 'mankind was one not because it was everywhere the same, but because the differences represented different stages in the same process'. And, he continued, 'by agreeing to call the process progress one could convert the social theory into a moral and political one'. The superiority of Europe, and of private property, was thus preserved in an era when old certainties were fast disappearing.[2]

In place of Benthamite deduction from the abstract principles of utility, Maine sought a scientific basis for his evolutionary social theory in what he called a 'comparative' and 'historical' method of analysis. By this reasoning India's ancient institutions, linked to those of Europe by their common Aryan origin, became the germs out of which the social and political systems of modern Europe had emerged. They were not merely curious anachronisms, of interest only to antiquarians, but successive phases of one on-going process of development. The old Aryan institutions had persisted in India, Maine argued, partly because of the country's geographical isolation, shut in by the Himalayas and the sea, and partly too because all subsequent migrations after that of the Aryans had affected Indian social organi-

---

[2] J.W. Burrow, *Evolution and Society: A Study in Victorian Social Theory* (Cambridge, 1966), especially pp. 98–100.

zation to only a superficial extent. With the people insulated from outside influences, 'Brahminical religion' and the system of caste had preserved 'in extraordinary completeness' the society's 'old natural elements', along with the institutions and ideas which were their 'appendage'.

Yet Maine's theory was hardly coherent. Despite his commitment to an evolutionary concept of history, his use of the 'comparative' method had the effect of undermining the theory it was meant to sustain. In order to justify making inferences from India's present to England's past, Maine had inevitably to assume that India had had no history since the time of the early Aryan invasions. The result was to sharpen the distinctions the Aryan theory was meant to contain. As he gave India with one hand a history linked to that of England, with the other he took it away. The dichotomy between India's static society and England's progress ultimately overwhelmed any sense of parallel development. Similarity was necessarily subordinated to difference. To account for this difference, other contemporary thinkers, as we shall see, preferred to speak of India's Aryan past not in institutional but in racial terms, and in the process devised yet other ways of explaining its unique history.

Central to Maine's analysis alike of India's similarity and its difference was his conception of the village community. By Maine's time the notion of the 'village community' had already acquired an extended history both in India and in Europe. Building upon the writings of German Romantics, who sought their national origins in the Teutonic forests, Victorian liberals, anxious to discern the origins of Britain's distinctive freedoms, conceived of the Saxon village community as the training ground for all subsequent self-government. From the Saxon freeman, these 'Germanists' argued, a line could be traced directly to the parliamentary system of their own era.[3]

The idealized Indian village community, derived from the same Romantic imagination, was described in much the same language, but served purposes of a very different sort. The conquests of the first decades of the nineteenth century first brought the British face to face with the fortified villages of Maharashtra and the North Indian plains. In 1830 Sir Charles Metcalfe, defending the award of revenue collect-

[3] J.W. Burrow, 'The Village Community and the Uses of History in Late Nineteenth-Century England', in Neil McKendrick (ed.), *Historical Perspectives: Studies in English Thought and Society* (London, 1974).

ing rights to these corporate village bodies, rather than to landlords or individual cultivators, wrote:

the village communities are little republics, having nearly everything that they can want within themselves, and almost independent of any foreign relations. They seem to last where nothing else lasts. Dynasty after dynasty tumbles down; revolution succeeds to revolution; Hindoo, Patan, Mogul, Mahratta, Sikh, English, are all masters in turn; but the village community remains the same ... If plunder and devastation be directed against themselves and the force employed be irresistible, they flee to friendly villages at a distance; but when the storm has passed over, they return and resume their occupations ... This union of the village communities, each one forming a separate little state in itself, has, I conceive, contributed more than any other cause to the preservation of the people of India through all the revolutions and changes which they have suffered, and is in a high degree conducive to their happiness, and to the enjoyment of a great portion of freedom and independence.[4]

As a Company official, Metcalfe's objectives were in large part fiscal and administrative. It was easier to rule by incorporating rather than destroying such entrenched institutions. Yet Metcalfe's romanticized vision of the village was difficult to reconcile with the community it purported to describe. Although the disruptions of the later eighteenth century had enforced a great degree of self-reliance upon the Indian village, it was at all times much less isolated, from state and market alike, and much less egalitarian than Metcalfe's rhetoric implied, for the community of cosharers rarely encompassed the entire population. Nevertheless, Metcalfe's text resonated through the years. Neither the decline of romanticism, nor that of the independent village community itself, which by mid-century had been incorporated into a system of law and a colonial economy that offered little scope for the exercise of its alleged virtues, much affected the way the village was perceived. Even the utilitarians, who disparaged the village community as an impediment to their plans for an agrarian revolution in India, spoke of it in terms that acknowledged its cohesion and independence.[5]

In the later nineteenth century policy and theory together combined to embed the 'village republic' ever more deeply into the ideology of the Raj. With the shift after the Mutiny to a bulwarking of what were seen as traditional and stable elites, and the consequent desire to

---

[4] Cited in Dewey, 'Images of the Village Community', pp. 296–97.

[5] Louis Dumont, 'The "Village Community" from Munro to Maine', *Contributions to Indian Sociology*, vol. 9 (1966), pp. 77–89; Dewey, 'Images of the Village Community', pp. 307–28; Ronald Inden, *Imagining India* (Oxford, 1990), pp. 137–42.

dampen the pace of social change, the 'village community' came to define an ordering of Indian society which was at once unchanging and unthreatening. Indeed, almost paradoxically, one might argue, as the village community altered to accommodate the requirements of an increasingly interventionist state, the simultaneous need for a secure agrarian order evoked an ever more urgent ideological assertion of its enduring permanence. At the same time, from the 1860s onward, with the growth of evolutionary thought, the Indian village community took on a new, and larger, meaning. In 1871 Maine published *Village Communities in the East and West*. In this work he described India's villages, with their patriarchal clans and communal tenures, as marking out the earliest phase of an evolutionary process whose end point was to be found in contemporary England. India was, he insisted, 'the great repository of verifiable phenomena of ancient usage and ancient juridical thought'; he went on to pronounce its present village communities 'identical' with the 'ancient European systems of enjoyment and tillage'. Like Metcalfe's vision of the 'village republic', Maine's theory also had little place for the state or for caste; the latter, in his view, was 'merely a name for a trade or occupation'. The institutions of the village thus embodied for Maine that which at once most intimately linked, and yet separated, India and Europe.

Maine refused to let inconsistencies, whether in 'Germanist' theory or Indian practice, deter him from constructing a unilinear scheme of evolution for the village community. In large part this was because what mattered to him was in the end not India, but Europe. His principal objective was always to explain Europe's historical development in a way that inextricably connected 'civilization', progress, and private property rights. Not surprisingly, in consequence, Maine's views secured a wide and appreciative audience among Europe's privileged classes. As time went on, however, alternative views emerged. By the 1880s agrarian reformers, determined to secure occupancy rights for Irish, and for Indian, tenants, turned Maine's theory to their own purposes. They argued that the collective organization of property in these early communities justified placing restrictions on private property in their own day. Maine and his followers, in response, fearful of 'communistic' attacks on landed property, vigorously denied that joint property holding had ever existed in the early history of Europe, and so brought to an end the European career of the village community. At the same time in India, officials like B. H. Baden-

Powell, on the basis of the land settlement reports of the 1870s and 1880s, insisted that the Indian village community had never enshrined communal ownership of land and indeed owed little to the country's Aryan invaders. Patterns of landholding were, in this view, always heterogeneous, most often ryotwari, or household based; and they were shaped by the social requirements of indigenous Dravidian and aboriginal peoples. Still, the notion of the 'immemorial' village community remained as a compelling sign of the 'traditional' India which the Raj sought to sustain. Eventually this idealized village was appropriated in turn by India's nationalists, who saw in these communities evidence for the antiquity of an indigenous concept of democracy.

Insofar as he extended India's ancient past up to the present, Maine had of necessity, despite his evolutionary schema, to deny that India had ever passed through a 'feudal' stage comparable to that of medieval Europe. He acknowledged the possibility of a 'nascent' feudal development, but his need to leap directly from India's antiquity to its present foreclosed any further discussion. For many of Maine's contemporaries, however, India was *par excellence* a 'medieval', even a feudal society. The Indian official Alfred Lyall, for instance, in 1875, marching through Rajputana, wrote that 'Barring Oriental scenery and decorations, the whole feeling of this country is medieval; the Rajput *noblesse* caracoles along with sword and shield; the small people crowd round with rags and rusty arms; the king and his principal chiefs are lords of the country, and the peasant is at their mercy.'[6] As one of the most philosophically and historically minded members of the Indian civil service, Lyall was to play a major role during his career in India in shaping an ideology for the late Victorian Raj.

Much in the description of India as 'medieval' was simply an extension of the 'picturesque' vision, attracted by the colourful and the exotic, which found such comparisons to be the most satisfactory way of coming to terms with India's difference from Victorian England. Nevertheless, the 'medieval' vision of India had much in common with that of the idealized village community. In each case one group was made to represent the whole: as the Jat community of the northern plains embodied the Indian 'village', so too did the princely states of Rajputana (now Rajasthan) personify a 'medieval' India. In the

6 Mortimer Durand, *Life of the Right Hon. Sir Alfred Comyn Lyall* (London, 1913), pp. 181–82.

princely state, as in the village, time stood still. The Rajput states, as Lyall wrote, had 'managed to preserve unaltered much of their original structure, built up out of the needs and circumstances of primitive life'. No other 'political fabric' in Asia, he insisted, had changed so little in the preceding 800 years. In this way, as India's princes were shaped to fit the needs of the Raj, India's past was once again created anew.[7]

The idea that the Rajput principalities represented an Indian feudal order took shape along with the British conquest of this desert region. In the 1820s, as Colonel James Tod negotiated the treaties which brought the Rajput chieftains under British suzerainty, he ordered their past as well as their present. In his *Annals and Antiquities of Rajasthan* Tod laid out in over a thousand pages of print the customs and lore of all the major Rajput states, and he did so with such authority that nearly a century and a half later the old Brahmin guide taking tourists through the Chitor fort would refer to Tod as 'our historian'. For Tod 'the leading features' of government among peoples in the 'same stages of society ... must have a considerable resemblance to each other'. The 'martial system' of the Rajputs, with its feuds and rivalries, its ties of lordship and vassalage, was similar, he wrote, lumping all these peoples together as medieval, to that of the ancient German tribes, the Franks, and the Gothic races. Hence, the Rajputs too had to possess a feudal order. Indeed, anxious to turn aside the 'contempt for all that is Asiatic' which, he said, too often marked 'our countrymen in the East', he proudly insisted upon Rajput participation 'in a system hitherto deemed to belong exclusively to Europe'. Despite 'general decay' during long periods of Muslim rule, Tod argued, much still remained of these 'ancient institutions', especially in such places as Mewar, which was 'worthy of being rescued from oblivion'.[8]

Other officials extended this 'feudal' analogy to princes outside Rajputana. George Campbell, for instance, compared the eighteenth-century Sikh states in the Punjab to the princes of medieval Germany. It was, however, he said, a 'puzzle' how these Sikh Jats, who had 'for many hundred years' never seen anything except their village communities, should create a 'complete and fully organized feudal system'. The only explanation Campbell could offer was that 'the same feudal

---

[7] Alfred C. Lyall, *Asiatic Studies*, vol. 1 (London, 1884), p. 208.
[8] James Tod, *Annals and Antiquities of Rajasthan*, 2 vols. (reprinted, London, 1914), pp. 108–15, 155–58.

system which prevailed in Europe is a sort of natural instinctive habit of the Aryan race when they go forth to conquer'. Only a racial ideology could undo what the same ideology had created in the Aryan 'village community'![9]

One of the more attractive features of this Indian feudalism for the British was the way its dispersed sovereignty served as a check on 'Oriental despotism'. Lyall, for instance, contrasted the Maratha ruler Sindhia, 'a despot of the ordinary Asiatic species, ruling absolutely the lands which his ancestor seized by the power of a mercenary army', with the Rajput states, where the 'feudal lords' counterbalanced the sovereign power of the prince, 'exactly as the barons of Europe did, and very effectively prevent him from becoming an arbitrary despot'. As a result, he said, although the peasantry were often reduced to near serfdom, the 'feudal system of Rajputana' was 'the only free institution of India'. A system of government that could be described by analogy with that of Europe, even the Europe of the Middle Ages, was by definition superior to a system which was purely 'Oriental' in character.

The 'feudal' view of princely India did not go wholly unchallenged. By the 1880s many officials, including Lyall himself, had determined that the political system of the Rajput states was shaped not by ties of vassalage but by those of kinship. The Rajput chief, Lyall argued, was 'the head of a clan which has for many centuries been lords of the soil which now makes up the State's territory'. Critics pointed out that such central feudal elements as the fief and the manor, homage and the knight's service, were all lacking in India. Although he emphasized Rajput participation in the larger feudal order, Tod was himself aware that in many of these states the 'vassal chiefs' claimed 'affinity in blood' to their sovereign. This 'tribal' ideology found its fullest expression, as we shall see later, in accounts of the society of the neighbouring province of the Punjab.[10]

The reconstruction of Indian 'feudalism' as a social order based on ties of blood and kinship inevitably implied that it was fundamentally different from any European form, and so called into question the possibility for India of any evolution, of the sort that had taken place in Germany, from a medieval to a fully modern state. Still, the notion

---

[9] George Campbell, *Memoirs of My Indian Career*, vol. 1 (London, 1893), pp. 46–47.
[10] Lyall, *Asiatic Studies* (1884), pp. 224, 244; Charles Lewis Tupper, *Our Indian Protectorate* (London, 1893), chapters 10–11; Tod, *Annals*, pp. 107–9.

of the Indian state system as medieval served important political purposes. Like the India of the idealized village community, a 'feudal' India lived in a past that extended into the present, yet one tied to elements of Europe's own past; it possessed its own indigenous institutions of self-government, yet needed the British to secure the larger order that warring principalities could not by themselves bring about.

Not only India's princes, but the Raj itself, so the British believed, exhibited 'striking analogies' to the medieval world. Such resemblances were not accidental. They reflected the powerful appeal of the medieval ideal in Britain. A number of elements converged to create this enthusiasm for the Middle Ages: the search for the picturesque, the Romantic creation of a national past, the Anglo-Catholic religious revival, and the abandonment of classical for Gothic forms in architecture. All, however, expressed an overriding nostalgia for what has been called 'the world we have lost'. In an age of industrialism and individualism, of social upheaval and *laissez-faire*, marked by what were perceived as the horrors of continental revolution and the rationalist excesses of Benthamism, the Middle Ages stood forth as a metaphor for paternalist ideals of social order and proper conduct. Though they had no intention of repudiating the material benefits which progress had brought to Britain, the medievalists looked to the ideals of chivalry, such as heroism, honour, and generosity, to transcend the selfish calculation of pleasure and pain, and recreate a harmonious and stable society.

Not surprisingly, the medievalist conception of an ordered society, together with its idealization of character in contrast to mere material wealth or intellect, made it an attractive vision for both the landed classes in Britain and the civil servant in India. Indeed, as the public schools by mid-century were propagating the virtues of the chivalrous 'gentleman', even people of middle-class origin could hope to join this elite. Whether at home or in the empire, and also in relations with women in the masculine world of Victorian Britain, like knights in armour, the noble were to protect, and cherish, the weak. Medievalism thus sustained the Raj not just by portraying India as itself a 'medieval' society of hierarchy and deference, but by holding forth an ideal of benevolent paternalism derived from ostensibly 'medieval' virtues.

As this medievalist ideal helped shape Disraeli's toryism, it is no surprise that in India the medieval fantasy reached its fullest flower in the 1877 Imperial Assemblage, when Disraeli's creation of Victoria as empress was proclaimed to India's princes. The viceroy, Lord Lytton, a romantic medievalist and member as a youth of Disraeli's Young England group, determined to use this occasion to give India's 'feudal nobility' a firm institutional basis, and to secure for the British Crown as 'the recognized fountain of honour' a visible place 'as its *feudal* head'. He sought to set up an Indian Privy Council which would bring together the 'great ruling chiefs' in a common body with the viceroy and high British officials, while he established a College of Arms at Calcutta to order the Indian 'peerage'. In this way, Lytton argued, the 'Imperial supremacy of the British Crown' could be associated with all hereditary ranks and titles.

In addition, Lytton designed for the major princes large banners emblazoned with coats of arms. The armorial bearings, devised by a Bengal civil servant and amateur heraldist, embodied European notions of the 'history' of the various princely houses. The presentation of these banners to the attending princes formed the central event of the Imperial Assemblage. The decoration of the viceregal pavilion erected for the ceremony also invoked a lush Victorian version of the 'medieval' idiom. The shafts holding the canopy, for instance, were festooned with satin bannerets displaying the Cross of St George and the Union Jack, while the frieze hanging from the canopy displayed the rose, shamrock, and thistle, with the lion of India, embroidered in gold and silver. Silver shields, with strips of red and white satin, decorated with fleurs-de-lis and gilden lances, completed the decorative ensemble. To open the Assemblage, announced by a fanfare from six trumpeters in medieval costume, the viceroy entered the arena to the strains of Wagner's 'March from Tannhäuser'.

Although the Assemblage represented India as having at once a feudal past and a medieval present, the organizing principles of the Assemblage were not consistently 'medieval'. The selection of Delhi as the site for the event was shaped by a desire to create for the Raj a Mughal past, while the orderly layout of the British camp announced a strategy of colonial mastery whose message did not go unheeded. As Sindhia's prime minister Dinkar Rao reported after viewing the imperial camp from Flagstaff Tower, anyone who notices 'the method, the order, the cleanliness, the discipline, the perfection of the whole organization ... will recognize at once the epitome of every title to command and govern which one race can possess over others'. The use of banners also attracted Lytton, not only as a way of representing

India as a 'feudal' society, but as part of a larger 'Orientalist' strategy of rule. In his view the Indian peasantry were an 'inert mass' capable of being moved only by their native chiefs and princes, and these princes in turn responded most effectively to symbol and 'sentiment'. The 'further East you go', he wrote, 'the greater becomes the importance of a bit of bunting'.[11]

Lytton's use of 'feudal' imagery nevertheless raised awkward questions about the direction of India's political development. The secretary of state, Lord Salisbury, warned Lytton, in making announcements about the proposed 'native peerage', to avoid the 'technical expressions applied to similar institutions in Western Europe'. The plan for a Privy Council, above all, he insisted, had to be abandoned. Such a body might evoke memories of the 'great power' once exercised by the English Privy Council and give rise to 'expectations' which could not be realized. More generally, Salisbury argued, the 'constitutional bodies' of medieval England could not be introduced into India because they formed part of a 'very different system of government'. India's 'feudalism', in sum, was not, like England's, to be a stage on the road to a modern nation state. Hence, Lytton had to be content with the naming of twenty 'Counsellors of the Empress' – a title with no meaning for a body which never met.[12]

The medievalist vision also found expression in the creation of orders of knighthood. In India, as throughout the empire, such orders, and with them the numbers of knights, grew throughout the later nineteenth century. Four years after the Mutiny, in 1861, as we have seen, the first Indian order, the Star of India, was created. By 1877 there were several hundred holders, British and Indian, of its three ranks; and in 1878 it was joined by a new order, the Order of the Indian Empire, established on the occasion of the Imperial Assemblage. For British officials in India the coveted knighthood represented the capstone of a successful administrative career. Few among them, however, in keeping with the medieval ideal, could hope after the age of conquest to join the ranks of imperial heroes, or win a chivalric title in the manner of James Outram, whose tomb in Westminster Abbey proclaimed him the 'Bayard of India'. Of necessity,

---

[11] For imperial assemblage, see Bernard Cohn, 'Representing Authority in Victorian India', in Hobsbawm and Ranger, *The Invention of Tradition*, pp. 189–207; Lady Betty Balfour, *The History of Lord Lytton's Indian Administration* (London, 1899), pp. 106–33.

[12] Lytton to Salisbury, 5 October 1876, Salisbury to Lytton, 20 November 1876, and address of 1 January 1877, in NAI For. Pol. A, December 1877, no. 286–496.

therefore, the princes, and above all the Rajputs in their desert fastnesses, given knightly rank, were made to take up the role of 'proud
nobles'. In strikingly similar fashion, the Scottish Highlanders, newly
bedecked in kilt and tartan, were created as a brave people with an
ancient Celtic lineage. It is no accident that Victoria was herself drawn
strongly to both the Highlands and to India's princes.[13]

Yet, as in the case of Lytton's proposed Privy Council, Indian
membership of orders of knighthood on the British pattern forced
India's rulers once again to confront the question of what it meant to
describe that society as 'feudal'. Although the government endeavoured to maintain a rough parity in numbers between the British and
the Indian members of the Indian orders, Indian initiates were rarely
'dubbed' as knights when they were invested with the insignia of the
order. On this ground – and also because financial contributions were
considered 'quite unsuited to India and Indian ideas' – the customary
fees charged for the conferment of knighthood were remitted. But in
consequence, as they were not properly 'knights', so officials such as
H. M. Durand at the Foreign Office argued, the Indian members of
these orders were not entitled to be called 'Sir'. In the end such an
invidious distinction between the races in the mode of address could
not be sustained, and the Indians were addressed by the usual titles.[14]

Hostility to the incorporation of Indians in ritual forms derived
from medieval Europe nevertheless persisted, and even grew more
intense as time went on, as we shall see in a subsequent chapter. The
British peerage, for instance, with only a handful of exceptions,
remained at all times closed to Indians. As Curzon wrote when he was
planning his own durbar in 1902, however 'illustrious' the Indian
chiefs, their traditions did not require, for their conservation, 'the
varnish of a purely European invention'. I do not think, he continued,
that 'Maharajas or Rajas will be any the better or the happier for being
converted into Dukes, Marquises, Earls and Barons'. Such titles, with
coats of arms of the sort Lytton had devised, represented ideas that
were 'essentially foreign to Indian history and practice'. In similar
fashion, Curzon eschewed a 'medieval' for what he regarded as a

---

[13] Mark Girouard, *The Return to Camelot: Chivalry and the English Gentleman* (New
Haven, 1981), pp. 220–29; Hugh Trevor-Roper, 'The Invention of Tradition: The
Highland Tradition of Scotland', in Hobsbawm and Ranger, *The Invention of Tradition*,
pp. 15–41.

[14] See note of H.M. Durand of 7 February 1889, and correspondence in NAI files For.
Secret-I, March 1889, no. 56–76, and For. Intl-A, June 1887, no. 356–66.

Mughal, or 'Saracenic', decorative scheme for his durbar. As he wrote disdainfully of Lytton's banners and flags, 'so far as these features were concerned, the ceremony might equally well have taken place in Hyde Park'. In his view, Britain ought to represent its empire as Indian, not its Indian subjects as Europeans.[15]

Whatever its manifestations, medieval nostalgia was invariably shot through with irony. By its very nature it involved an effort to preserve that which the British were in the process of destroying, and indeed, as they built their empire, could not help but destroy. This destruction was visible, if with an ample measure of self-deception, to those engaged in the colonial enterprise itself. Tod, for instance, insisted that British 'generosity' had 'rescued' the Rajputs 'from impending degradation and destruction' at the hands of their Afghan and Maratha neighbours. Yet, he said, the British alliance was itself 'pregnant with evil', liable to 'lay prostrate' these 'ancient relics of civilization'. Tod nevertheless maintained that by a scrupulous policy of non-interference in the internal affairs of these states it was possible to restore the 'harmony and continuity' which had once existed, and so 'perpetuate this oasis of ancient rule'. Lyall, fifty years later, in similar fashion spoke of British rule as having 'rescued' the Rajput states from the anarchy that had followed the decline of Mughal rule. He recognized as well that the 'listless security produced by our protection' had brought about a 'rapid deterioration' in the effective functioning of the Rajput states. Yet he too clung to the hope, if not the expectation, that these 'ancient political structures' could be preserved.[16]

At one level, of course, such yearning for the past, and the consequent desire to keep 'the past' alive in India in the present, represented a disenchantment with Victorian British civilization itself. This was particularly evident, as we shall see in the next section, in patronage of India's crafts. Yet medievalism concealed as much as it revealed. No one was prepared, above all, to give up the 'progress' that had secured Victorian England its predominance, much less the Indian Empire itself, in pursuit of what can only be called a medieval fantasy. Renato Rosaldo has argued that 'imperialist nostalgia uses a pose of "innocent yearning" both to capture people's imaginations and to conceal its complicity with often brutal domination'.[17] Medievalism

---

[15] Minute of 11 May 1902, NAI For. Secret-I, September 1902, no. 1–3.

[16] Tod, *Annals*, pp. 100–5, 155–58; Lyall, *Asiatic Studies* (1884), pp. 204, 261–63.

[17] Renato Rosaldo, *Culture and Truth* (Boston, 1989), chapter 3, especially pp. 68–74.

can perhaps best be seen as a form of theatre which was meant, through insistence upon the persistence of the past, to obscure, from the British themselves as much as from the Indians, the extent of change which occurred under British rule, and perhaps even the fact of colonialism itself. Certainly its theatrical character was readily apparent at the time to outside observers. As the painter Val Prinsep wrote with disgust of the arrangements for the 1877 Assemblage, 'They have been heaping ornament on ornament, colour on colour ... They have stuck pieces of needlework into stone panels, and tin shields and battleaxes all over the place. The size ... gives it a vast appearance, like a gigantic circus.' Of the ceremony itself he said, 'it was what is called a splendid sight, but so was Batty's hippodrome, and so is Myers's circus'. At its conclusion, he wrote simply, 'The curtain falls ... Turn down the lights.'[18] This grand assemblage, one might suggest, was not so different from the famous Eglinton Tournament of 1838, when a spectacular recreation of the Middle Ages, with armour, costumes, and horses, was brought to an abrupt halt by a downpour of rain that forced the knights to lower their lances and unfurl their umbrellas.

Lytton's 'medieval' India was not a sham in the manner of Eglinton, for the princes were being shaped to play a central role in the colonial order. What the British sought, one might say, was not to turn the clock back but rather to create a simulation of the Middle Ages, in which its institutions remained apparently intact even as they were fundamentally altered to suit the requirements of the new order. In so doing, perhaps, the British could convince themselves that they had bridged the gap between Maine's 'two longitudes'. In the end, however, medievalism illuminated only Britain's present, not India's past.

LANGUAGE, RACE AND HISTORY

Although the antiquity of India's past had been brought to light by the Oriental scholars of Warren Hastings's time, the process of recovering its rich and lengthy history was inevitably long drawn out. The path-breaking studies of the Sanskrit language undertaken by such men as Jones, Halhed, and Colebrooke in the 1780s and 1790s were followed in the first decades of the nineteenth century by exciting new discoveries. Among these were the decipherment of the Brahmi script,

[18] Val C. Prinsep, *Imperial India* (London, 1878), chapter 3.

which revealed the existence of the third century BC Asokan era; the uncovering of Gandharan art in the northwest, which pointed to ties linking India and classical Greece; and the translation of the account by the Chinese pilgrim, Fa Hsien, of his tour in the fifth century AD, which, together with the discovery in 1819 of the Ajanta caves, gave historical depth to the Gupta Empire and the Buddhist experience in India. Although much remained unknown, above all the existence of the Harappan civilization, by the middle of the nineteenth century the major outlines of India's history had been established.

Confronted with this history, the British could not simply dismiss India as a land of 'changeless' villages and feudal principalities. India's extended past had at once to be explained and made subservient to the needs of the Raj. The British could, of course, assert their own superiority, as James and J.S. Mill had done, by pointing to the values, such as individualism and liberty, embedded in Western culture. They could also recite evidence of their technological prowess. By this measure Britain's superiority was palpable. The British had, after all, conquered India; and by the 1850s they were engaged in building railway and telegraph networks whose principles had been devised in Europe, not India. As Michael Adas has argued, this technological superiority was taken, even by such a sympathetic observer of indigenous societies as the traveller Mary Kingsley, as a justification for imperial dominance. On her return from West Africa, Kingsley wrote that she was ready to embrace 'the first magnificent bit of machinery' she came across as 'the manifestation of the superiority of my race'.[19] Kipling too, despite his sympathy with much in Indian culture, in *Kim* proclaimed the 'te-rain' and even the museum keeper's spectacles, so gratefully received by the lama, as evidence of the West's superiority.

Yet the mere celebration of technology provided no way of explaining the course of India's history. Britain's mastery of nature – so long as one chose to accept technology as the appropriate measure for judging the worth of cultures – could perhaps be seen as marking out differing levels of achievement between itself and India, but by themselves such differences gave no indication of why India had been left stranded so far behind. To explain this apparent discrepancy many Victorian theorists in the latter half of the century turned to the Aryan theory of race, which joined England and India in a compelling discourse at once of history and of science. Initially, as Sir William

[19] Michael Adas, *Machines as the Measure of Men* (Ithaca, 1989), pp. 146–53, 175–77.

Jones conceived it, what was to become the Aryan theory amounted to no more than perceived affinities in certain key words and forms of grammar between Sanskrit and most European languages. On the basis of these similarities, Jones then speculated that the peoples who spoke these languages must have shared a common origin. But these speculations were no more 'scientific' in character, or widely accepted, than Jones's other more fanciful theories linking the ancient Hindus with peoples as widely scattered as the Ethiopians and the Scythians.[20]

As a diffusionist, Jones insisted upon a common origin for all peoples; and he made no attempt to connect language with race. Nevertheless, over time, as comparative philology became more sophisticated, especially through the work of the German scholar Max Muller, Jones's loosely linked language family took on a new ethnic coherence and was given an ancestral home in southern Russia, from which the Aryans (as they were now called) were believed to have spread out to conquer and colonize vast tracts of land from northern India to western Europe. In this process language, culture, and the physical biological features that distinguish race became inextricably linked; and the Aryans as a race became sharply demarcated from other races such as the Semitic and the black African.

For the German Romantics who devised the theory, Aryanism was part of the search for the origins of the German *Volk*. They saw India as a land of ancient wisdom and the cultural cradle of mankind. In England, although many questioned the validity of Aryan racial categories and were unhappy about the use of linguistic affinities to define biological descent, the Aryan theory still had a powerful attraction in that its 'scientific' character allowed the similarities and differences of the Indians and the English to be assessed systematically. As such, Aryanism participated in the growing appeal, from the 1850s onward, of racial theory in general. Yet it was fundamentally different in character from that 'scientific' racism which sought to measure anatomical features such as the size of the brain and the shape of the head. To be sure, such classificatory schemes were not without adherents in India, for the Victorians, as their power came to encompass the entire world, sought to order that world in a coherent and 'scientific' fashion. H.H. Risley, census commissioner and ethnologist, for instance, denied the existence of any correlation between head size or shape and intelligence, but sought to demonstrate that the social status of the

[20] Marshall, *Hinduism*, pp. 15–16, 252–54, 260–61.

members of the various caste groupings varied 'in inverse ratio to the mean relative width of their noses'. Nevertheless the greatest utility of such 'sciences' as craniometry lay elsewhere, above all in the effort to assess the racial characteristics of Africans, and blacks more generally. Africans, in the British view, were deemed to have no history at all, because they lacked written records and ancient monuments. Hence, they were regarded as mere 'savages', whose bodies alone could define their enduring nature. India's extensive past could obviously not be treated with the disdain directed towards that of the African peoples. A place too had to be found in any racial theory for India's similarity with, as well as its difference from, Europe. Hence, as the British set out to place India in a racial hierarchy, they used philology to constitute a history, not biology to constitute a 'primitive' state of being.[21]

Aryan racial theory was itself not free of troubling difficulties. If the Indians and the British were alike Aryans, then how could the Indian people be marked out as inferior? How, indeed, could the British Raj be justified? The answer was to be found in evolutionary theory. Unlike the properly Darwinian view, in which weaker species suffered extinction, among human races, with perhaps such exceptions as the Tasmanians, those who fell behind in the struggle for survival instead experienced racial degeneration. While the European branch of the Aryan peoples triumphed over those of other races, those who went to India, as the amateur ethnologist and civil servant George Campbell wrote, 'lost their purity of race' by 'intermingling with the aboriginal races, and by the innate decay of enervation by the climate'.

The notion of Aryan decline in India was of course wholly dependent upon the characterization given to India's non-Aryan peoples. Victorian philologists categorized these people under the terms Turanian and Dravidian. The latter encompassed the major language grouping of southern India, first subjected to serious study by Robert Caldwell, in his *Comparative Grammar of the Dravidian or South Indian Family of Languages* (1856); while the term Turanian was loosely used as a way of describing speakers of non-Aryan and non-Semitic languages, especially those of Ural-Altaic derivation. From mid-century onward these categories, like that of Aryan itself, took on racial connotations; and Turanian especially, perhaps because

---

21 For Aryan theory, see Joan Leopold, 'British Applications of the Aryan Theory of Race to India, 1850–1870', *English Historical Review*, vol. 89 (1974), pp. 578–603; Herbert Risley, *The People of India* (London, 1915; reprinted, Delhi, 1969), chapter 1.

of its inherent vagueness, was adapted to the need of creating within India a racial foil to the Aryan conquerors. Overlapping and incorporating the Dravidian speakers, it defined those low caste aboriginal races who served, and had corrupted, their Aryan superiors. They were, as Risley put it, the oldest and 'most primitive' of India's peoples; their 'birthright' was that of labour for those above them.

As the Aryans settled in India, a few favoured communities, especially in the country's northernmost reaches, were able to preserve themselves from this 'intermixture' with 'Turanian blood'. The Jats, for instance, were described by George Campbell as 'in no degree Tartar or Turanian, but on the contrary in every respect intensely Aryan in their features, in their figure, in their language, and particularly in their institutions'. Risley too insisted that the Aryans of the Punjab and Rajasthan, with their 'very light transparent brown' skins, retained a 'high degree of purity' distinct from the bulk of the Indian people. For the most part, however, as the Aryan invaders migrated down the Gangetic valley, they came in contact with the Dravidians. The results were disastrous. As the 'men of the stronger race took to themselves the women of the weaker', the amount of 'pure Aryan blood' flowing through the veins of India's peoples became ever less, until by the British colonial period it had become 'infinitesimally small'. As we shall see, this racial distinction between those of the northern plains and those of the lower Ganges was to have its counterpart in the category of gender, which opposed the 'martial' peoples of the north to the 'effeminate' Bengali.[22]

An account of India's evolution based on race created problems as well as solved them; for the Aryan thesis as applied to India's social institutions, by such men as Henry Maine, was used to deny that change of any sort had ever taken place. Far from declining, as we have seen, India's Aryan institutions, in Maine's view, remained as powerful at the end of India's historical development as at its beginning. Nevertheless, a racial theory had the great advantage that it could provide not only a 'scientific' account of the diverging paths followed by India and England, but it could also order England's 'progress' in relation to India's 'decline', and so mark out the precise stages of India's downward course. Despite the incompatibility of institutional 'changelessness' with racial 'decline', each served important purposes, and so their theoretical contradictions had to be ignored.

[22] Campbell, *Memoirs*, vol. 1, pp. 59, 194–95.

Similarly, in their depreciation of racial 'mixing' the British were not always consistent. They took pride after all in the mixture of racial strains from across northern Europe which were supposed to have given the British themselves their exceptional vitality. Nor was India all that different. Campbell himself admitted that the 'modern Hindoos' were 'in fact, taken as a whole, a mixed race like ourselves, with much the same varieties of features that are found in Europe'.[23] What was at issue, then, was clearly not race itself, but processes of history and culture for which 'race' was a convenient marker. These inconsistencies are readily visible in the history, at once racial and cultural, that the British constructed for India.

For the racial theorists, the spirit of the Turanian or the Dravidian stood opposed in every way to that of the Aryans. The Turanian peoples, above all, had never declined, but rather, isolated in the jungles and hills of the south, they had 'preserved their nationality pure and unmixed'. Furthermore, the coming of Buddhism, from the fifth century BC, provided an occasion for these depressed peoples to rise up in opposition to Aryan, and Brahminical, domination. At the same time too, the era of Buddhist predominance, pre-eminently the two centuries before and after the coming of Christ, provided a new and attractive way of marking out India's ancient greatness. Untainted by the associations of Hinduism with 'superstition' and 'priestly despotism', which contributed so much to its disparagement at the hands of the Victorians, Buddhism had at its core a 'great teacher', who converted by persuasion to a 'rationalistic' faith. Buddhist art too, as revealed in such monuments as Sanchi, approached a European aesthetic which celebrated simplicity of design and a 'truthful' representation of nature. Impressed by the values associated with this 'classical' era, the British had to overlook the obvious paradox that those same people whom they had defined as racially inferior had created a religion, and an art, which represented the apex of India's cultural achievement.

The pre-eminence of the Buddhist era was further assured by the fact that one school of Indian Buddhist art, that of Gandhara in the far northwest, directly incorporated Western classical forms. As the art of European classical antiquity was for Victorians the measure of superiority for all art everywhere, art influenced by it had by definition to be superior to other Indian art. Alexander Cunningham, for instance,

[23] Ibid., vol. 2, pp. 2, 133.

who as first director of archaeology focussed his attention primarily on the excavation of Buddhist sites and the decipherment of Bactrian Greek coins, was convinced of the central role of Greece in providing inspiration for the finest Indian work. Vincent Smith too, with other historians, until well into the twentieth century argued for the superiority of the classically influenced Gandharan sculpture over that of Mathura and central India. In similar fashion, Alexander the Great's brief invasion of the Punjab in 326 BC was made the climactic moment of ancient India's history.[24]

The decay of Buddhism, together with the waning of Greek influence following the fall of the Bactrian kingdoms, enabled the Aryans, by now thoroughly mixed with the indigenous peoples, to reassert their dominance. They did so, however, only by adopting as their own 'the absurd fables and monstrous superstitions' of the Turanians. The result was the absorption of the 'pure' Vedic faith into these 'abominations', and the subsequent emergence of the two predominant Hindu sects of Shaivism and Vaishnavism. These, wrote the architectural historian James Fergusson bitterly, 'brought God to earth, to mix and interfere in mundane affairs in a manner that neither the Aryan nor the Buddhist ever dreamt of, and so degraded the purer religion of India into the monstrous system of idolatry that now prevails in this country'. Nor did the enduring encounter with the Dravidians shape religion alone. As Risley put it, 'By the stress of that contact caste was evolved ... and the whole fantastic structure of orthodox ritual and usage was built up.' In this view, contemporary Hinduism, as both a religion and a form of social organization, was the product of racial mixing and Turanian superstition. It had nothing to do with the 'genius' of the Aryan race. To be sure, some, with Fergusson, echoing Maine, insisted that the influence of Aryan 'intellect' remained 'powerfully impressed on every institution of the country'. Nevertheless, its racial history made India a fundamentally different place from Britain. As a society whose Aryanism had been overwhelmed by too intimate a contact with debased Turanians, it could never hope to emulate on its own the achievements of Europe.[25]

India's downward trajectory was most visibly manifested in its art

[24] Vincent A. Smith, 'Greco-Roman Influence on the Civilization of Ancient India', *Journal of the Asiatic Society of Bengal*, vol. 58 (1889), pp. 112–37.
[25] James Fergusson, *History of Indian and Eastern Architecture* (London, 1876; 2nd edn, 1910), pp. 10–12, 34–47.

and architecture. Unlike the obscure and difficult Sanskrit texts, whose study in Victorian times was confined primarily to German scholars like Max Muller, the looming temples and intricate carvings which the English found all about them in India were easily accessible, even, with the invention of photography, in Britain itself. As Fergusson put it, announcing his study of India's monuments, they could be regarded 'as a great stone book, in which each tribe and race has written its annals and recorded its faith'. Architecture, one might say, provided, with philology, another language in which could be read the story of India's decline. The Turanians, in this view, though incapable of producing great literature, were 'extensive and enthusiastic builders', and so inaugurated India's architectural traditions. The results were, however, as Fergusson described them, not very impressive. All the south Indian builder sought, he wrote, was 'a place to display his powers of ornamentation, and he thought he had accomplished all his art demanded when he covered every part of his building with the most elaborate and difficult designs he could invent'. Nowhere was there to be found 'those lofty aims and noble results which constitute the merit and greatness of true architectural art'. The logic of decline further demanded that later structures be more 'degraded' than those of earlier times, so that the seventeenth-century Madurai temple became 'the most barbarous, it may be said the most vulgar' building to be found in India. Nor, in this degenerate period, could even borrowing from the West, of the sort undertaken by the later nawabs of Avadh, redeem Indian design. The Western forms would themselves only be tainted by, and so further degrade, a 'dying art'.[26]

These judgements were informed not only by a theory of history, but by arguments drawn from the science of aesthetics. From the time of the Renaissance onward, Europeans had conceived that there existed a universally valid aesthetic shaped by certain principles of balance and proportion. By this standard India's architecture, above all such structures as South India's temples, were judged wanting. Instead of a 'tall central object to give dignity to the whole', most of them possessed lofty gateways surrounding inconspicuous central shrines. Such an arrangement of architectural elements was, as Fergusson asserted flatly, 'a mistake which nothing can redeem'. In the end, the lessons of science and of history were the same: temples that

[26] Fergusson, *History*, pp. 323–24, 341–42, 362–65, 604; see also Thomas R. Metcalf, *An Imperial Vision: Indian Architecture and Britain's Raj* (Berkeley, 1989), chapter 2.

housed the deities of a 'degraded' faith were, not surprisingly, constructed according to 'false' principles, while the use of a 'false' architectural design testified to the existence of a 'degraded' civilization.[27]

Nor was architecture alone seen as flawed. George Birdwood, the premiere patron of India's arts in late-nineteenth-century Britain, argued that while the creative spirit had flourished in the era of India's 'archaic beginnings', it had then been stifled by Turanian influence. As a result, the 'nobler lovelier forms of flowers and trees' inherent in the Aryan 'love and worship of nature' were discarded in favour of a meaningless elaboration of form. Only on those rare occasions, above all during the Buddhist era and subsequently during the years of Islamic predominance, when the artist was free of the 'trammels' of Puranic mythology, could India's art escape what John Ruskin in 1858 called its wilful and resolute opposition to 'all the facts and forms of nature'. Yet the accurate representation of 'Nature' was hardly the real issue. What was at stake, in the discussion of art as much as of architecture, was not aesthetics, but politics. Neither India's art, nor the larger culture in which it was embedded, could be allowed to challenge Britain's, and Europe's, predominance.

In this historiography only intervention from without could halt India's spiral of decline. '*Ex Occidente Imperium*', as Risley put it, 'the genius of Empire in India has come to her from the West.' This was the 'determining factor' both of India's ethnology and its history. Yet no set of invaders could for long remain aloof from India's peoples, and its institutions. 'As each wave of conquerors', Risley wrote, 'Greek, Scythian, Arab, Moghul, that entered the country by land became more or less absorbed in the indigenous population, their physique degenerated, their individuality vanished, their energy was sapped, and dominion passed from their hands into those of more vigorous successors.' Even those warriors who seemed to emerge from within India, like the Marathas, could claim their 'individuality of character and tenacity of purpose' only as part of an inheritance which had come to them from supposed 'Scythian ancestors'.[28]

India's Muslim conquerors, above all, were made to share with the Aryans the task of revitalizing a decadent society. To be sure, these

---

[27] Partha Mitter, 'Western Bias in the Study of South Indian Aesthetics', *South Asian Review*, vol. 6 (1973), pp. 125–36.
[28] Risley, *People of India*, pp. 53–61.

men were 'Oriental despots', subject to the 'effeminacy and corruption inherent in Eastern dynasties'; so that each of the Muslim states of India, despite a 'brilliant beginning', gradually sank into 'inevitable decay'. Still, as both Muslims and conquerors, their perceived role in shaping India's history was markedly different from that of the indigenous Hindus. For Europeans, as we shall discuss more fully in chapter 4, Muslims were always, unlike Hindus, a worthy adversary. As Lord Napier insisted, 'the progress of Mahomedanism was not entirely destructive'. Throughout the Muslim world its rulers, he argued, despite conquest and rapine, discovered 'generous abilities and tastes', which made their courts centres not only of warfare but of artistic patronage. These men adhered as well to a rigorous monotheism that was 'no vain superstition, but a true religion', and hence was deserving of respect.

The Mughal dynasty which preceded the British conquest was accorded an exceptional status. It contained 'liberal and humane' rulers such as the emperor Akbar; and these men constructed such buildings as the Taj Mahal, an architectural 'jewel' Fergusson considered almost, though not quite, on a level with that masterpiece of Western art, the Parthenon. Yet precisely because it had reached such illustrious heights the collapse of the Mughal Empire was all the more devastating. As Alfred Lyall wrote, 'assaulted by foreign invaders from outside, and distracted by internal revolts, it fell with a crash, and was torn to fragments by usurpers, successful rebels, and military adventurers'. In the 'anarchy' that resulted during the eighteenth century the Indian people were left a 'masterless multitude swaying to and fro in the political storm, and clinging to any power, natural or supernatural, that seemed likely to protect them'. In short, Lyall concluded, 'the people were scattered without a leader or protector; while the political system under which they had long lived was disappearing in complete disorganization'. Eventually, as the Viceroy Lord Lytton told the Imperial Assemblage in 1877, 'Providence' called upon the British to 'replace and improve' the 'constantly recurrent' anarchy of its strife-torn predecessors. India, in other words, had to be saved from itself.[29]

Critically important in this creation of a history for India was not, of course, the mere fact of decline. What mattered, and what set the

---

[29] Alfred Lyall, *The Rise and Expansion of the British Dominion in India* (London, 1894; reprinted, New York, 1968), pp. 62–65.

late-Victorian theorists apart from those, say, of the eighteenth century, was the description of this decline in racial, rather than environmental or cultural, terms. This alternative mode of explanation had far-reaching consequences. As the effects of racial degeneration could never be eradicated, India's peoples, even though Aryan in origin, had now to remain forever distinct, different, and inevitably inferior. Asserting 'difference' in such terms provided powerful theoretical underpinning for the larger post-Mutiny disillusionment with liberal idealism. Science and history together, so this ideology seemed to say, made all thought of reform pointless. Such ideas, in particular, reaffirmed the sense of Christianity, not as a faith to be shared with the world, but as a sign of England's intrinsic superiority. This took visible form in Indian church architecture. Even as the British were devising an architecture that endeavoured to represent the Raj as Indian, through the use of 'Saracenic' forms, church architecture remained rigidly confined within European, and particularly English Gothic, styles. The few attempts to create structures for Christian worship adapted to Indian forms, such as that of F.S. Growse in Mathura or the Cambridge Brotherhood in Delhi, provoked only a fury of opposition. As one correspondent wrote, criticizing the Delhi college of the Cambridge Mission, 'I cannot but regard as fatal the idea of carrying on Christian teaching in a building entirely surrounded with symbols, suggestions and associations which are opposed to Christianity.' The parallels the British delighted to find between themselves and the Romans were also shaped to the same end. Few of the British by the 1870s and 1880s expected what they called the 'ancient polytheism' of India to give way, as had occurred in the Roman Empire of antiquity, to Christianity. As Alfred Lyall put it, 'the seasons and the intellectual condition of the modern world are unfavourable to religious flood-tides'. In practice, Christianity was a faith meant for Europeans, to be housed in European-styled structures. In the India of the Raj, race and faith went hand in hand. India had to be accepted, and ruled, as it was.[30]

India's decline from an ancient Aryan glory did not, in the view of the late Victorians, degrade all elements of its culture. To the contrary, as men such as John Ruskin and William Morris argued, India kept alive in its crafts, as in its villages, cherished values of a shared past. Fergusson exulted that India's architecture was a 'living art' practised

[30] Lyall, *Asiatic Studies* (1884), pp. 159–60; Metcalf, *Imperial Vision*, pp. 98–104.

on the principles which caused its 'wonderful development in Europe in the twelfth and thirteenth centuries', while Morris praised India's art works for being 'founded on the truest and most natural principles'. In so doing these men expressed a growing British disillusionment with the fruits of the industrial revolution. Although its industrial might had raised Britain to the position of the most powerful nation on earth and secured their own prosperity, it had at the same time, the crafts enthusiasts argued, enshrined the making of money, degraded English taste with its mass-produced ugliness, and isolated the labourer from pride in his work. 'Degrading' labour, as Morris wrote, must be replaced with work conceived in the spirit of the village blacksmith or carpenter. In its condemnation of Victorian individualism the crafts movement inevitably participated in the larger 'medievalist' critique of contemporary society. Although Morris as a socialist sought a revolution to usher in a new communal society, his romantic and backward-looking vision brought him close to those who sought to preserve distinctions of status and custom, and to assert the authority of the Crown, the landed elite, and the state.

The crafts enthusiasts' vision of India's past closely paralleled that of men like Henry Maine. The art critic Birdwood, in opposition to Maine, insisted that the perpetuation of the past in India was not a product of the growth of unwritten custom, but arose directly from the Code of Manu. This body of ancient Sanskrit law, in Birdwood's view, established both the caste system and the enduring village communities. Yet the end result was identical. Caught up in an ordered system which provided 'place and provision' for everyone, India's craftsmen had no 'stimulus to individual exertion', and so had handed down the industrial arts of antiquity 'through 5,000 years to modern times'. India was a land which had escaped an unattractive industrial order, yet remained confined within an 'invincible immobility' that disabled the country from participating, like England, in the 'advancement of art'.[31]

Despite their hostility to industrialism, the crafts enthusiasts in no way emancipated themselves from the fundamental assumptions that sustained the imperial enterprise. They fully accepted the Victorian belief that the 'whole organization of social life in India', as Birdwood put it, was 'theocratic' in character, with, at its centre, the 'monstrous

---

[31] George Birdwood, *The Industrial Arts of India* (London, 1880), pp. 136–40; Metcalf, *Imperial Vision*, chapter 5.

shapes' of Hindu idolatry. Imbedded in this religion, India's art inevitably expressed its values. Truly creative art was therefore inconceivable. In 1910, reflecting on his 'experience of seventy-eight years' in the study of Indian art, Birdwood asserted that he had never found any work that sought to give 'perfected form to the artist's own ideals of the good, the beautiful and the true'; and he went on, in a memorable phrase, to compare an image of the Buddha to a 'boiled suet pudding'. For Ruskin and his associates, as much as for their opponents, aesthetics remained bound to the service of politics. No matter how much they might criticize their own society, the crafts enthusiasts were never prepared to abdicate their moral superiority, and with it the predominance of Europe. The work of the artisan craftsman alone, safely contained within the village order, posed no threat to the supremacy of the Raj, and so could secure unstinting praise. Everything else – whether of art or architecture – of necessity expressed only the 'barbarism' of a debased land.

Whether India's history was described in terms of 'decline' or of 'invincible immobility', in either case, then, the outcome was the same. Contradictions within the ideologies of race and language were ignored; the similarities demanded by the Aryan theory were accommodated; while difference was accentuated and shaped to insure a space in India for the Raj. Invariably, India was linked to Europe's past only in antiquity, and only where the ties to Europe were constituted within an unthreatening village society. The creation of an enduring 'traditional' India, in its crafts as in its village communities and among its princes, as we shall see later, carried with it as well a rigorous enclosure of the 'native' within this 'traditional' space. As the prince had to play the role of feudal 'vassal', so too did the craftsman have to work within what the British 'experts' who controlled the Schools of Art and the lavish *Journal of Indian Art* had determined was a properly 'traditional' style. In no way did the preservationist ideal simply involve the preservation of what existed.

GENDER AND THE COLONIAL ORDER

The British conceptualized the difference between Great Britain and India in terms not only of history and race, but also gender. Such distinctions had a long history. As far back as the 1750s, Robert Orme had entitled a chapter of his account of India, 'Effeminacy of the

Inhabitants of Indostan'. As he wrote, 'we see throughout India a race of men, whose make, physiognomy, and muscular strength convey ideas of an effeminacy which surprizes when pursued through such numbers of the species, and when compared to the form of the European who is making the observation'.[32] With the growth of empire, gender, like race, helped define the contrast between ruler and ruled, and so provided a way to order Britain's relations with its Indian subjects. Throughout, though the two are not identical, the categories of gender intersected with those of race. As a result, British men, British women, Indian men and Indian women were all fitted for distinct roles within the ideology of the Raj. Together they were made to enact a set of gendered notions of India's 'difference'. Yet these distinctions could be sustained only by rigorously containing, even disowning, the similarities of gender, of male and female, that cut across the hierarchy of race and rule.

Distinctions based on gender gained an avowedly 'scientific' rigor with the growth of a powerful domestic ideology in Britain during the early nineteenth century. According to this theory, innate and demonstrable biological differences defined a fundamental difference between male and female. By their very nature women were fragile, passive, and emotional, in contrast to men, who were held to be strong, active, and intellectual. These differences in the structuring of the body, in turn, dictated differing patterns of behaviour for men and women. Men were to be active in the public world, competing against each other for power and wealth; while women, from the sanctuary of the home, were to nurture their husbands and children, and so uphold the society's values. Women possessed great power, for their task was the moral regeneration of society; but it was a power that made itself felt indirectly, by shaping the consciences of men.

The existence of empire sharpened these distinctions of gender. By its very nature the British imperial experience, as Ashis Nandy has written, brought into prominence the 'masculine' virtues – such as control, self-discipline, and the like – and de-emphasized the 'feminine' virtues, such as tenderness and feeling, which were expressive of 'the softer side of human nature'. The everyday life of the British in India, with women for the most part secluded, though, as we shall see, by no means inactive, in darkened bungalows, and with men engaged

[32] Robert Orme, 'Effeminacy of the Inhabitants of Indostan', in Of the Government and People of Indostan, pp. 42–43.

in the work of empire in court and camp, reinforced the distinctions between home and the world, and between the private and the public, which lay at the heart of the British domestic ideology. The experience of the British in India under the Raj in this way reinvigorated dichotomies of 'masculine' and 'feminine', which then returned to England to nourish further the ideology of separate spheres.[33]

Although domestic ideology defined coherent, if contested, gender roles in Britain, the construction of gender within the empire did not take shape in any explicit formulation. Rather, theories of gender, though forming a consistent set of assumptions and expectations, were embedded in the ideology of the Raj in a variety of often only half-recognized ways. Hence, each must be examined separately. It is necessary to look in turn at British ideas of their own masculinity as they sought to 'rescue' India's 'degraded' women; at the notion of India as a 'feminized' land, at once seductive and dangerous; at the presumed effeminacy, as Orme described it, of Indian men; and at the ambiguous role of the white woman, caught up in the centre of the hierarchies of race and gender. For the most part, for obvious reasons, the voice that enunciated this vision was not only British but male.

For the Victorians, as heirs of the historical anthropology of the Scottish Enlightenment, the distinctive gender roles of their own domestic ideology were markers by which progress in civilization everywhere could be measured. The more 'ennobled' the position of women in a society, the 'higher' its civilization. By this measure, not surprisingly, India lagged far behind Britain. In contrast to the 'pure' and 'modest' demeanour presumed to define English women, India's women were not 'ennobled' by their men but instead 'degraded'. This state of moral degeneration, as we will see, was visibly represented by the *zenana* and the veil. Confined to a life of languid idleness in closed rooms, hidden from view, India's women were seen as suffused with an unhealthy sexuality and a disabling passivity. As India's men, so the British conceived, did not properly order their households – much as the country's previous rulers had failed to provide proper governance for the society as a whole – the British determined that they themselves should act as the protectors of India's women. In so doing they could not only, as they saw it, 'rescue' these unfortunate creatures; they could also make manifest their own 'masculine' character and proclaim their moral superiority over the Indian male.

[33] Ashis Nandy, *The Intimate Enemy* (Delhi, 1983), pp. 31–34.

3 *Lord William Bentinck*, by Richard Westmacott (1835). This full length bronze statue of Bentinck, portrayed as aloof and serenely self-confident atop a circular drum, announces Britain's new commitment, recorded in an inscription on the rear of the base, to 'elevate the moral and intellectual character' of its Indian subjects. In the *sati* scene an Indian woman, oblivious to the cries of her children, is shown as she prepares to mount the pyre.

Few of their activities in India gave the British greater satisfaction than this vision of themselves as the reformers of Indian morality, which left as its legacy a range of enactments from the abolition of sati in 1829, through the Hindu Widow Remarriage Act of 1856, to the Age of Consent Act of 1891, and beyond. Though these acts were very different in character, none of them immediately affected large numbers of people. Satis, for instance, when enumerated in Bengal during the 1810s and 1820s, though sufficiently numerous to be readily visible at 500 or 600 a year, involved only an infinitesimal fraction of the millions of people in that province alone; while enforced widowhood and child marriage remained at least as prevalent after the enactment of British reform legislation as before. Yet the dramatic representation of these 'evils' was essential to the self-image of the Raj. The statue of Bentinck, for instance, erected soon after his departure from India in 1835, praised him for 'abolishing cruel rites'; on the base is depicted an affecting bas-relief of a half-clothed woman, her baby pulled from her exposed breast, being led to the funeral pyre. (See fig. 3.) None of Bentinck's other achievements, which include the introduction of Western education, gained such graphic representation.

From the earliest days of the Raj sati compelled widespread attention. Despite its infrequent occurrence, the fascination with this event is not surprising. With its immolation of a living woman in a raging fire, sati, even more than the public execution, catered to the English obsession with death as spectacle. In the British imagination the event was also highly sexualized. The scene on Bentinck's statue evoked a salacious mixture of sex and violence, for it showed the woman's sari slipping from her hips and her bare breasts, now rubbed smooth, pushing forward on the curved pedestal at the centre of the composition, while the governor-general presided majestically above. It was easy, as well, to conceive of sati as emblematic of much that was wrong with Indian society. Whether the widow walked by herself in a trance-like state onto the pyre or was pushed from behind by relatives and priests, the act of sati represented the Indian woman as the helpless victim of a blood-thirsty and superstitious faith. India, sati seemed to say, was at once an exotic and a barbarous land.

Yet the representation of sati as an embodiment of India's difference could succeed only by the suppression of similarity. This was not an easy task. In the late eighteenth century, and in the first years of the

4 *An Indian Woman Burning Herself on the Death of her Husband* (date
and author unknown, but probably *c.* 1810). A product of the late eighteenth
and early-nineteenth-century romanticized depiction of the Hindu widow's
self-immolation as a heroic act, this drawing shows the widow, as the funeral
pyre is lit, pouring oil over herself, while three British officers calmly watch
from on horseback.

nineteenth, the British had frequently romanticized, as an ideal of conjugal fidelity, the self-sacrifice of the bereaved widow who selflessly braved the flames. Several paintings even show the widow as a heroic figure nobly transcending death in the manner of Captain Cook in Hawaii. (See fig. 4.) Nineteenth-century domestic ideology too, as it took shape in the 1810s and 1820s, presented the ideal woman as not only moral and innocent, but imbued with a spirit of self-renunciation. She was not to think of 'self-development', but was meant to sacrifice herself for her 'high and lofty mission' in society. For the British themselves, however, such female 'self-renunciation' was not meant to be that of the sati who followed her husband onto the pyre. From this act the British recoiled in horror. It was, nevertheless, as the ultimate 'self-sacrifice', not so far removed from the 'self-abasement' or 'self-annihilation' that, especially for feminist critics, defined the core of the domestic ideology. In a Britain where gender roles were contested, the existence of a connection between Indian self-immolation and the ideals of domesticity could not be avowed. To the contrary, only a vigorous attack on sati could effectively deny such similarities by displacing them onto an India seen as barbaric and inhumane. The suppression of sati had to be made an affirmation of Britain's superiority, and with it that of Christian civilization. Such a task fell with special urgency upon evangelicals, for they had played a central role in creating the notion of women as morally pure and self-sacrificing. Hence, from the outset, they took the lead in the campaign against sati, and they used the representation of its 'horrors' to induce English audiences to support evangelicalism. In time, as a 'moral' India was constructed in accordance with the ideals of Victorian liberalism, its women would presumably adopt an 'appropriate' mode of self-sacrifice – as 'angels in the house', not as victims upon the pyre.

Among British officials in India a different perspective informed the campaign against widow burning. Unlike the British at home, they sought to challenge sati from within Indian tradition, and so make themselves the masters of that tradition. In India sati's opponents and supporters alike accepted the assumption, a product in large part of late eighteenth-century Orientalist scholarship, that India was a society ruled by 'scripture' and the self-interest of Brahmins, and that its people were so tightly bound by the constraints of religion that they possessed little independent agency. Thus, on the one hand, those who opposed the abolition of sati argued that the practice was a cherished element of the Hindu religion with which it would be unwise, if not foolhardy, to interfere; while those who supported abolition equally denied any intention of introducing into India 'modernizing' notions of 'individual rights'. Instead of imposing outright their own ideals, so Bentinck and his supporters argued, they sought only to establish a 'purer morality' within forms of legitimation shaped by a vision of Britain as an indigenous Indian ruler. As Bentinck said, disavowing any intent to convert Indians to Christianity, 'I write and feel as a legislator for the Hindus and as I believe many enlightened Hindus think and feel.' Authority for suppression had thus to be found in Brahmanic 'scripture'. The British approached various pandits, and from them secured interpretations of selected Sanskrit texts which they used to support a claim that sati was not an essential part of the Hindu religion. In either case, the will of the widow mattered not at all; what was 'proper' was what could be defined as 'scriptural'. Bentinck's decision to outlaw sati was therefore, as he saw it, a 'restorative act' meant to enable Indians to act according to the 'purest' precepts of their religion. In practice, of course, this 'restoration' involved the introduction of 'modern', which is to say colonial, notions of the country's past and its religion. In the process too, not surprisingly, Hinduism was meant to give way to a 'higher' religion.[34]

The central assumptions of the sati debate continued in the later-Victorian era to inform legislation for the reform of Indian morals. Always, as in the case of sati, discussion of the condition of Indian women involved an outraged expression of horror at Indian degradation, and the consequent need for the British to save the Indians from themselves. The 1891 Age of Consent Act, for instance, which prohibited the consummation of marriage for girls below the age of twelve, provided an opportunity, as Mrinalini Sinha has written, for the British to 'demonstrate their liberal intentions in the face of the "uncivilized" and "unmanly" practices of the Bengalis'.[35] Similarly, in these later discussions, whether of widow remarriage or the age of marriage, 'scripture' always mattered more than custom, with the oldest texts accorded the greatest authenticity. At the same time, while

[34] Lata Mani, 'Contentious Traditions: The Debate on Sati in Colonial India', in Kumkum Sangari and Sudesh Vaid (eds.), *Recasting Women* (New Delhi, 1989), pp. 88–126.
[35] Mrinalini Sinha, 'The Age of Consent Act', in Tony Stewart (ed.), *Shaping Bengali Worlds, Public and Private* (East Lansing, 1989).

religion was seen as permeating Hindu society, those practices the British sought to discountenance were defined as marginal to, if not wholly outside, its core traditions. As the viceroy, Lord Lansdowne, told the legislative council in the Age of Consent debate, early consummation of marriage was not one of the 'great fundamental principles' of the Hindu religion, but one of a number of 'subsidiary beliefs and accretionary dogmas which have accidentally grown up' around it.

Much in this reformist ideology was internally inconsistent, if not contradictory. Although the British looked to ancient texts to define their ideal Hindu society, in fact the practice of the courts, inasmuch as they enforced Brahminical norms, encouraged precisely the kind of behaviour, such as avoidance of widow remarriage, that the government sought to discourage through its legislation. Similarly, although not accorded an independent voice of their own, Indian women were viewed at one and the same time as the passive vessels of 'tradition', and the site on which colonial officials, and with them upper-caste Hindu reformers, proposed to constitute a reformed society more closely fitted to Victorian ideals. Despite their avowed concern to avoid unsettling Indian religious belief, British reformers were in no doubt that there existed an absolute standard of 'morality', and that where, as Lansdowne insisted in the debate on the Age of Consent act, 'religion' and 'morality' were in conflict, the former had to give way. In their vision of themselves as moral reformers, as in their attitude towards Indian society more generally, the British could not escape the enduring contradiction between their self-imposed 'civilizing mission', with its ideal of an India remade in Britain's image, and their insistence upon maintaining an imagined India of enduring 'difference'.[36]

As India's Hindu women, so the British conceived, were degraded by their sexuality and their vulnerability to priestly influence, so too was their religion itself feminized in its character. Above all, the British looked on in horror at a Hinduism that venerated female deities imagined as vicious and licentious in nature, such as Kali. Further, many Hindu devotional practices, especially those of India's

---

[36] Rosalind O'Hanlon, 'Issues of Widowhood: Gender and Resistance in Colonial Western India', in D. Haynes and G. Prakash (eds.), *Contesting Power* (California, 1991), pp. 62–108; Lucy Carroll, 'Law, Custom, and Statutory Social Reform: The Hindu Widows' Remarriage Act of 1856', *Indian Economic and Social History Review*, vol. 20 (1983), pp. 363–88; *Proceedings of the Imperial Legislative Council*, vol. 30, 19 March 1891, pp. 146–50.

peasantry, were stigmatized as 'mother goddess' cults. Drawing on the gender stereotypes of Victorian England, M. Monier-Williams described such 'guardian mothers' as 'more easily propitiated by prayer, flattery, and offerings', yet 'more irritable, uncertain, and wayward in her temper' than male salvation gods. At the same time, such deities, related, some thought, to Mesopotamian mother-goddesses, expressed the innate degeneracy characteristic of Dravidian peoples. Together, these characterizations, as they linked the discourses of race and gender, defined for the British a religion of unashamed sensuality and shallow emotionalism. This system of belief, by its very nature, stood in sharp contrast to the Protestant British conception of Christianity. Lacking the coherent belief and principled conviction that was taken to mark Christianity, Hinduism was of necessity effeminate because it was degraded, and degraded because it was effeminate. The Brahmin priesthood alone exercised authority within the religion. But theirs was not the self-mastered command of the properly masculine elite. It was only the guileful concealment and dissimulation of the weak.[37]

The contrast between India's degraded sensuality and the masterly redemption of the British nourished a larger, enduring, opposition between an ordering Europe and a feminized 'Orient'. Such an Orient, with its erotically charged excitation, was perhaps most visibly manifested in the French painting of the imagined world of the harem and the shapely figure of the odalisque. Though John Frederick Lewis created such scenes for English audiences, he, with the French 'Orientalist' painters, worked almost exclusively in the Middle East. In paintings of India, though the landscape was often evoked in soft and yielding tones, representations of the erotic were infrequent, and confined for the most part to scenes of the 'nautch', or dance. Colonial officials, especially in the early years of British rule, participated as observers in dance performances given by Indians; and to some degree the 'nautch' dancer in colonial painting can be seen as a sexual being presented for the privileged, and controlling, gaze of the European male viewer. Yet the British response to Indian dance, particularly in Victorian times, was ambivalent. Many, like G.O. Trevelyan, found the nautch 'extravagantly dull', while others reported that the dancers were, 'as usual, ugly'. At best, as one observer recounted a visit to Lucknow, 'the dancer slinks to and fro with panther steps on her white

[37] Inden, *Imagining India*, pp. 115–22.

cloth, raises her eyes to the heavens before closing them to smack her lips together, and sings verses from a sleepy lullaby, sways beneath her veils, stretches out her arms, writhing like a serpent in paradise until the highlight of her act is over, and another girl, more supple even than her ... takes her place and sways to and fro in her turn'.[38]

In the creation of a feminized India the figure of the prostitute took centre stage. For the British, the prostitute, alluring and dangerous, at once symbolized India's degradation and generated a set of practical problems of regulation and control. As a result, in contrast to the voyeurism common to the male European vision of the Middle East, where the British, on the outside looking in, were free of the day-to-day responsibility of maintaining order, in colonial India the play of male erotic fantasies had for the most part to be contained within the confines of a moralized imperial authority. Even so, an India seen as suffused with sensuality offered ample scope for the imagination; and the imagination, in its turn, often shaped administrative action. One arena, not surprisingly, in which the existence of prostitution revealed itself was the Hindu religion. There it took the shape of the devadasis, women married to a god and dedicated to his service in the temple. Unable, or unwilling, to conceive of a religious system in which the erotic and the spiritual could be joined together, the British called this practice 'temple prostitution'. Through the use of such a term the unimaginable could be contained, and so controlled, and appropriate righteous indignation mounted against its existence. Even though a Hindu petitioner in Madras claimed that girls dedicated to a temple lead a life 'very similar with that class of females called nuns in Roman Catholic churches', while British critics from their side captiously compared the 'immorality' of such women with that of 'ballet-girls' on the London stage, the Indian authorities insisted on India's essential difference. Temple prostitution, they argued self-righteously, was 'equally immoral and immemorial'. Unlike English ballet girls, who sometimes 'preserve their virtue in spite of trials and temptations', in 'the case of the pagoda girl prostitution is the object of her dedication to the temple, and practice it she must to the end of her existence'.[39]

Anxiety about the prostitute loomed largest in connection with the military. As British troops in India were not allowed to marry, and the

[38] Sten Nilsson and Narayani Gupta (eds.), *The Painter's Eye: Egron Lundgren and India* (Stockholm, 1992), p. 128.
[39] See correspondence in NAI Home Judl.-B, May 1874, no. 169–74.

scourge of venereal disease regularly incapacitated large numbers of soldiers, the military authorities endeavoured to make available in cantonments a supply of prostitutes subject to medical inspection. This policy, formalized in the Contagious Diseases Act of 1868, modelled upon that in force for British ports, brought down upon the government the wrath of moralists at home, who disliked the official recognition of prostitution which these acts implied. Their opposition, together with that of British feminists, secured the reluctant repeal of both the British and the Indian Acts by 1888, although the Indian military authorities, ever anxious to contain the spread of venereal disease, managed to circumvent much of the effect of repeal by the promulgation of 'sanitary' regulations for cantonment areas.[40]

More was at stake in these controversies, however, than the simple provision of prostitutes for soldiers. Especially when contrasted with the comparable British acts, the Indian regulations make clear how the treatment of Indian prostitutes at once constituted, and was informed by, assumptions about enduring Indian 'difference'. In Britain, for instance, moral reformers, with their feminist allies, fought for the right of women, even as prostitutes, to be free of coerced bodily searches and registration; and they endeavoured to 'rescue' 'fallen women' by exhortation and recuperative treatment. No such concern for women's civil liberties cumbered the Indian debates, nor was there talk of redemption or 'rescue'. The Indian reformers were concerned only to secure an appearance of 'purity' in the behaviour of the British themselves. Prostitution itself mattered only where European women were involved, for their 'immoral' behaviour, by inverting the 'proper' hierarchies of race and gender, would bring discredit on the Raj. The fate of the common Indian prostitute evoked no interest. Prostitution was, after all, so the British commonly believed, an hereditary caste profession, recognized in the Hindu law books.

Furthermore, the Indian acts extended to major urban areas throughout the country, not just to selected ports, and hence implied that prostitution was a widely spread menace to the security of the Raj. While 'respectable' British women might openly traverse the city streets, if only in certain times and places, no such secure public arena existed for her Indian counterpart. Almost any Indian woman outside the seclusion of the zenana could thus potentially be suspect as a

---

[40] Kenneth Ballhatchet, *Race, Sex, and Class Under the Raj: Imperial Attitudes and Policies and their Critics, 1793–1905* (London, 1980), especially chapters 1–3.

prostitute, and a bearer of disease. As Lord Kitchener, the commander-in-chief, warned his troops in 1905, 'the common women as well as the regular prostitutes in India are all more or less infected with disease.' Venereal disease in India was regarded, moreover, as not just an unfortunate infection, but rather as a symptom of a 'diseased' society. As Kitchener wrote, 'Syphilis contracted by Europeans from Asiatic women is much more severe than that contracted in England.' It assumes, he continued, 'a horrible, loathsome and often fatal form'; and he proceeded to list an array of frightening symptoms, above all that of the body rotted and eaten away by 'slow, cankerous, and stinking ulcerations'. India was a land in which sexuality, disease, and degradation were linked together, and inscribed on the bodies of its women.[41]

The notion of a sexualized India was not, of course, exhausted by the figure of the prostitute. As we shall see later, in discussing Rudyard Kipling's Indian stories, the seductive attraction of India was by no means wholly contained by its enmeshment in the administrative concerns of the Raj. Furthermore, the contradiction between the vision of the prostitute as a contaminated being, and the urgency with which the government endeavoured to make prostitutes available to its soldiers, pointed to another fear, unacknowledged but haunting – that of homosexuality. Such an 'effeminate' pattern of behaviour among the members of the ruling race had to be avoided at all costs. Nevertheless, in the hyper-masculine society of the Raj, a barely suppressed homosexual tension can be seen shaping much of the erotic attraction of India. Such was the case, above all, in the British association with the 'martial' tribes of the Frontier. There alone, one might argue, did the British find in India a sense of excitement comparable to that aroused by the veil and the harem of the Middle East.

A society defined by sensual indulgence created, in the British view, 'effeminate' men as well as 'degraded' women. Indeed, the very opposition of a 'feminized' India to a 'masculine' Britain had as a central object the devaluing of the Indian male. Insofar as the British claimed for themselves the right to protect Indian women from the evil effects of 'tradition', Hindu males, denied a claim on 'masculinity', were reduced to a helpless ineffectuality. The growth of the idea of Indian 'effeminacy' can be traced in part to eighteenth-century theories of

---

[41] Philippa Levine, 'Venereal Disease, Prostitution and the Politics of Empire: The Case of British India', *Journal of the History of Sexuality*, vol. 4 (1994), pp. 579–602.

climatic determinism, in which heat and humidity were seen as conspiring to subvert manliness, resolve, and courage. As Orme wrote, 'Satisfied with the present sense of ease, the inhabitant of Indostan has no conception of anything salutary in the use of exercise.' Diet reinforced this preference, for the Indian, in Orme's view, ate only rice, which was an 'easily digestible' food, obtained with little labour, and thus 'the only proper one for such an effeminate race'. The most famous depiction of the debilitating effect of India's climate is surely that of Macaulay, who wrote of the languor and indolence produced by the 'constant vapour bath' in which the Bengali spent his days. The result, not surprisingly, was that his 'physical organisation' was 'feeble even to effeminacy'. There had never perhaps existed, Macaulay tellingly concluded, 'a people so thoroughly fitted by habit for a foreign yoke'. Reprinting this passage in his authoritative *India* some fifty years later, John Strachey concurred. Bengal remained as Macaulay had represented it.[42]

The experience of Bengal, the area which they conquered first and knew best, powerfully shaped British views of Indian effeminacy. Not only the climate, but much in Bengali dress and customs confirmed this stereotype. The Bengali male's voluminous *dhoti* could easily be deprecated as a woman's dress; Bengalis, perhaps more than those of other regions, were devoted to female deities, among them Kali and Radha; and male devotees sometimes assumed the dress and demeanour of women as a mark of their submission to the god. In all of this, of course, the British, knowing little and caring less about Bengali belief, saw what they wished to see. Conquest itself reinforced this gender stereotyping. If not a land *of* women, for the 'sturdy' peasant gained British respect, India was a land ruled *by* women, or rather womanly men, who ran from battle, and so deserved their subjugation. To be sure, as their conquests reached northern India, the British encountered groups whom, as we shall see in chapter 4, they called 'martial races'. But praise of Punjabi 'manliness' did not eradicate the stereotype of Indian effeminacy. It only carved out an exception, which cast the larger Indian, and especially Bengali, 'effeminacy' ever more sharply into relief.

Within Bengal the British detested, above all, the English-educated Indians, known collectively as 'babus'. This term of respect among Indians, comparable to that of 'gentleman' in Britain, became in

[42] Orme, *People of Indostan*, pp. 42–45; Strachey, *India*, pp. 334–35.

British usage a title of disparagement denoting those, unworthy of respect, who sought to ape British ways. Behind this condescension lay unvoiced, anxious fears. By his mimicry of English manners, the babu reminded the British of a similarity they sought always to disavow; and, steeped in English liberalism, he posed by implication, if not by outright assertion, a challenge to the legitimacy of the Raj. As the seductive female had to be repudiated, so too, even more urgently, had the educated Indian male to be contained within the gender stereotype that portrayed him as no more than a caricature Englishman. He might be, as Kipling wrote in his story 'The Head of the District', filled with 'much curious book-knowledge of bump-suppers, cricket-matches, hunting-runs and other unholy sports of the alien'; but his 'extraordinary effeminacy' made it unnecessary to treat seriously his 'political declamations'. Possessed of manly self-control, the Englishman alone stood apart from, and so could legitimately rule, the peoples of India.

Characterization of the Indian male, especially the English-educated Bengali, as 'effeminate' gained further strength from Indian opposition to such measures as the Age of Consent Act. While many educated Indians, from Rammohun Roy onward, had joined the British in seeking reformation of Hindu society, others, as early as the time of the sati debate, sought to exclude the colonial government from what they regarded as their domestic and religious affairs so that they might carve out an autonomous arena which they could call their own. At the same time, educated Indians often accepted the British insistence upon a connection between the 'status of women and that of the country in general'. *The Hindu* of Madras was even prepared to admit, as its editors announced on 15 September 1890, that Britain's 'power and prosperity' dated from 'the time when women were accorded a higher status than is implied in the present Hindu conception of women's privileges and rights'. Hence, questions of the proper role for women, and of men's responsibilities toward women, evoked strong feelings on all sides.

By 1890, with the proposal to prohibit consummation of marriage for girls under the age of twelve, hostility to British interference had spread across India from Maharashtra, where the nationalist leader B.G. Tilak took the lead in mobilizing public opinion, to Bengal. Opposition was most intense in Bengal because the educated classes there commonly practised, in the *garbhadan* ceremony, consummation of marriage at the time of a girl's puberty. Appalled, the British sought explanations for this 'debased' sexual behaviour in a variety of racial and climatic factors, including most prominently, as the secretary of the Calcutta Public Health Society put it, the fact that Bengalis were not, like the residents of northern India, a 'more purely Aryan population'. Whatever the cause, however, for the British the effects of this early sexual activity were readily apparent in the 'degeneracy and deterioration' of Bengali society. Hence, opposition to raising the age of consent only strengthened their conviction that Indian men, above all Bengalis, were weak and 'voluptuous', and lacked 'manly self-control'. The argument was, of course, circular: for not only were effeminate men prone to premature sexual intercourse, but effeminacy, and with it the larger 'enervation' of the people, was itself a product of 'unnatural' early sexuality. In any case, such 'unmanly' men, like women, required the protection of a paternal superior.

The British refused to accept as legitimate not only arguments based on the character of the *garbhadan* as a religious ceremony, but those grounded in the belief, widespread among Indian men, that female sexual desire, if not satisfied within marriage immediately after puberty, would seek 'some other course' to satisfy its needs. For the British, female sexuality, at least among respectable women, simply was not supposed to exist. Similarly, Bengali protests that their 'male honour' was challenged by British infringements on their rights as husbands had to be ignored: not, of course, because the British refused to accept the notion of male superiority, but because the Bengali could not be allowed to claim more than a 'caricature' of masculinity. Even though it was clear from the outset that the Age of Consent Act could not be effectively enforced – the government openly acknowledged that its effect would be 'mainly educative' – this enactment nevertheless enabled the British effectively to display their superiority as rulers who were at once 'masculine' and moral.[43]

The discourse on gender in colonial India had to accommodate English women as well as English men. Although women had no formal place as rulers in the colonial order, Victorian ideology, with its exaggerated opposition of 'masculine' and 'feminine', shaped a central place for them, as sign and signifier, in the discourse of colonialism. Pure and virtuous, superior to 'degraded' colonial races of either sex,

[43] Sinha, 'Age of Consent Act'; and Correspondence relating to the Act in NAI Home Judl., October 1890, no. 210–13, and January 1891, no. 1–42.

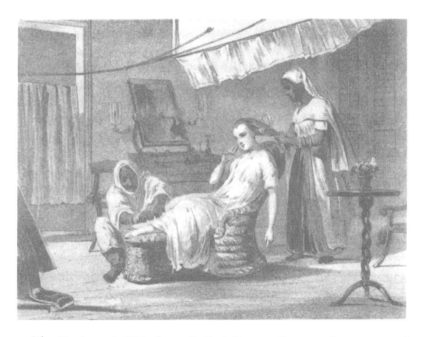

5 *The Magistrate's Wife*, from G. F. Atkinson, *Curry and Rice ... or the Ingredients of Social Life at our Station in India* (1859). This drawing represents the enduringly popular vision of the English woman in India, surrounded by servants, as idle and self-indulgent.

the Englishwoman was meant to enact Britain's moral superiority. In so doing, her 'true' femininity showed forth most visibly in contrast to that of the Indian zenana woman. Hardly less than a prostitute, so the British conceived, the secluded woman of the zenana typified India's moral degeneracy in her behaviour. Not only did she live a life of idleness in closed and unhealthy rooms, but her entire existence was seen by many observers as suffused with sensuality. The 'sexual function', as Flora Annie Steel wrote, was necessarily 'the central topic of lives confined to twelve square feet of roof'.[44] Ironically, even the Indian woman's veil, which for her male relatives signified her inviolability, and for the woman herself, as Lady Mary Wortley Montagu had appreciated long before, made possible an exhilarating freedom of

[44] Flora Annie Steel, *The Garden of Fidelity: The Autobiography of Flora Annie Steel, 1847–1929* (London, 1930), pp. 246–47.

movement, suggested to the British what it was meant to hide – her sexuality. The English woman, by contrast, veiled in modesty, remained vigorous but delicate, active but demure. (See fig. 5.)

In these circumstances British women established space for themselves in a variety of ways – by writing, by travelling, and, most commonly, by undertaking religious and philanthropic activity. Such activity, seen as helping their 'degraded' colonial sisters, appealed especially to liberal Victorian feminists, for it gave them scope for independent action, without presenting a frontal challenge to the ideologies of either domesticity or empire. Nonetheless, such activity inevitably blurred gender roles. The 'lady missionary', or the 'lady doctor', was needed because she alone could visit the women's quarters of Indian homes and care for Indian women. Yet she ran the risk by virtue of her independent movement of being implicated in 'indelicate' behaviour with men, or simply of being seen as acting 'improperly'. The negotiation of such conflicting demands was never easy. Most successful perhaps was Florence Nightingale, who, as she created a nursing corps, acted out a dominant 'masculine' role in the imperial arena, yet as the nurturing 'lady with the lamp' participated in the creation of a 'mythic' figure compatible with Victorian domestic ideology. In the process she could further represent an aggressive English imperialism in the guise of a mother's curative care for the 'sickly child' that was India.[45]

Even the English woman who did not venture outside her bungalow, as we shall see later, could not wholly escape a similar conflict. While embodying the ideals of Victorian womanhood, she had also in practice to enact within the bungalow a role similar to the one her husband played outside – that of a masculine assertion of ordering rationality in the face of an India where disease and disorder raged unchecked. This was especially evident in the disciplining of Indian servants, who, 'accustomed to it for thousands of years', as Flora Annie Steel wrote, needed to be treated firmly. By pitting against each other the extremes of decorative seclusion and vigorous activity, the female roles set out within the Raj enforced upon the white woman exceptional tensions of race and gender. Caught between masculine assertion and feminine modesty, between identification with English men and with Indian women, the English woman, within the private

[45] Mary Poovey, *Uneven Developments: The Ideological Work of Gender in Mid-Victorian England* (Chicago, 1988), chapter 6.

sphere she presided over, bore the unenviable responsibility – what one may call the 'white woman's burden' – of both representing the virtues of domesticity and extending the authority of the Raj.

Some few English women sought to create a space for female authority within an India free of colonial domination. The arena in which this took place was the practice of spiritualism. Although English spiritualists sought to portray themselves as properly 'feminine', still by its very nature female mediumship, or spirit possession, as Alex Owen has put it, 'effected a truly radical subversion' of nineteenth-century femininity.[46] Such 'subversion' came to encompass India with the founding in 1875 of the Theosophical Society. Through a set of occult practices drawn in large part from Hinduism, women like Madame Blavatsky, and subsequently Annie Besant, defiantly asserted a power of their own. Building upon, but inverting, the stereotypes which depreciated India as a 'spiritual' land, and women as 'religious', they challenged the accepted discourses of both empire and gender. Establishing the headquarters of the Theosophical Society at Adyar, near Madras, Blavatsky openly consorted on an equal footing with Indian males, whom she accepted as disciples; while Besant, with her support of Home Rule in the early decades of the twentieth century, extended the challenge from the realm of the spirits to that of nationalist politics. In so doing these women gave the creation of 'difference' a new meaning – as a set of values that could be used against the Raj as well as on its behalf. Nor was it long before Indians were to do the same, above all under the leadership of Gandhi, as he appropriated for the purposes of the freedom struggle the 'feminine' virtues assigned to India by the Raj. Such strategies of inversion nevertheless invigorated, rather than overturned, the gendered assumptions that had fortified the Raj.

Together with the construction of a distinctive history that sustained them, ideas of gender and race, then, were employed to constitute a set of fundamental differences between India and England. There existed a 'changeless' India inhabiting a past that endured in the present; an India of racial 'decline' marked by the triumph of Dravidianism and the anarchy of the eighteenth century; and an India of a gendered 'effeminacy' which made its women and men alike dependent on a benevolent British 'masculinity'. Each of these descriptions of India's difference had its own theoretical, even 'scientific', rationale;

[46] Alex Owen, *The Darkened Room* (Philadelphia, 1990), chapters 1 and 8.

each too was rent with deep contradictions both within itself, and in relation to the others. Above all, race and gender provided explanations of very different sorts for India's plight. The theory of racial decline announced a process of irreversible physical deterioration brought about by the mixing of blood, while the degeneracy defined by effeminacy was one of character and morals.

In each case the creation of difference involved an acknowledgement, either avowed or implicit, of similarity as well as of difference. These similarities were then reconstituted to secure the results which the British required of them. Least troubling was Aryan racial theory. Though it implicated the British with the Indians in a common origin, the similarities were sufficiently distant, and India's subseqent history of 'decline' sufficiently convincing, that, whether examined in terms of language, architecture, or religion, India's racial history clearly stood apart from that of Britain. This distance was less apparent in the context of the village community and Indian feudalism. The ideal of the village community, in particular, resonated with nostalgia for the 'world we have lost'. Medievalism too was an English category imposed upon India to serve the requirements of English nostalgia as much as those of empire. Hence, this vision of India's past could not escape being caught up in a conflict between the need to 'civilize' India, and the opposing desire to preserve a still 'medieval' land. As the elements of this 'traditional' India were fitted into the working of the Raj, as we will see in chapter 4, they consorted uneasily with a commitment to progress which could not be disowned without disavowing the empire itself.

The British were much less willing to accommodate similarities of gender than of race or history. In part this was because gender distinctions were tangled in deeply seated British self-perceptions. Unlike Aryan racial theory, where similarities could be acknowledged and then shaped to the needs of empire, contested notions of women's roles in Britain, shaped by ideals of purity and domesticity, made impossible any acknowledgement of a shared female sexuality or the larger implications of women's self-sacrifice. Similarly, the reluctance of British men to acknowledge the feminine side of their own nature, or to accord Indian men more than a caricatured masculinity, meant that similarities of gender among males were consistently masked or denied. At once psychologically and politically threatening, any avowal of such shared ties was unthinkable. Conceptions of gender therefore found expression not so much in a coherent ideology as in the ways they were enacted in British relations with their Indian subjects. Despite their inherent contradictions, however, all these varied notions of Indian 'difference' were made to fit together; and all alike helped to define the British as a 'superior' race. Sustained by Victorian 'masculine' and 'feminine' virtues, they possessed an incontestable right to rule over India's peoples.

CHAPTER 4

THE ORDERING OF DIFFERENCE

The strategies devised by the British to comprehend India were never simply intellectual exercises, nor were they meant only in some general way to justify British rule over the subcontinent. Always these theories, whether of race or gender, of an unchanging or of a feudal India, found meaning as they were used to order India's peoples and their past. Through them what the British conceived of as India's enduring difference was given shape in administrative practice. This process of ordering India was not driven wholly by political objectives. It was also part of the larger Enlightenment endeavour, by observation and study, to understand the world outside Europe, as Europeans came to know it more fully. A relentless need to count and classify everything they encountered defined much Victorian intellectual activity. For the most part too, as they set out to order the peoples who inhabited their new Indian dominion, the British sought to fit the categories they used to the society they purported to describe. Indeed, Indians themselves, especially the Brahmin informants and assistants who worked with the British, by the information they provided shaped much of the ethnographic project. Still, under the Raj the knowledge the British amassed can not be separated from its role in the successful working of colonial rule. India was 'known' in ways that would sustain a system of colonial authority, and through categories that made it fundamentally different from Europe.

The theories of 'difference' the British devised, as we have seen, despite their claims to scientific precision, were never wholly coherent, nor were they free of internal contradiction. As they were deployed by India's colonial administrators, these contradictions became ever more difficult to contain. Often mutually inconsistent theories were cobbled together to achieve particular political purposes, and controversy frequently erupted over how best to fit the ungainly facts of India's social order into the 'proper' modes of explanation. Inevitably, the endeavour to create a coherent social order involved the creation everywhere of what could only be called 'exceptions'. Furthermore, as the colonial sociology of India was tied to a system of power, the British necessarily eschewed at once those categories which would announce India's similarity to Britain and those which might threaten the colonial order. To be sure, classificatory schemes familiar to the British at home were not entirely absent. Occupation, for instance, played an important role in the British ordering of Indian society. Nevertheless, categories meant to denote India's difference, above all those of caste, community, and tribe, were placed at the heart of the country's social system. Class, by contrast, which Victorian Englishmen regarded as the great divide in their own society, was nowhere to be found in British accounts of India's peoples. Despite its inconsistencies and its subordination to the needs of colonial rule, the British ethnographic enterprise had far-reaching consequences, for these various categories – of caste and community, of race and sect – informed the ways in which the British, and in time the Indians themselves, conceived of the basic structures of their society.

ORDERING INDIA'S PEOPLES

Initially, as they first came to know India in the late-eighteenth and early-nineteenth centuries, the British described its peoples through a variety of classificatory systems in which occupational and caste rankings jostled with one other. There was unanimity on little more than the superior position of the Brahmin. Such views gained force from the textual studies of the early Oriental scholars, who adopted as their own the Brahminical view of India as a land whose peoples were forever fixed into positions defined by the four great *varna* categories of Brahmin, *ksatriya*, *vaisya*, and *sudra*, with the untouchables set beneath them all. By the turn of the nineteenth century, however, above all in the wake of the conquests of Lord Wellesley, when the British began to make their way into the Indian countryside, direct observation began to assume greater importance in the gathering of information on Indian society. The extensive tours of Francis Buchanan through Mysore and eastern India, and of Colin Mackenzie throughout southern India, can be said to have inaugurated the era of 'scientific' understanding of India based on detailed local knowledge.

Both Buchanan and Mackenzie amassed vast amounts of information on the working of Indian society. In his survey of Bihar, Buchanan collected statistics on housing, health, occupation, family size, and education, among other subjects, and even attempted to

6   Detail from *A Company Officer About to Sketch a Ruined Temple*, in the collection of Colin Mackenzie, *c.* 1810. Emblematic of the British determination to master India, this drawing shows a massive, once richly ornamented temple, now in ruins, with a tree rending the stone structure. A British officer, perhaps Mackenzie, with native assistants bearing a portfolio, ink, and a chair, has come to draw the ruined temple and so preserve it from India's inexorable decay.

estimate standards of living for various classes of labourers. So detailed are his statistics that modern researchers have sought to use them as a baseline from which to measure changes in economic well-being in the subsequent colonial era. In similar fashion, with the help of Brahmin assistants, Mackenzie collected local histories, religious and philosophical texts, coins, images, and antiquities, and made extensive plans and drawings wherever he went. Mackenzie's collecting enthusiasms far exceeded even the requirements of the colonial state, which remained always dubious of the value of his vast hordes of material. Although his collections announced Britain's control over India,

Mackenzie's activities participated as much in the omnivorous empiricism characteristic of nineteenth-century British amateur science. (See fig. 6.)

Neither Buchanan nor Mackenzie, as they toured India, paid much attention to what was later to define India's distinctiveness – the caste system. References to caste in the work of both men are haphazard and unsystematic. For Buchanan occupation largely defined the nature of caste, while Mackenzie's local histories for the most part recount the origins and doings of the chiefs and rajas of southern India, not its castes. The British in India in these years of discovery also commissioned extensive collections of drawings of various castes and peoples of India. But these too, informed by romanticism and the cult of the picturesque, sought primarily to capture the likenesses of colourfully dressed soldiers and courtiers, itinerant merchants, and exotic holy men, as well as those, identified by occupation, with whom the British came into daily contact, such as their own vast array of household servants. These lists and drawings were, moreover, highly idiosyncratic. No attempt was made to organize them into a coherent caste 'system'.

The lack of interest in a systematic ordering of caste during the early decades of the nineteenth century was not surprising. Engaged as they were in conquering the country, the British sought, above all else, immediately useful information about India's resources and the character of those chieftains whom they were endeavouring to subdue into revenue-paying subjects. While the drawings in such collections as Mackenzie's made India's 'difference' readily visible, British notions of the character of that 'difference' were not as yet clearly established, so that caste existed as no more than an ethnographic curiosity. Insofar as it claimed any meaning for the men of the generation of Macaulay and Trevelyan it was as an emblem of India's degradation, and as a barrier to its improvement.

As British rule by mid-century became increasingly secure, and as the reforming impulse waned, the colonial search for knowledge took on a new shape. After the Mutiny, anxious to rule India without disrupting its established social institutions, and driven by an ever more compelling commitment to 'scientific' understanding, the British set out to reduce to a comprehensible order what they saw as the baffling variety of India's myriad peoples. By the 1860s, as we saw in chapter 3, ideas of 'difference' defined an India that had become a 'laboratory of mankind' or 'living museum', where ancient customs, habits, and practices endured up to the present. Denied a history of their own, the peoples of India were defined by unchanging racial and cultural identities. The most important of these, by far, was caste. As Bernard Cohn has written, for late Victorian anthropologists 'a caste was a "thing", an entity which was concrete and measurable; above all it had definable characteristics – endogamy, commensality rules, fixed occupation, common ritual practices'; and these 'things' could be ascertained and quantified for reports and surveys. Once fitted together in an organized hierarchy, this 'system' could be taken as providing a comprehensive and authoritative understanding of Indian society. India was, in this view, no more than the sum of its parts, and the parts were castes. Of course, as we shall see, the apparent rigor was deceptive, for this 'system' had to accommodate kinship and 'tribe', and at times 'religion' as well.[1]

This increasing systematization of caste was intimately connected with the development of photography. As much of the effort of ethnological classification was directed by a search for 'scientific' precision, the recording of 'exact' images by photography logically complemented the compiling of statistical information. Insofar as different castes were conceived of as representing distinct racial types, a photograph of a 'typical' member of an ethnic group could be used to identify the precise characteristics, of physiognomy, dress, and manners, that defined the group as a whole. Although photography had been used to record the 'ethnic types' of India from the early 1850s, the first full scale compilation was *The People of India*, an eight volume work of 468 photographs published by the Government of India in 1868. Initially conceived by the governor-general, Lord Canning, and his wife as a collection of souvenirs for their own personal use, the work was transformed by the Mutiny of 1857, with its challenge to Britain's presumed knowledge of India, into an official project. Accurate information about India's peoples now mattered as never before.

Although *The People of India*, like earlier collections, idiosyncratically mixed caste, varna, and occupational categories, and occasionally

[1] Bernard Cohn, 'Notes on the History of the Study of Indian Society and Culture', in Milton Singer and Bernard Cohn (eds.), *Structure and Change in Indian Society* (Chicago, 1968), pp. 3–25, especially pp. 15–16; Nicholas Dirks, 'Castes of Mind', *Representations*, no. 37 (Winter 1992), pp. 56–78; and his 'Colonial Histories and Native Informants', in Breckenridge and Van der Veer (eds.), *Orientalism*, pp. 279–310.

7 *Brinjara and Wife*, from J. Forbes Watson and J. W. Kaye, *The People of India* (1868).

betrays what Christopher Pinney calls the 'moral preoccupations' of the reforming era, for the most part the work marked out a stage in the transformation of ethnological curiosity into 'a structured framework – the sort of "grid" to be found in museums and exhibitions – in which scientific theory and normalizing judgment predominate'. In its initial request for photographs, for instance, the Foreign Department asked the provincial governments to supply likenesses of 'characteristic specimens' of each tribe within their jurisdiction, and to include for each not only the 'peculiar characteristics of costume' but 'the exact tint of their complexion and eyes'. Nor did the photographs stand alone. Each was accompanied by a brief account of what purported to be that group's essential character. Gujars, for instance, were described as 'given to indiscriminate plunder in times of disturbance', while Banjaras had 'a reputation for perfect honesty'. (Consistency, however, was always elusive, for the Banjaras were later classified as a 'criminal' tribe.)[2] (See fig. 7.)

Those, above all the educated Indians, who rejected the notion of their country as an ethnographic 'museum', vigorously endeavoured to distance themselves from this collection. Shown the volumes in the India Office in 1869, Sayyid Ahmad Khan was horrified to see his countrymen portrayed as 'the equal of animals'. With considerable embarrassment, his son Sayyid Mahmud told an inquiring official that, while he was a Hindustani, he was 'not one of the aborigines'. What, Sayyid Ahmed reflected sadly, could the young English official on his way to India think 'after perusing this book and looking at its pictures, of the power or honour of the natives of India?'[3]

As time went on Indian ethnography asserted ever more rigorously its scientific claims. Its categories, embedded in censuses, gazetteers, and revenue records, became ever more closely tied to the administrative concerns of the colonial state. At the heart of this ethnography remained always the study of caste. As H.H. Risley pronounced with vigour, in his own account of *The People of India*, caste 'forms the cement that holds together the myriad units of Indian society'. Were

---

[2] Christopher Pinney, 'Classification and Fantasy in the Photographic Construction of Caste and Tribe', *Visual Anthropology*, vol. 3 (1990), pp. 259–88; and C.A. Bayly (ed.), *The Raj: India and the British 1600–1947* (London, 1990), p. 254–55; see also the correspondence in NAI For. Dept. Part A, June 1861, no. 278–79, and Home General A, December 1861, No. 43–45.

[3] G.F.I. Graham, *The Life and Work of Sir Syed Ahmed Khan* (1885. Reprinted, Karachi, 1974), p. 129; and David Lelyveld, *Aligarh's First Generation: Muslim Solidarity in British India* (Princeton, 1978) pp. 4–6.

its cohesive power withdrawn or its essential ideas relaxed, he continued, the change 'would be more than a revolution; it would resemble the withdrawal of some elemental force like gravitation or molecular attraction. Order would vanish and chaos would supervene.'[4]

Despite this general agreement on the centrality of caste as an organizing principle for Indian society, what caste actually consisted of remained always a source of controversy. Several ethnographers, among them J.C. Nesfield and William Crooke, argued that castes were defined by the occupations pursued by their members. Others, most notably Risley, insisted on a physical basis for caste. In his view, by contrast to other areas such as Europe, where 'anthropometry has to confess itself hindered, if not baffled, by the constant intermixture of types obscuring and confusing the data ascertained by measurements', in India 'the process of fusion has long ago been arrested, and the degree of progress which it had made up to the point at which it ceased to operate is expressed in the physical characteristics of the groups which have been formed'. Caste, that is, like race, was immutably inscribed on the bodies of India's peoples, and could be ascertained, so Risley argued, by measuring the nasal index. If, he said, 'we take a series of castes . . . and arrange them in order of the average nasal index, so that the caste with the finest nose shall be at the top, and that with the coarsest at the bottom of the list, it will be found that this order substantially corresponds with the accepted order of social precedence'.[5]

While few were as confident as Risley of the explanatory value of particular measures such as the nasal index, most late-nineteenth-century ethnographers, in India as elsewhere, accepted the notion that anthropometric research had some value. Almost all measured skulls – if only, as the case of Crooke, to contest Risley's more extravagant claims – took casts and photographs, and developed techniques of fingerprinting to identify criminals. In similar fashion, British ethnographers universally insisted that, whatever their defining characteristics, castes were discrete and distinct; and until after the First World War their mapping remained an enduring preoccupation. Nevertheless, despite the enthusiasm which drove forward the process of

---

[4] Risley, *People of India*, p. 278.
[5] Ibid., pp. 25–29; for William Crooke's criticism of Risley's views, see his introduction to the second edition, pp. xvi-xxii, and his own *Tribes and Castes of the Northwest Provinces and Oudh*, 4 vols. (Calcutta, 1896).

measurement, in administrative practice caste proved to be an awkward and unwieldy classificatory category. Even the mere enumeration of castes in the decennial census was a project of formidable difficulty. Constant efforts had to be made to reduce the bewildering array of caste names returned by individuals to a consistent order, and to fit all enumerated individuals properly into the assigned categories. Nor was it a simple matter to devise systems of classification which could contain the vast array of caste data.[6]

Most controversial was the effort to arrange castes hierarchically by 'social precedence'. In the various provincial 'Castes and Tribes' volumes, the authors sidestepped this nettlesome question by arranging the entries alphabetically. The 1891 census made some effort within larger occupational categories to list groups in accordance with their 'social estimation', but the self-confident Risley, as census commissioner a decade later, determined to secure an accurate ranked listing. To aid his own research, and to insure that his lists accorded with 'native public opinion', he even consulted a wide array of Indians. The prescriptions found in Sanskrit legal textbooks, together with the opinions of Brahmin pandits, shaped the responses of most of these informants; while the whole enterprise generated a vast outpouring of claims to higher status, especially among the members of middling castes such as Kayasthas and Khatris who felt entitled to rank as ksatriya. Risley, however, had long since made up his own mind. What mattered was race. On the first page of the *Tribes and Castes of Bengal*, Risley illustrated a stone panel from the Buddhist stupa at Sanchi depicting three women at prayer in front of an altar. In the background 'four stately figures ... of tall stature and regular features ... look on with folded hands in apparent approval'. The whole shows us, as Risley interpreted the scene, the 'higher' Aryan race on friendly terms with the 'lower' Dravidian, but 'keenly conscious of the essential difference of type'. 'Race sentiment', he concluded, resting upon a 'foundation of fact which scientific methods confirm', at once 'shaped the intricate grouping of the caste system, and has preserved the Aryan type in comparative purity throughout Northern India.'[7]

---

[6] Bernard Cohn, 'The Census, Social Structure and Objectification in South Asia', *Folk*, vol. 26 (1984), pp. 25–49; Frank Conlon, 'The Census of India as a Source for the Historical Study of Religion and Caste', in N. Gerald Barrier (ed.), *The Census in British India* (Delhi, 1981), especially pp. 107–17.

[7] Herbert Risley, *Tribes and Castes of Bengal*, vol. 1 (Calcutta, 1891), pp. i–ii; Risley, *People of India*, pp. 5, 109–20.

The persistence of fragmented ethnic identities at the heart of Indian society, in the view of most British ethnographers, foreclosed any effective unity amongst the country's peoples. Risley certainly was in no doubt about the political implications of a racially based caste system. Because castes, he insisted, were in India so sharply demarcated from each other, there existed 'no national type and no nation or even nationality in the ordinary sense of these words'. Risley nevertheless endeavoured to define a way by which India's castes could be reshaped so that they would play a role in the country's future political development. It may be said, he wrote, that the caste system 'with its singularly perfect communal organization, is a machinery admirably fitted for the diffusion of new ideas; that castes may in course of time group themselves into classes representing the different strata of society; and that India may thus attain, by the agency of these indigenous corporations, the results which have been arrived at elsewhere through the fusion of individual types'. The caste system, in this vision, could constitute a kind of civil society for India, which taught its peoples to work together. Ultimately, unlike the English language, confined to a tiny elite, caste might even help form a larger structure of shared values for the subcontinent. But Britain's presence would be needed for the foreseeable future to provide unity and leadership. In the end, of course, as the British patronage of caste helped embed it within Indian politics, Risley's vision found substantial realization in what has increasingly become independent India's caste-based political system.[8]

The valorization of caste difference as fixed and immutable found perhaps its most striking expression in the creation of the two opposed groups of 'criminal tribes' and 'martial races'. The notion that certain caste groups practised crime as a hereditary profession – that, as one British official wrote, 'crime is their trade and they are born to it and must commit it' – followed logically from the assumptions that sustained the British view of the caste system, and more generally of Indian society. As there existed those destined to be carpenters or cultivators, so too were there those 'destined by the usage of caste to commit crime and whose dependents will be offenders against the law'. Many of these so-called criminal tribes, furthermore, as wanderers and vagrants, were outside the normal networks of sedentary society; hence they were believed to challenge British efforts to

[8] Risley, *People of India*, pp. 26, 278–301.

order and control their Indian dominion. The outcome was the Criminal Tribes Act of 1871.

The notion that there existed groups in India predisposed to crime originated in the campaign against the thags during the 1830s. The thags, as we have seen, with their mysterious rituals of murder and worship directed to the goddess Kali, exerted a powerful fascination for the British, and so came to embody the 'mysterious' East. Inasmuch as thags were conceived of as being fundamentally different from ordinary criminals, W.H. Sleeman, as he set out to eradicate thagi, decided that no effort need be made to prove that a given individual had committed a particular crime. On the basis of thag genealogies which he put together, he argued that thagi was hereditary. Hence, it was sufficient for conviction to prove that an individual was a member of a thag gang. Although Sleeman successfully demonstrated the ability of the Raj to extirpate such gangs, largely through the use of informers' testimony, in the process the notion of distinct 'criminal communities', with its challenge to liberal ideas of individual responsibility and the procedural guarantees of the 'rule of law', became embedded in the legal framework of British India.[9]

In the wake of the 1857 uprising, the British determined to subdue all remaining low-status, wandering groups. Such concerns were not of course unique to India, for European governments had long been suspicious of gypsies and wandering vagabonds of all sorts. But for the Raj of the 1860s it was a matter of special urgency, as only a settled village society, wholly under the supervision of a conservative landed elite, could guarantee the British the security they required. In the process, the spectre of thagi was revived and blown up to ever greater proportions. As the inspector-general of the North-Western Provinces Police wrote in 1867, 'It must be remembered, in dealing with the wandering predatory tribes of India, that the fraternities are of such ancient creation, their number so vast, the country over which their depredations spread so vast, their organization so complete, and their evil of such formidable dimensions, that nothing but special legislation will suffice for their suppression and conversion.' Now, however, as part of the new ethnography, caste affiliation, not the fictive kinship of gang membership, defined collective criminality. The

[9] Sandria Freitag, 'Crime in the Social Order of Colonial North India', *Modern Asian Studies*, vol. 25 (1991), pp. 227–41; Radhika Singha, 'Providential Circumstances', pp. 83–146.

1871 act listed four tribes as criminal, out of some twenty-nine proposed by the police, and provided a mechanism through which additions could be, and were, made to their numbers in subsequent years. The members of such tribes were registered, and their movements restricted by a system of passes and roll-calls. Those found outside their prescribed place of residence were liable to arrest without a warrant.[10]

This effort to define specific 'criminal tribes' did not escape criticism. Several officials, among them the judges of the Punjab Chief Court, committed to the procedure of the ordinary criminal law, with its denial of Indian 'difference', urged that only individuals should be registered, and then restricted in their movements only when charged with crimes actually committed. Others pointed to the likelihood that such legislation would confound the innocent with the guilty, and might even drive those deprived of their customary livelihood to take up crime, as well as offering the police great opportunities for abuse of their power. Further, the avowed goal of reforming these criminals by settling them in special colonies under surveillance stood sharply at odds with the theory, underlying the act, of a hereditary predisposition to commit crime. Nevertheless, as time went on, the act was extended to include ever more 'tribes', and was finally repealed only after independence.

The ideology sustaining the notion of 'criminal tribes' was not wholly a product of the colonial environment. Even in Victorian Britain the government feared the so-called 'dangerous' classes, who were conceived of as threatening public order. Hence in 1869, while discussions regarding the 1871 act were underway in India, the Habitual Criminals Act incorporated into English law exceptional powers for the surveillance and control of those denominated 'habitual offenders'. Throughout the first half of the nineteenth century, during the unsettled decades from Peterloo to Chartism, fear of the lower orders as inherently revolutionary was widespread among the members of 'respectable' society. By the 1860s, with the extension of the franchise, as we have seen, the regularly employed working class began to be brought into the constitution. There remained only the

[10] NAI Home Judl., April 1870, no. 9–14, and July 1870, no. 55–59; Legis. Dept. Papers Relating to Act XXVII of 1871. For a full account, see Sanjay Nigam, 'Disciplining and Policing the "Criminals by Birth", Part 1: The Making of a Colonial Stereotype – The Criminal Tribes and Castes of North India', *Indian Economic and Social History Review*, vol. 27 (1990), pp. 131–64.

'habitual offenders'. Conceived of as a separate criminal class, perhaps even biological degenerates born to a life of crime, these men required a separate coercive apparatus for their control. Yet the category of the 'habitual offender' remained always sharply differentiated from its Indian counterpart. Despite the notion of a genetic predisposition to criminal behaviour, the English legislation encompassed only those already convicted of a crime, and never their children. It involved, that is, the identification of individuals, not the proscription of defined 'tribes'. Even the assertion that criminal behaviour was 'racially' grounded was far removed from the stigmatizing of everyone in a 'racial' group as a criminal. Despite the superficial similarity of the two enactments, the Indian Criminal Tribes act marked out a distinctively colonial ethnography. Even India's criminals were not similar to England's.

Incongruous though it might appear, the 1871 act included among the 'dangerous' classes not only the so-called criminal tribes, but eunuchs as well. James Fitzjames Stephen, as Law Member drafting the act, insisted that there existed 'an organized system of sodomitical prostitution, of which these wretches are the managers', and that no measure to force them to adopt 'honest pursuits' would be too severe. Although the subsequent discussion on the bill evoked much righteous indignation with regard to the eunuchs' alleged kidnapping and castration of children, what clearly disturbed the government as much as criminal behaviour, and what the act forbad, was the practice of eunuchs appearing in public dressed in female attire. Everyone, so the act implied, had not only to adopt a settled livelihood, but to conform to accepted gender roles. Sexual ambiguity could no more be tolerated than a life of 'wandering without leave'.[11]

Far more consequential were India's 'martial races'. Although these groups never achieved full statutory definition, in the years after the Mutiny a perceived sense of a distinctive martial fitness came to distinguish various peoples of northern India from those elsewhere, above all in Bengal. This process was driven by the imperatives of the military, who sought an army organized 'with a view to the full development of race efficiency.' Inbred martial skill, as G. F. MacMunn wrote in his definitive study of India's armies, defined one of the 'essential differences between the East and the West'. In the

[11] Stephen, Note of 4 July 1870, Home Judl., July 1870, no. 55–59; and Papers Relating to Act XXVII of 1871.

'East' only 'certain clans and classes can bear arms; the others have not the physical courage necessary for the warrior'. In Europe, by contrast, 'every able-bodied man, given food and arms, is a fighting man of some sort', and hence capable of serving his country in time of war.[12]

Initially, as Clive and his successors recruited an army for the East India Company, considerations of racial ability mattered little. Many regiments, especially in the southern armies, accepted all recruits and intermixed them without concern for caste or religion. The Bengal Army after 1800 in large part confined its recruitment to the higher castes, above all Brahmins and Rajputs, whose customs the British took care to conserve, and it drew the bulk of its soldiery from rural Oudh and Bihar. Though the upper castes, regarded as generally superior within Indian society, might be presumed to be better soldiers, and though 'a fine physique and martial appearance' might gain an individual the attention of the recruiting officers, no attempt was made to portray the men of these castes or regions as inherently better suited than others for military service.

After 1857 the mutinous Bengal regiments were disbanded, and the recruiting grounds shifted to the north, to the area from Delhi across the Punjab to the frontier. Simultaneously, mixed regiments were largely abandoned in favour of those organized on a systematic grouping of men by 'race and sept and clan'. This transformation was not the result of any historical experience, apart from the Mutiny itself, nor was it wholly a matter of tactical considerations of 'divide and rule'. Madrasis, Marathas, and the sepoys of the Bengal Army had fought well, both for the Company and against it, over the preceding half-century; and even during the upheaval of 1857 the mixed regiments of the southern armies had remained loyal. As a result, following the recommendations of the Peel Commission in 1859, many officers argued for a mixture of castes within units in order to avert exclusive combinations that might once again lead to mutiny. Yet so compelling was the logic of 'martial races' that by the 1880s almost the entire army was organized into units based on caste or ethnicity.

The notion of 'martial races' drew sustenance from a variety of elements in the cultural baggage of late Victorian England. As the Aryans had once conquered northern India, it was assumed that those races descended from them possessed superior military capabilities.

[12] G.F. MacMunn, *The Armies of India* (London, 1911), pp. 2, 129.

The Dogras, isolated in the hills, for instance, were presumed to retain the 'old Aryan Hindu stock'. Other groups, such as the Afridis, with close cropped fair hair and blue eyes of a 'distinctly European appearance', could well, so MacMunn reasoned, have kept intact 'traces' of Alexander's Greek soldiers. Where race failed – for MacMunn acknowledged that most 'martial' groups had lost their distinguishing racial characteristics – environment supplied an alternate explanation. Their 'hardy, active, and alert life' in a land of cold winters and often rugged mountains had 'inured' these northern peoples to hardship and thus fitted them for military life. A presumed camaraderie along the frontier, which we shall soon discuss more fully, also mattered. As MacMunn wrote of the Pathans, 'to the best type of Englishman their open, irresponsible manner and delight in all exercise and sport, with their constant high spirits, appeal greatly'. Whether defined by race, climate, or personality, 'martial races' were those who most closely resembled what the British imagined themselves to be. In similar fashion, 'martial races' existed in contrast to the Bengalis. Indeed, one might argue, the 'extraordinary effeminacy' of the Bengali, whom 'no necessity would induce to fight', alone gave meaning to the notion of 'martial races'. They were what the Bengali was not.[13]

In keeping with the larger principles informing the British idea of the caste system, each 'martial' race was conceived of as possessing its own distinctive set of characteristics – Jats, for instance, were 'proverbially thick in the uptake, but have served with distinction' – and these traits were all meticulously detailed in the various regimental recruiting handbooks. One group, however, that of the Sikhs, was not merely enrolled in the list of 'martial races', but came to predominate in the army, and in the process found their community transformed. As Richard Fox has made clear in his study of the 'Lions of the Punjab', the British, from the very outset, determined that only 'pure' Sikhs should be recruited. The British 'laboured hard to insure the religious conformity of the Sikh recruit', and not just to any version of Sikhism, but to what the British conceived was proper Sikh belief and practice. Potential recruits had to be baptised into the Sikh faith, while regimental commanders insisted upon a strict observance of those customs associated with reformed monotheistic Sikhism, among them unshorn hair, the wearing of the dagger and steel bangle, and taking the name of

---

[13] Ibid., *Armies*, chapter 5.

'Singh', or lion. As MacMunn acknowledged, it was the 'British officer who has kept Sikhism up to its old [sic] standard'.

By distinguishing a select group of Sikhs in this way, the British believed they could keep Sikhism free of contamination by 'unorthodox' forms of Sikh belief and, more generally, by Hinduism. Sikhism, after all, as they saw it, was a religion distinct from Hinduism, and, as a monotheistic faith, superior. Hence, as one official wrote, 'with the relapse into Hinduism and readoption of its superstitious and vicious social customs, it is notorious that the Sikh loses much of his martial instincts and greatly deteriorates as a fighting soldier'. This 'colonially constituted Sikhism', as Fox describes it, was ostensibly marked out by religious belief, for in principle anyone could be baptised. Yet in practice it embodied British racial ideas as well. Only 'true' Sikhs, men of proper 'stock', which usually meant those of certain prescribed regions and classes, possessed the necessary martial skills; others, of lower class background or recent conversion to the faith, were of inferior or 'deteriorated' stock, and so, with a few exceptions, such as the Mazhbis, were not recruited into the army. As the British endeavoured to put their ideology into practice, in the army as elsewhere the categories by which Indian society was ordered inevitably became confused.[14]

The British did not view Indian society only through the prism of race and caste. Descent, or 'tribal' affiliation, mattered as well. For the most part such genealogical connections were important insofar as they facilitated the resolution of disputes over landholding and inheritance among individual families. Settlement officers, and the courts, needed to know the principles by which estates were to be apportioned among heirs or princely thrones awarded to claimants. In the Punjab, however, the British made kinship the organizing principle of the entire society. This reflected, in part, their perception that in a province with a Muslim majority, 'caste', as an inherently Hindu phenomenon, could not by its very nature appropriately order rural society. In part, too, the constitution of Punjabi society on a unique basis was a logical continuation of the 'Punjab school' style of governance, based on direct and personal rule, and with it the use of local customary law, rather than the Bengal regulations, with their

---

[14] Richard G. Fox, *Lions of the Punjab: Culture in the Making* (Berkeley, 1985), chapter 8, especially pp. 140–52; MacMunn, *Armies*, pp. 133–40.

Sanskritic uniformities, for the adjudication of disputes. This determination to rule, so far as possible, in accordance with indigenous principles gained further strength from the unsettling experience of the 1857 rising, from which the Punjab had for the most part been exempt. Many officials, indeed, attributed this fortuitous escape from rebellion to the province's unique system of rule. As the British in the 1860s and 1870s studied the organization of Punjab society, the 'native institution' they found at its heart, as C. L. Tupper argued, while preparing his compendium of 'Punjab Customary Law', was the 'tribe', which he defined as a patrilineal descent group encompassing those who preserved the memory of a common ancestor. The British set out accordingly to define and systematize this 'tribal system', and so build it into their own imperial order. In so doing, so they believed, they could not only present themselves as legitimate indigenous rulers, presiding over an unaltered 'traditional' society, but they could also harness the Punjab's distinctive social forms, above all in the settlement of canal colonies, to the creation of a prosperous land.

Much in this endeavour involved an effort at self-delusion, for tradition, once systematized and enforced as 'tradition' in the courts, defined a new mode of governance far different from that which had gone before. Furthermore, even though the notion of a 'tribally' based Punjab was self-consciously grounded in British perceptions of local practice, it did not wholly accord with the social realities it purported to describe. Structures of descent varied across the face of the Punjab, as they did elsewhere; while few of the so-called 'tribes', especially in the central and eastern Punjab, had managed to preserve recognized traditions of leadership in the face of hostile Mughal and Sikh rulers. As a result, to provide an institutional footing for local leadership the British created the administrative unit of the *zail*, a grouping of five to forty villages found only in the Punjab. *Zaildars*, as heads of these local units, were meant to be simply existing leaders of locally dominant 'tribes' and 'clans', but in practice they were often created as the British sought to make Punjab society resemble the ideology that informed their conception of it. Nevertheless, by the end of the century, building upon existing patterns of contiguous settlement, grounded in bonds of solidarity among local kin groups, and reinforcing them where necessary by institutional means, the British had successfully brought into being a rural elite whose influence, as David

Gilmartin argues, 'was tied to the "ideology" of imperial authority on which the British had built their regime'.[15]

The final stage in the creation of a distinctive 'tribal' Punjab took place with the creation of the category of 'agricultural tribes' in the Land Alienation Act of 1900. The problem of land alienation, or, more precisely, the sale of land for debts owed to moneylenders, perceived as 'outsiders' in village society, had long concerned the British, in the Deccan and the Gangetic valley as well as in the Punjab. Though recent research has brought into question the scale and character of such transfers, their existence forced upon the British at the time an agonizing choice between, on the one hand, the 'modernizing' ideology of an India transformed by the free working of natural economic laws, which encouraged the transfer of property from the hands of 'unenterprising' owners, and, on the other, the ideal of a stable agrarian order kept in place by 'traditional' elites. In the Punjab there was little dissent from the notion that this strategic border province and recruiting ground for the army had to be preserved from agrarian upheaval. Hence, in a far-reaching assault on the privileges of those whom they saw as outsiders, the British prohibited the sale of land to anyone other than a member of a registered 'agricultural tribe'.

With the passage of the Land Alienation Act the British transformed the 'tribal' structure they had built up during the previous half-century. Grouped together into a single unit for the entire province, the 'agricultural tribes', as Gilmartin has pointed out, denoted no social reality, as each did to some degree in its own locality, but only a category which the British used to define who would have the right to own land, and hence the right to wield power within the colonial order. Despite its highly artificial character, however, the notion of 'agricultural tribes' soon took on a life of its own. Under the banner of the Land Alienation Act the province's rural elite, in cooperation with the British, successfully controlled Punjab politics throughout the first half of the twentieth century. Both the organization of the Unionist Party and the Punjabi response to Muslim nationalism before 1947, and even afterwards in Pakistan, demonstrated the enduring power of the ideology of a 'tribal' Punjab. No more than that of 'caste' could the notion of 'tribe' be contained within the colonial ideology that had originally shaped it.

---

[15] David Gilmartin, *Empire and Islam* (Berkeley, 1988), chapter 1.

8   *Monument to Warren Hastings*, by Richard Westmacott (1830).

SHAPING COMMUNITIES

Richard Westmacott's 1830 statue of Warren Hastings, now in the Victoria Memorial, shows him accompanied by two Indians, who flank him on either side, but stand well below the toga-clad imperial ruler. (See fig. 8.) One of the flanking figures, a tall, classically proportioned Brahmin with a shaven head and topknot, represented Hinduism; the other, a seated *munshi* or scribe, bearded and turbaned, and gazing thoughtfully at a book, was meant to stand for India's Muslim peoples. Both figures, garbed as scholars, were treated respectfully, and so reflected Hastings's sympathetic view of India's culture and its religious traditions. Yet they also announced what was to be Britain's enduring insistence that India was divided into two religious communities – those of Hinduism and of Islam.[16]

Division of India's people into Hindu and Muslim was not of course new in Hastings's time. The earliest British travellers even in Mughal times had been struck by the distinctive characteristics of the adherents of what they then called the 'Gentoo' faith. As Ralph Fitch, Queen Elizabeth's emissary to the emperor Akbar in 1584, wrote of the Hindus, 'They be the greatest idolators that I ever sawe.' Nor was his perception at all sympathetic; the idols, he declared, were 'blacke and evil favoured, their mouthes monstrous, their eares gilded, and full of jewels'. Such perceptions went back even further in time, to Marco Polo, who toured southern India, and to Alberuni and the medieval Muslim conquerors, as they contemplated the difference between themselves and those over whom they ruled. Yet the term 'Hindu', though of Perso-Arabic origin, was not used in Muslim texts to mark out a religion, but rather referred generally to the inhabitants of the Indian subcontinent, the lands across the Indus river. Even when the term 'Hindu' was used to set off those adhering to a non-Islamic faith, the perception each group had of the other, as Romila Thapar has written, 'was not in terms of a monolithic religion, but more in terms of distinct and disparate castes and sects along a social continuum'. From the Indian, or Hindu, side, the Central Asian invaders were

---

[16] For British statuary, see Barbara Groseclose, 'Imag(in)ing Indians', *Art History*, vol. 13 (1990), pp. 488–515.

demonized, but, Sheldon Pollock has pointed out, as incarnations of the evil Ravana, or as Turks, not as Muslims.[17]

Only with the coming of British rule, from the late eighteenth century on, did the notion that there existed distinct 'Hindu' and 'Muslim' communities in India take on a fixed shape. In part this was simply a product of administrative convenience, as the British sought to devise comprehensive systems of law that would at once respect the customs of their new subjects and yet reduce them to a manageable order. It is altogether appropriate that Hastings, who set on foot the codification of 'Hindu' and 'Muslim' law, should be commemorated by a statue showing him with a Brahmin pandit and a Muslim munshi. Yet from the outset distinctions of religion were seen as shaping those of character. Dow and Orme, as we have seen in chapter 1, had defined the basic differences demarcating the two religious groupings: Muslims were violent, despotic, masculine; Hindus were indolent, passive, effeminate. One fought by the sword; the other by cunning and litigation. However much William Jones and James Mill may have disagreed in evaluating the accomplishments of India's peoples, together they accepted without question their division into Hindu and Muslim. By the early nineteenth century authoritative conceptions of the two faiths, and the character of their adherents, had been set firmly in place.

More importantly, the British came to believe that adherence to one or the other of these two religions was not merely a matter of belief, but defined membership more generally in a larger community. To be Hindu or Muslim by itself explained much of the way Indians acted. Riotous behaviour, for instance, no matter what its actual character, as Gyan Pandey has made clear in his account of British reportage on riots in Banares, was often made to express enduring antagonisms between two opposed and self-contained communities.[18] In early nineteenth-century Britain too, of course, religious affiliation mattered intensely. Anglicans, Dissenters, and Catholics, from the time of the Reformation onward, had been set apart from each other by

---

17 W. Foster (ed.), *Early Travels in India, 1583–1619* (New York, 1921), especially pp. 14–23; Romila Thapar, 'Imagined Religious Communities? Ancient History and the Modern Search for a Hindu Identity', *Modern Asian Studies*, vol. 23 (1989), pp. 209–31; Sheldon Pollock, 'Ramayana and Political Imagination in India', *Journal of Asian Studies*, vol. 52 (1993), pp. 261–97.

18 Gyanendra Pandey, 'The Colonial Construction of "Communalism": British Writings on Banares in the Nineteenth Century', in Ranajit Guha (ed.), *Subaltern Studies VI* (Delhi, 1989), pp. 132–68.

Sabbath observance, attitudes to liquor, marriage networks, and education, with each community maintaining its own schools. Until well into the nineteenth century the state awarded the right to vote on the basis of religious affiliation, and even the 1870 act, which committed the state to support of education, authorized only the disbursal of funds to religious bodies. Yet, however much religion may have informed British life, it was never imagined, apart from the exceptional case of Ireland, as having the power to shape the entire society into opposed 'communities'. Symptomatic perhaps of the difference was the prominence given to religious affiliation as a 'fundamental category' in the Indian census, while in Britain the census, apart from one survey in 1851, never recorded data on religion. The centrality of religious community, along with that of caste, for the British marked out India's distinctive status as a fundamentally different land.

British 'understanding' of Hinduism, unlike that of Islam, developed only with the discoveries of the Oriental scholars in the late eighteenth century. Whereas Europeans had since medieval times created a rich descriptive tradition for Islam, perceived as an enemy and an alternate religious system known from bitter experience, Hinduism long remained obscure, a mysterious faith of 'idols' and 'monstrosities'. Furthermore, as the British scrambled to understand Hinduism, they created for that religious system a degree of coherence that it had not possessed before. Indeed, one might almost say, by imposing their 'knowledge' upon it, the British made of Hinduism, previously a loosely integrated collection of sects, something resembling a religion – although, as they saw it, a religion that was not a 'proper' religion. To the present day scholars of religion still remain at odds over the extent to which the Hinduism of pre-colonial India can be described as a 'religion', with an orthodoxy that defines the faith of a set of believers, as distinct from a set of beliefs and practices embedded in India's larger social order.

Initially, the British sought an organizing principle for Hinduism in the Brahmin community. As the highest caste, as priests, and, in Jones's time, as collaborators in the study of the ancient Sanskrit texts, Brahmins were naturally perceived as the focal point of the faith, and with it of the Hindu community. Ever since Fitch's time commentators had singled out for notice the habits and customs of the Brahmins, whether their wearing of the sacred thread or, as Fitch announced, that they 'eatt no flesh, nor kill any thing; they live of rice, butter, milke, and fruits'. For James Mill, the Brahmins, creators of the caste system, were a primary cause of the country's 'degradation'. 'By a system of priestcraft', he wrote, 'built upon the most enormous and tormenting superstition that ever harassed and degraded any portion of mankind', the minds of the Hindus 'were enchained more intolerably than their bodies'. In all such descriptions of Hinduism, Victorian commentators, steeped in Protestantism, turned inevitably to Catholicism, with its practices ranging from 'popery' to saint worship, as providing a European parallel, and an appropriate vocabulary through which the Hindu faith might be understood.

As time went on Europeans extended and refined their knowledge of the texts that embodied the Hindu faith. Much of this was the work of German Indological scholars, from the philospher Hegel and the Romantic idealist Friedrich Schlegel to the Sanskritist Max Muller. Together these men fitted India's ancient philosophical texts into a larger vision in which, as Ronald Inden has indicated, Mill's 'more or less disconnected examples of Hindu irrationality and superstition' gave way to a view of Hinduism as a system of 'dream-like knowledge' dominated by a 'creative imagination'. These German scholars did not, of course, construct their philosophical systems with the aim of advancing the administrative objectives of the Raj. Nevertheless, as their world view made of the Indian mind, 'imaginative and passionate', a foil for Christian and Western 'rationality', it necessarily carried with it the assumption that the Hindus, unable to supply this element themselves, required an externally imposed 'rationality' to order their day-to-day lives. Hence, Germanic Indology, though never directly a part of the ideology of the Raj, by creating a coherent vision of the 'Hindu mind' that at once incorporated it into a larger ordering of the world and yet subordinated it to the West, played a critical role in sustaining the intellectual assumptions that bulwarked Britain's Indian Empire. The vision of a 'spiritual' India, in contrast to a 'materialist' West, was never incompatible with the existence of the Raj.[19]

Simultaneously, during the middle decades of the nineteenth century, the British in India endeavoured to come to terms with the variety of Hindu religious experience they were encountering on the ground. The attempt to comprehend contemporary Hinduism was, however, a frustrating enterprise. Alfred Lyall, one of the more careful

[19] Inden, *Imagining India*, chapter 3, especially pp. 89–96.

students of Indian religion in the government, came close to throwing up his hands in despair. We can scarcely comprehend, he wrote, 'an ancient religion, still alive and powerful, which is a mere troubled sea, without shore or visible horizon, driven to and fro by the winds of boundless credulity and grotesque invention'. The range and diversity of worship, with beliefs undergoing 'constant changes of shape and colour' within an 'extraordinary fecundity of superstitious sentiment', made Hindu India, in his view, unlike anywhere else in the world.[20]

The British sought to make sense of this 'religious chaos' in two ways. First, rather like Maine's account of the village community, the British saw in Hinduism a 'survival' of the ancient world. Even Mill had argued that, 'by conversing with the Hindus of the present day, we, in some measure, converse with the Chaldeans and Babylonians of the time of Cyrus; with the Persians and Egyptians of the time of Alexander'. For Lyall the popular Hinduism of his day was very similar to the polytheism of the Roman Empire. Indeed, he wrote, 'We perceive more clearly what classic polytheism was by realizing what Hinduism actually is.' The second strategy was to insist upon the centrality of 'Brahmanism' as the historic core of the Hindu faith, and to regard so-called popular, or devotional, Hinduism as a 'whole vegetation of cognate beliefs sprouting up in every stage of growth beneath the shadow of the great orthodox traditions and allegories of Brahmanism'.

But why had Hinduism not progressed beyond ancient polytheism to a 'true' monotheism? To some extent men like Lyall found an answer in the absence of a central ecclesiastical structure capable of disciplining popular practice. But for a larger explanation the British turned to Aryan racial theory. Popular Hinduism, in this view, was the inevitable outcome of the settling of the Aryan invader in a tropical land, where his 'pure' faith became mixed with the fertility cults and superstitions of the subcontinent's aboriginal peoples. Contemporary Hinduism was, as the Sanskrit scholar Monier-Williams described it, using the metaphor of the jungle, 'Brahminism run to seed and spread out into a confused tangle of divine personalities and incarnations. The one system is the rank and luxuriant outcome of the other.' Lyall in similar terms compared religious practice in India to the 'entangled confusion of a primeval forest, where one sees trees of all kinds, ages, and sizes interlacing and contending with each other'. Above the tree

[20] Lyall, *Asiatic Studies* (1884), chapter 1, and the revised edition (London, 1904), chapter 5.

tops a 'glimpse of blue sky' symbolized the 'illimitable transcendental ideas' of Brahmanic speculation above and apart from earth-born conceptions. India's essential Dravidianism, its 'femininity', and its popular Hinduism, were all the same and interchangeable; and together debarred forever any recovery of its former Aryan self.[21]

Such attempts at ordering Hinduism achieved only a partial success. Even Lyall's detailed account of the 'religion of an Indian province', that of Berar, where he had served in the 1860s, though it served as a model for subsequent studies of popular Hinduism, did little more than catalogue some eleven modes of religious practice, ranging from the worship of stones and animals to that of deceased persons and local heroes. In the late eighteenth and early nineteenth century, with the Brahmins as collaborators, and the ancient texts to guide them, the British, and subsequently the German Indologists, had constructed a coherent notion of Hinduism, and of a Hindu community, that took shape in the codes of Hindu personal law. A century later, their knowledge of Hinduism no longer confined to a tidy set of texts, the British instead found themselves confronted with Lyall's 'tangled jungle of disorderly superstitions'. In such circumstances, to deploy the term 'Hindu', even as an overarching category, was always diffi-cult. The decennial censuses, which from 1881 onward marshalled the members of India's religions into 'communities', mapped, counted, and above all, as Kenneth Jones has noted, compared each with its rivals. Yet, even so, the category 'Hindu' remained exceptionally elusive. As the Punjab census commissioner reported in 1881, 'Every native who was unable to define his creed, or who described it by any other name than that of some recognized religion ... was held to be and classed as a Hindu.'[22]

In many ways it suited British purposes not to press forward too vigorously with the consolidation of Hinduism. The adherents of that faith, after all, a majority of India's population, if accorded an autono-mous sense of identity, posed a potentially menacing alternative to the Raj. The British thus turned instead to local custom and caste as more useful categories through which to make sense of Indian society. Though the codes of Hindu law still embodied the ideology of Hastings's time, more localized identities informed much of legal and

---

[21] Ibid., (1904), p. 318; Inden, *Imagining India*, pp. 109–22.
[22] Kenneth W. Jones, 'Religious Identity and the Indian Census', in Barrier (ed.), *The Census*, pp. 73–101.

administrative practice outside Bengal. This process was perhaps most visibly manifested in the recording and codification of Punjab customary law. Here overarching religious identities, whether of Hinduism or Islam, as we have seen, were set aside in favour of principles drawn from the secular ordering of kin and clan. Caste, in particular, was convenient, for it afforded (or so the British thought) a precise way of knowing, and so controlling, Indian society at the local level, and it could be seen in any case as incorporating much that was distinctive about Hinduism. With the rare exception of such reformist groups as the Brahmo and Arya Samaj, seen as hopeful portents of a 'purer' faith, the late-nineteenth-century ethnographic enterprise was based upon caste, rather than sect. In many reports and statistical tables a commonly used heading was 'Caste if Hindu, otherwise religion'. The shaping of a compelling sense of 'Hindu' identity was to be a product only of the twentieth century, and the work of Hindus themselves.

Islam, by contrast, possessed for the British (if not always for its adherents) an established coherence. The long and intimate connection of Islam with Europe, from the time of the Crusades onward, had provided Europeans with an assured sense of 'knowing' Islam, and Muslims, that did not exist as they endeavoured to understand Hindus and Hinduism. As James Mill noted, 'With the state of civilization in Persia the instructed part of European readers are pretty familiar.' This contrasted sharply with the 'mysterious, and little known' state of civilization among the Hindus. One might argue that in India two different Orientalist discourses met: one derived from the European encounter with the Muslim Middle East; the other an attempt to describe distant Asian lands where a tropical climate shaped passive and effeminate peoples. Insofar as India's pre-colonial states were frequently constituted as Islamic polities, and Muslims provided the dominant elite within them, it was easy to project the stereotypes constructed in the Middle East upon India's Muslims. In so doing, Muslims were inevitably distinguished sharply from their Hindu neighbours, and included within the alternate set of Orientalist notions of the 'East'. Shaped by these two contrasting discourses, the two communities found themselves counterposed, at first imaginatively and then in the strife of 'communalism', one against the other.[23]

The distinguishing features of India's Muslims, as we have seen,

---

[23] Mill, chapter 10, esp. p. 304; see also Ronald Inden, 'Orientalist Constructions of India', *Modern Asian Studies*, vol. 20 (1986), especially pp. 404–8, 423–24.

were laid out by Dow and Orme in the mid-eighteenth century. With 'despotism' as the central representational mode, the country's Muslims not surprisingly were depicted as fierce invaders, who as rulers alternated arbitrary violence with indolence and self-indulgence. While the Mughals, perceived as 'mild and humane' rulers, were largely exempted from severe criticism, such was not the case with their eighteenth-century successors. These, whom the British set out to supplant as they extended their own rule, had to be painted in the darkest colours. The archetypical representative of Islam in this period was unquestionably Tipu Sultan of Mysore (ruler from 1782 to 1799). As both a Muslim sovereign and an implacable opponent of the British Raj, he was portrayed (with no factual basis) as a man driven by a zealous fanaticism, while his regime was described as 'the most perfect despotism in the world'. In keeping with the differing characterizations projected onto Muslims and Hindus, his 'Mahommedan tyranny' was contrasted unfavourably with the 'ancient Hindoo constitution' allegedly enjoyed by Mysore before Tipu's father Haider Ali took over the throne in 1761. Tipu's fall at Seringapatnam in 1799 unloosed an orgy of self-congratulation among the British at their triumph, and seemed to justify alike British rule over India and the depiction of Muslims enunciated a half-century earlier by men like Alexander Dow.[24]

As Britain's Muslim opponents in India were either displaced or reduced to the status of pensioners, condemnation of their 'despotic' rule receded into the background, where it took its place as a part of the larger historiography of the 'misrule' and 'decadence' of the eighteenth century. Suspicion nevertheless continued to shape much of the way the British conceived their Indian Muslim subjects. Throughout the first half of the nineteenth century the British remained convinced that resentment at their supersession as rulers had generated among Muslims an inevitable and implacable hostility toward their successors. Hence, the 1857 revolt, though it originated in the army and found supporters among Hindus and Muslims alike throughout northern India, was widely viewed as a product of enduring Muslim animosity. The young Alfred Lyall, less than two years in India at the time, in the midst of the uprising wrote that 'the whole insurrection is a great Mahometan conspiracy, and the sepoys are merely tools in the hands of the Mussulmans'. He went on to differen-

[24] For British representations of Tipu, see Bayly, *Raj*, pp. 152–60.

tiate between the behaviour of Muslim and of Hindu rebels. For Hindus 'plunder always seems to be their chief object, to attain which they will perform any villainy, whereas the Mahometans only seem to care about murdering their opponents, and are altogether far more bloody minded'. These last, he insisted, 'hate us with a fanatical hate that we never suspected to exist'.[25]

Such hostility was not, however, so the British conceived, simply a product of the grievances of former rulers. As Lyall concluded of India's Muslims, 'there is something in their religion that makes warriors of them'. In similar fashion John Lawrence spoke of the Muslim mutineers as possessing 'a more active, vindictive, and fanatic spirit' than their Hindu compatriots; but, he argued, this was only to be expected, for these traits were 'characteristic of the race'. Such behaviour, that is, had its origin in the very nature of Islam as a religion, and it could be traced back to the religion's beginnings in Arabia. As William Muir, later author of a life of Muhammad, wrote in October 1857, among Muslims 'all the ancient feelings of warring for the Faith, reminding one of the days of the first Caliphs, were resuscitated'.[26]

Such views did not dissipate with the suppression of the uprising. Into the 1860s and 1870s this aura of suspicion remained a powerful force shaping British conceptions of their Muslim subjects. Constantly on the alert for outbreaks of violence, the British saw above all in the so-called 'Wahabi' movement, which sought a return to a purified Islam, evidence, as the Punjab government wrote in 1862, of the gathering together of 'the tribes of Islam' to 'wage a holy war against the Faringhi'. Increasingly, however, monolithic notions of Muslim hostility gave way, in part because the British began to enter into dialogue with Muslims themselves, and in part also because varied notions of who the Muslims were, and what interests they represented, began to emerge. The result was an ambivalence which at once revealed the contradictory visions of Islam the British themselves possessed, and opened the way to one of the more enduring imperial myths – that of the 'Frontier'. This re-evaluation was provoked by the publication in 1871 of W.W. Hunter's *The Indian Mussalmans*, a

---

[25] Letters to his father, 11 July and 30 August 1857, in IOL MS. Eur. F132/3.
[26] Cited in Peter Hardy, *The Muslims of British India* (Cambridge, 1972), chapter 3, especially pp. 62–63, 71–73.

volume which posed in stark terms the question of whether these British subjects were 'bound to rebel against the Queen'.

Hunter opened his account with a stirring vision of seething discontent among India's Muslims. For years, he said, 'a Rebel Colony has threatened our Frontier; from time to time sending forth fanatic swarms, who have attacked our camps, burned our villages, [and] murdered our subjects'. From this 'hostile settlement', he continued, 'a network of conspiracy has spread itself over our Provinces', so that 'the bleak mountains which rise beyond the Punjab are united by a chain of treason depots with the tropical swamps through which the Ganges merges into the sea'. This 'fanatic colony', Hunter asserted, owed its origin to the reformer Saiyyid Ahmad Barelvi, whose preaching of a purified Islam during the 1820s, after his return from the pilgrimage to Mecca, had roused 'frantic enthusiasm' among those 'most turbulent and most superstitious of the Muhammadan Peoples', the Pathan tribesmen of the northwest. No one could predict, he wrote, 'the proportions to which this Rebel Camp, backed by the Musalman hordes from the Westward, might attain, under a leader who knew how to weld together the nations of Asia in a Crescentade'. Here, within his first pages, Hunter evoked a number of what were subsequently to become central elements in British imagery as it related to India's Muslims: an obsession with 'conspiracy', an acknowledgement of the power of reformist preaching, and an assertion of a unique character setting off the Pathans from the other Muslim peoples of the subcontinent.

The central objective of Hunter's work was to urge upon the government a policy toward Muslims less unyieldingly hostile than the condemnation that had marked the period from Tipu Sultan to the Mutiny. In so doing Hunter sought to distinguish between the 'fanatical masses', and the 'landed and clerical interests'. The latter, he insisted, 'bound up by a common dread of change', had no interest in the reformist enthusiasms of the Wahabi movement, for such 'dissent' was necessarily 'perilous to vested rights'. Hence by a more equitable treatment of these classes, especially in Bengal where a century of dispossession had stored up a host of grievances, they could be prompted to support the British government. More generally, Hunter urged upon the government a broad support for Muslim education, and held out the vision of a 'rising generation' of Muslims, no longer 'imbued solely with the bitter doctrines of their own medieval Law, but tinctured with the sober and genial knowledge of the West'.

Despite its obsession with 'conspiracy', Hunter's *The Indian Muss-almans* laid out a new policy initiative that, pushed forward by the successive viceroys Mayo and Northbrook, was to lead to a new alliance with India's Muslim elites, above all with men such as Sayyid Ahmad Khan, whose Cambridge-styled Aligarh college gave visible shape to Hunter's vision. Yet this vision was not itself free of ambivalence. Though Hunter sought an alliance with the 'comfortable classes', those 'of inert conviction and some property', for he appreciated that the support of these men was essential for the stability of the Raj, at the same time he could not shake off a sympathy for the Frontier reformers themselves. As representatives of 'the bravest races in the world', they had from their mountain fastnesses time and again successfully defied the 'combined strategy and weight of a civilized Army' sent to subdue them. It was, he said, 'inexpressibly painful' that these, 'the best men', were not 'on our side'. Nor was their religious zeal, with its cry for a purification of Islamic practice, wholly unattractive. In Hunter's view the Wahabi faith was a 'simple system of puritanic belief', whose adherents devoted themselves to bringing their countrymen to a 'purer life and a truer conception of the Almighty'. Expressing his own Protestant sympathies, Hunter compared the Wahabis, engaged in the 'great work of purifying the creed of Muhammad', to Hildebrand's monks, who had 'purged the Church of Rome'.

Islamic reform, then, represented an ideal both of faith and of practice toward which, even as they denounced it, the British found themselves drawn. In part this attraction involved a romantic yearning for a simpler life of the sort they imagined to have existed in the 'merry England' of old, and which they sought now, as we shall see presently, to reconstruct on the Frontier. But Islam exerted an appeal of its own. The spread of Western education would, to be sure, help make Muslims 'less fanatical', and so propel them away from a 'mistaken' religion to a 'higher level of belief' in Christianity. Yet it also would mean, as Hunter saw it, that the Islamic faith, like that of his own Christian contemporaries, would become 'less sincere', with the educated sons 'less earnest' in their belief than their untutored fathers. Such a transformation was an occasion not only for rejoicing but for regret; for among late-Victorian Englishmen, who doubted their faith but still wished to believe, the rigorous monotheism of the Wahabi preacher offered a reassurance they could no longer find in themselves. As Alfred Lyall wrote, 'The Mahomedan faith has still at least a dignity, and a courageous unreasoning certitude, which in western Christianity have been perceptibly melted down ... by long exposure to the searching light of European rationalism.' The 'clear, unwavering formula of Islam' by contrast 'carried one plain line straight up toward heaven like a tall obelisk pointing direct to the sky'.[27]

Lyall was critical of Hunter's insistence that British policy had antagonized India's Muslims. The Muslims were, he argued, by the very nature of their faith 'distinctively aggressive and spiritually despotic', prejudiced against Christians by 'the religious rivalry of a thousand years'. For this reason there was no point, as Hunter had suggested, in endeavouring to conciliate them. All that the British could profitably do was 'to keep the peace and clear the way' for the 'rising tide of intellectual advancement'. As for himself, Lyall never ceased being mistrustful of Muslims. As he wrote in his poem 'Badminton':

> Near me a Mussalman civil and mild,
>> Watched as the shuttled cocks rose and fell;
> And he said, as he counted his beads and smiled,
>> 'God smite their souls to the depths of Hell.'

Still, unlike the effeminate Hindus, the Muslims were 'worthy' opponents. Hence, despite his administrator's pride in the 'progress' the Raj had brought to India, Lyall could not resist the romanticized vision of the 'sturdy' Muslim who defied Hindu and Christian alike. In 'The Pindaree' he expressed this enduring tension through the voice of an old warrior who had fought the British in Central India, but who now saw his children in school and the 'Settlement Hakim' come 'to teach us to plough and to weed'. As Lyall wrote in the final verse of the poem:

> And if I were forty years younger, with my life before me to choose,
> I wouldn't be lectured by Kaffirs, or bullied by fat Hindoos;
> But I'd go to some far-off country where Musalmans still are men,
> Or take to the jungle, like Cheetoo, and die in the tiger's den.

Others too, as they confronted Islam, found themselves torn between condemnation and admiration. Sir Richard Temple, for instance, described Islam bitterly as a religion that 'withers human

[27] Lyall, *Asiatic Studies* (1904), p. 289.

character as with a blight, warps all the feelings and sentiments ... and rivets all customs and opinions in a groove'. Still, he acknowledged, 'there remains something of grandeur about it'. Though 'really opposed to human progress', he wrote, echoing Hunter and Lyall, 'yet it reigns in the affections of many millions of bright-eyed and strong-handed men'. Above all, it had not 'the many absurdities about it which Hinduism has'.[28] Thus this faith, and its adherents, were inevitably set apart, with Christianity, from the 'vast swamp', as Lyall called it, of Indian religious belief. Islam in the end was a religion which commanded respect, even a covert envy, among the British in India. From the views of men like Lyall it was but a short distance to the Islamic enthusiasms of Sir Richard Burton and Wilfred Scawen Blunt.

As Hunter urged upon the government a policy of conciliation toward India's Muslim elites, at the same time his writing gave new life to the idea of the Frontier as a land set apart, where conspiracy and 'fanaticism' flourished. To be sure, this vision of 'conspiracy' was grounded in the reality of a frontier always hard to control. Many frontier districts, left in the hands of tribute-paying chiefs, were never fully subdued, and two Afghan wars, in 1838–42 and 1879–80, had cost Britain dearly. Very rarely, however, did Islamic movements by themselves, even that of the Wahabis, pose a significant threat to the Raj. As James Fitzjames Stephen observed, by the time Hunter's book was published the Wahabi movement had been in existence 'for forty years more or less and would probably become formidable only if it came to be connected with other causes of disaffection'. Yet, as he pointed out, on the one recent occasion when their participation might have made a difference, that of the 1857 Mutiny, these 'conspirators' had remained aloof.[29] Nevertheless, the romanticized 'myth' of the Frontier grew ever more compelling as the years went by. The young Winston Churchill, for instance, described the origin of the 1897 rising in the following terms: 'Messengers passed to and fro among the tribes. Whispers of war, a holy war, were breathed to a race intensely passionate and fanatical.' Curzon too spoke of the frontier tribes as 'inured to religious fanaticism and hereditary rapine'.[30]

---

[28] Richard Temple, *Oriental Experience* (London, 1883), pp. 147, 315.
[29] Cited in Hardy, *Muslims*, p. 87.
[30] David B. Edwards, 'Mad Mullahs and Englishmen: Discourse in the Colonial Encounter', *Comparative Studies in Society and History*, vol. 31 (1989), pp. 649–70; Curzon of

Behind the fascination with the Frontier lay of course the looming menace of a Russian advance into Central Asia, and the consequent necessity to secure a friendly Afghanistan as a buffer state. Yet, even in Tashkent, the Russians were far away, separated from India by the towering Hindu Kush mountains. Considerations of strategic rivalry alone therefore cannot wholly account for the imaginative appeal of the Frontier. Rather, one might argue, the Frontier embodied, in compelling fashion, the enduring tension between the ideas of similarity and difference that shaped the British vision of India. This tension is perhaps most clearly captured in Kipling's famous poem 'The Ballad of East and West'. The opening stanza insists on difference, and yet, in the context of the Frontier, on similarity as well:

> Oh, East is East, and West is West, and never the twain shall meet,
> Till Earth and Sky stand presently at God's great Judgment Seat,
> But there is neither East nor West, Border, nor Breed, nor Birth,
> When two strong men stand face to face, though they come from the ends of the earth!

The poem goes on to describe the pursuit of an Afghan horse thief by a young British officer. Led deep into rebel held territory, the officer is spared by his antagonist, who in turn entrusts his own son to his charge. In the end:

> They have looked each other between the eyes, and there they found no fault.
> They have taken the Oath of the Brother-in-Blood on leavened bread and salt:
> They have taken the Oath of the Brother-in-Blood on fire and fresh-cut sod,
> On the hilt and the haft of the Khyber knife, and the Wondrous Names of God.

Upon this imagined Frontier the Pathan, while continuing to express much of the religious zeal the British saw as characteristic of Islam, was made also to play a distinctive role as a foil to the British themselves. Initially, in the years immediately after conquest, the Pathans, their hardy defiance sustained by remote mountain retreats, were portrayed as 'bloodthirsty, cruel, and vindictive', or as Richard Temple put it, 'thievish and predatory to the last degree'; and they

Kedleston, *Speeches on India Delivered while in England in July–August 1904* (London, 1904), pp. 8, 16.

were granted only a grudging recognition of their 'courage and gallantry'. Soon, however, the positive elements in this 'mixture of opposite vices and virtues' came to be ever more enthusiastically embraced. As men moved by passion rather than reason, the Pathans might possess the qualities belonging to 'savages', but they were a type of the 'noble savage'. If the Bengali, as Lewis Wurgaft has argued, was the 'spoiled child' of British India, the Pathan was, by contrast, the 'natural' child. In his 'barbarity and utter disregard for instinctual limitations' he embodied a 'fierce and admirable independence of spirit'. On the Frontier, so the British believed, they and their opponents, like the British officer and the Afghan of Kipling's poem, could look each other in the eye, and, moved by codes of heroism and honour, fight as men. Whereas the Bengali threatened the Englishman by caricature, the Pathan was an idealized alter-ego, the 'half-barbarian' warrior lurking in himself.[31]

This insistence on the Frontier's unique character, set apart from India, extended to the landscape itself. At once harsh and beautiful, 'indescribeable in its clarity and contrast with the barren emptiness that went before', its climate marked by 'sharp, cruel' extremes, this land, 'woven into the souls and bodies of the men who move before it', as the Frontier governor Olaf Caroe wrote, moved the British by its contrast with a 'soft' and 'civilized' India. As much of the attraction of Islam was its similarity to the faith they wished they still possessed, so too did the Frontier, even as the British denounced its 'savageness', evoke a romantic ideal of simplicity, together with an untrammelled masculinity. On the Frontier it was possible to escape the confining life of rules and regulations, of artifice and effeminacy, of the India of the plains. The 'clean, manly, vigorous life' of the frontier, as Wurgaft has put it, where women were altogether absent, and where Englishman and Pathan confronted each other in open warfare, 'allowed the most unconflicted expression of male aggressiveness'. At the same time, away from the 'dust and stink' of an India suffused with a debilitating female sexuality, the Frontier provided an arena where a suppressed homoerotic excitement might find an outlet.

The purely male world of the Frontier evoked too for the British the days of their boyhood. The Frontier, so they believed, like the public school, 'tested the man'. Its encounters, in this view, were like games,

---

[31] Lewis Wurgaft, *The Imperial Imagination: Magic and Myth in Kipling's India* (Middletown CT, 1983), chapter 1.

in which one fought to win, but in which there was no malice when the whistle blew and the game was over; it was 'our chaps' versus 'your chaps'. On a larger scale, involving the Afghans and the Russians, the Frontier was of course the locale of the 'Great Game', of which Kipling wrote so evocatively in *Kim*, and whose ideal Pathan was Mahbub Ali the horsetrader, wild yet tamed to the service of the Raj. The Pathan's own code of behaviour, as the anthropologist Akbar Ahmed has shown, was of crucial importance in facilitating the enactment of these schoolboy fantasies; for the concepts of honour, courage, and loyalty which shaped Pathan life were not wholly at odds with those the British cherished themselves. Hence it was possible to conceive of the Pathans as 'someone not at your school but who could take a beating in the boxing ring or rugger without complaining, who could give as good as he got'. For the Pathans, however, the colonial encounter was no game, but a struggle for survival. They did not play it as a matter of choice.[32]

Even for the British, the 'Great Game' was never just a game, for death was always possible on the recurrent border raids. Apart from the two deadly Afghan Wars, however, there was never desperate combat on the frontier. Fantasies could thus be safely indulged, conspiracies imagined, and tribal risings confronted with a display of manly heroism. The Muslims, eternally plotting on the border, even the occasional raids themselves, provided a *frisson* of excitement not to be found in the dull round of life in court and camp. They provided a distraction too from the onerous task of coming to terms with the challenge posed from within, after the 1880s, by the educated Indians. One might argue that the existence of a safely distant threat gave the British a necessary sense of duty, validating the Raj in its self-appointed task of securing the peace of the subcontinent.

At once opponents and allies, a romanticized Self and a threatening Other, the Muslims were, during the later decades of the nineteenth century, shaped into a community strikingly different from India's Hindus. This vision was never free of ambivalence, nor did it accord at all closely with that of the Muslims themselves. While Hunter saw in the Wahabi reformers men of a 'pure' faith, Sayyid Ahmad Khan, as a self-styled 'cosmopolitan' Muslim, found nothing attractive in these

---

[32] Akbar S. Ahmed, 'The Colonial Encounter on the North-West Frontier: Myth and Mystification', *Journal of the Anthropological Society of Oxford*, vol. 9 (1978), pp. 167–74.

'wild denizens of the hills', worshippers of tombs and saints. Muslims, he insisted, should work peaceably alongside the British as they 'purified' their faith. Yet Sayyid Ahmad, with Hunter and the British, accepted as fact the existence of enduring differences between 'the two races' of Hindus and Muslims. By the end of the nineteenth century, this insistence that India was divided into two opposed religious communities shaped the way not only the British, but increasing numbers of Indians, viewed their society. Nor did even those liberal dissenters who refused to abandon the ideals of an India remade ever question the country's division into Hindu and Muslim, or challenge the stereotypes defining these communities. For E.M. Forster, as much as for Lyall or Hunter, Hindus and Muslims were set apart from one another. The characters of Dr Aziz and Godbole in *A Passage to India* represented conventions of descriptive writing about the two communities whose origins could be traced back to Alexander Dow.

ORDERING INDIA'S PAST – AND ITS PRESENT

As part of their larger project of defining the enduring elements of India's society, the British set out to order its past, and its present. It was not enough simply to assert the existence of a continuing 'decline' from antiquity, nor to insist upon the recurrence of 'anarchy' whenever the strong hand of the invader was lifted. The British were determined not only to recover India's past, as part of the larger Victorian fascination with the ancient world, but to order this past into a coherent narrative that extended up to the present. In so doing, the British could, or so they imagined, create a secure and usable past in India for themselves. They were to be at once invaders from outside, and rulers from within. India's history was to comprehend alike the stupa of Sanchi and the ruins of the Lucknow Residency, India's enduring 'difference' and Britain's 'civilizing' mission.

At the heart of this enterprise was a massive archaeological survey in which all of India's ancient sites and monuments were to be authoritatively described, evaluated, and related to each other. The earliest archaeological work, in the years before the Mutiny, was at once haphazard and driven largely by individual expectations of unearthing objects of rarity and value. Likely looking mounds were dug open, while coins and statues were removed to private collections even by British officials. The East India Company's government, preoccupied with conquest and administration, paid little attention. As the viceroy, Lord Canning, wrote in 1862, when establishing the post of archaeological surveyor, the Indian government had neglected the 'duty' of 'placing on record, for the instruction of future generations', the 'early history of England's great dependency'. It will not be to our credit, he argued, 'as an enlightened ruling power, if we continue to allow such fields of investigation as the remains of the old Buddhist capital in Behar, the vast ruins of Kanouj, the plains round Delhi, studded with ruins more thickly than even the Campagna of Rome, and many others', to remain unexplored and unprotected. During the subsequent four years, until 1865, Alexander Cunningham, military officer and self-made archaeologist, undertook the series of tours which marked the beginning of organized archaeological activity in India.

On his tours Cunningham determined to 'follow the footsteps' of Alexander the Great and the Chinese Buddhist pilgrim Huen Tsiang, who travelled in India in the seventh century AD. For the first two years, starting at Mathura, Cunningham followed Huen Tsiang down the Gangetic valley; then in 1863–4 he began in the western Punjab near the Indus river, and gradually 'worked my way to the eastward in company with the Macedonian soldiers of Alexander'. Cunningham justified this selection of routes by arguing that they would lead him directly to the great sites of antiquity. Yet in following Alexander he clearly sought as well to associate the British, though they had conquered India from the east and south, with the historic invaders of the subcontinent, who, in his view, had brought it enlightenment and order, and had 'entered India from the West'.[33]

In retracing these ancient routes Cunningham inevitably let the Chinese pilgrim and the Greek conqueror determine the places of historic importance in northern India. As he wrote of the Punjab, the 'most interesting subject of enquiry' was 'the identification of those famous peoples and cities whose names have become familiar to the whole world through the expedition of Alexander the Great'. In similar fashion, he argued, the 'travels of the Chinese pilgrim' hold 'the same place in the history of India which those of Pausanias hold in the history of Greece'. The sites visited by these two ancient travellers, and thus described by Cunningham, were largely those associated

[33] Archeological Survey of India, *Four Reports Made During the Years 1862, 1863, 1864, and 1865 by Alexander Cunningham*, 2 vols (reprinted, Delhi, 1972).

with the era of Buddhist predominance in India. Cunningham's pre-occupation with such sites was, however, not surprising; for, as we have seen, the great Buddhist monuments, especially those of the far northwest influenced by Greek aesthetic ideals, defined for the British of the Victorian era the high point of ancient India's civilization. The Buddhist monuments too, as the Harappan civilization was as yet unknown, marked out the oldest sites to be found in India, and hence claimed the attention of a British public fascinated by the search for origins.

After his 1865 tour Cunningham was dismissed and sent home by a government, that of John Lawrence, loath to spend money on such pursuits. During the subsequent few years the provincial governments sponsored photographic tours by various amateurs, such as Captain Edmund Lyon in Madras, and drew up extensive lists of 'ancient architectural structures or remains' within their territories. During these years too the government sought to make available for the British public the finest of India's antiquities. From among the ruins of Sarnath, for instance, some sixty-five objects, deemed to 'possess the greatest interest and throw the most light on the manners and habits of former ages', were set aside for shipment to England by the East India Company directors in 1858. Enterprising officials devised schemes as well to take casts of the largest monuments. Most ambitious was the complete casting of one of the massive gates of the Sanchi stupa. Bearing orders from three British museums and the French and Prussian governments, Lt. H. H. Cole came to India in 1869 accompanied by some 28 tons of gelatin and plaster of paris. From Jabalpur, at the end of the railway line, the material was conveyed to Sanchi in 60 carts, and the whole casting, when completed, consisted of 112 separate pieces. The subsequent year Cole returned to India with the aim of casting portions of the Qutb Minar at Delhi and the sculpture of Fatehpur Sikri, but the Government of India refused to support the project. The government also denied Cole permission to take away to England the gates of the temple of Somnath, which had been retrieved from their previous Muslim captors with great fanfare by Lord Ellenborough, but were then left to languish in the Agra Fort. Henceforth India's antiquities were to remain in India, where, displayed in museums newly established from Calcutta to Lahore, they announced Britain's mastery over the country's past.

In 1871 the archaeological survey was re-established with professedly scientific objectives. As the Government of India told Cunningham, appointing him to the permanent post of director-general, he was to undertake a 'complete search over the whole country' and to compile a 'systematic record and description of all architectural and other remains that are remarkable either for their antiquity, or their beauty, or their historical interest'.[34] This survey was of course hardly shaped by scholarly concerns alone. Above all, these monuments, preserved in a state of arrested decay, testified to Britain's self-proclaimed role as guardian of India's past. Indeed, as Lord Curzon put it in a speech to the Asiatic Society in 1900, 'a race like our own, who are themselves foreigners, are in a sense better fitted to guard, with a dispassionate and impartial zeal, the relics of different ages, than might be the descendants of warring races or the votaries of rival creeds'. Even the palace of the Burmese kings at Mandalay, less than half a century old, had to be preserved, as at once a mark of respect for Burma's past sovereignty and a 'reminder that it has now passed forever into our hands'. Mute witnesses to a past whose achievements had been superseded by those of the Raj, India's antiquities could not be allowed to crumble into oblivion; nor, despite Lord Napier's endeavour to install district offices in the Tirumal Naik palace at Madurai, and so make it a 'machine of civilized administration', were they meant to be put to use by the British government.

The British conceived that India's buildings provided the best, if not the only, book from which long periods of its history could 'satisfactorily be read'. These structures, as the Royal Asiatic Society put it, told of 'the rise and fall' of the different religions of India, of the 'ethnological relations' of its various tribes and races, and of the ebb and flow of power as the north and south contended for mastery. Not surprisingly, the British insisted always that India's historic architecture, like its peoples, were 'naturally' divided, as Cunningham put it, into 'the two great classes of Hindu and Muhammadan, which are widely distinct from each other'. The first for Cunningham comprehended Buddhist and Jain, as well as Brahmin, structures; the Buddhist among them, as the 'earliest specimens of Hindu architecture', deserved complete protection. Among the Muslim buildings he singled out for recognition the imposing structures of the great capital cities of medieval India. The 'majestic beauty' of the Qutb Minar, the

[34] See NAI Home Public, 28 May 1870, no. 88–89, and 18 February 1871, no. 28–29.

'stern grandeur' of Tughlaqabad, the 'elegance' of the Taj Mahal, all commanded the attention of the new archaeological survey.[35]

More than antiquity or 'elegance' was, however, at stake in these discussions. Each site had its role to play in the drama whose final act was the coming of the British Raj. Delhi's Qutb Minar, for instance, told of the 'bold and daring' 'first Mussalman conquerors', who endeavoured by constructing this 'lofty column' to 'humble the pride of the infidel ... and to exalt the religion of the prophet Muhammad'. The Asoka pillar in the Firoz Shah Kotla provided Cunningham with an occasion for a tirade against what he saw as 'the unblushing mendacity' still too common in India. 'Almost everywhere', Cunningham wrote, 'I have found Brahmins ready to tell me the subject of long inscriptions of which they could not possibly read a single letter.' Always the triumphs of Indian art were ascribed to the influence of foreign invaders. Curzon, for instance, insisted in his speech to the Asiatic Society that the 'majority' of Indian antiquities, those of medieval times as well as those of the Buddhist era a thousand years before, were 'exotics, imported into this country in the train of conquerors, who had learnt their architectural lessons in Persia, in Central Asia, in Arabia, in Afghanistan'. Echoing Cunningham forty years before, he saw the British themselves, 'borne to India upon the crest of a later but similar wave', as the agents of a similar process of architectural transformation.[36]

Despite their insistence on classifying India's historic architecture in communal terms, as 'Hindu', 'Muslim' or 'Buddhist', the British did not in practice always find it easy to fit these categories to the buildings they were meant to describe. The architecture of north India's rulers from the sixteenth to the eighteenth centuries, above all, created intractable problems of classification. As many of the buildings in the Mughal emperor Akbar's capital at Fatehpur Sikri were, so British critics argued, 'thoroughly Hindu' in outline and details, so too, by contrast, were the structures erected by the Hindu rulers of the surrounding region powerfully influenced by contemporaneous Mughal architecture. Difficulty of classification, as in the simultaneous

---

[35] See NAI Home Public, 30 July 1870, no. 204–16, and June 1874, no. 10–13.
[36] Archeological Survey, *Four Reports ... 1862–63 ... Cunningham*, pp. 163, 195; Curzon speech of 7 February 1900, in Sir Thomas Raleigh (ed.), *Lord Curzon in India* (London, 1906), pp. 182–94.

effort to order India's castes, bred controversy. While some, like Richard Temple, insisted, for instance, that the eighteenth-century palace of the Jat rajas of Dig, despite its 'Mohammedan' borrowings, was nevertheless a 'Hindoo' structure, others, with Cunningham, argued that the palace was in its architectural style 'purely Mahomedan', with 'very little if any trace of the real Hindu architecture about it'. For the most part, commentators like Fergusson, though with reluctance, classified these buildings as 'Hindu' because of the religious faith of their builders. Throughout these controversies no one ever questioned the assumption, so deeply embedded in the ideology of the Raj, that, as religious affiliation shaped India's society, so too must it – in timeless fashion – inform the elements of the country's architecture.

Alone among India's viceroys, Curzon devoted substantial energy to archaeological preservation. He reorganized the Archaeological Survey into an efficient administrative body and tirelessly toured India's ancient monuments. He was the first governor-general in eighty years to visit Gaur, Bengal's historic capital, and one of only two in a century of British rule ever to tour the Hindu shrines of Brindaban. Curzon's obsession, however, was the Taj Mahal, which he visited six times during the course of his viceroyalty. Convinced that the local engineers were 'destitute' of the 'faintest artistic perception', he set on foot a number of restoration projects, which he then supervised with a single-minded devotion to detail. Behind this commitment to precision lay, however, a world of 'Oriental' fantasy. Curzon dressed the hereditary custodians of the tomb, for instance, in the white suits and green scarf that he had decided was 'the traditional garb of Mogul days'; he ordered the removal of the 'garish English flowers' from the gardens and their replacement by a row of cypress trees framing the Taj at the end; and he determined to procure a hanging lamp for the domed chamber above the cenotaphs. As the style of the Taj was, in his view, Indo-Saracenic, 'which is really Arabic', he asked Lord Cromer, British proconsul in Egypt, to design a lamp for him modelled on those still to be found in the mosques of Cairo. Dissatisfied with Cromer's suggestion, Curzon then sought, unsuccessfully, to locate a copy of his childhood illustrated edition of 'The Arabian Nights' as a source for suitable designs. Finally, during his trip back to England, upon his retirement from the viceroyalty, he stopped in Cairo, where he selected the design for the lamp, installed in the Taj in 1906, which still hangs over the tomb chamber.[37]

Although the Taj always stood forth for the British as, so Curzon put it, a 'vision of eternal beauty', nevertheless even this great monument had to be made to fit into the appropriate categories of the British discourse on India's past. As the Taj was by definition a 'Saracenic' design, a lamp from Cairo – or even one drawn from a Victorian illustrator's 'Arabian Nights'! – could alone suitably complement its soaring domes and arches. What mattered was not the Indian reality of shared architectural forms, but an 'Orient' constituted of opposed 'Saracenic' and 'Hindu' elements. In its majesty the Taj evoked too the grandeur of empire, against which the British sought always to measure themselves. Although Curzon insisted, when he set out to build the Victoria Memorial in Calcutta, that there could be 'no greater rashness than to attempt a modern Taj', and though he scrupulously avoided elements of 'Saracenic' design, still at every stage of construction the Taj remained his animating ideal. Sometimes it presented an unreachable goal – he could not, he admitted, aspire to the eighteen-foot-high terrace of the Taj. Yet he took pride in the fact that he had made the Queen's Hall larger than the tomb chamber of the Taj, and he insisted, despite objections on grounds of cost, that the marble for Victoria's memorial be taken from the same quarry as Mumtaz Mahal's.

It was not always easy to secure the preservation of India's ancient monuments in the proper state of arrested decay. Curzon bemoaned the use of whitewash on the medieval mosques and tombs of Bijapur and the unwillingness of the British military to vacate the Delhi and Lahore forts. Climbing up a ladder outside the temple of Bhubaneshwar to inspect the restoration work for which his government was paying, he denounced the 'supposed prejudices' of its guardians, who excluded, as they still do, non-Hindus from the shrine. Where religious structures had already come into the possession of government, he determined not to 'hand them back to the dirt and defilement of Asiatic religious practices'. Where worship had to be permitted, the devotions should be of a sort appropriate, as the British saw it, to the history and character of the site. At Bodh Gaya, the place of the Buddha's enlightenment, the government was determined to restore

---

[37] For Curzon's architectural activities, see correspondence in IOL Curzon Papers MS. Eur. F111/621.

the main temple to what it 'is undoubtedly, and always has been primarily, a Buddhist temple'. That the site had been in the control of a Hindu mahant since 1727 the Bengal authorities dismissed with the assertion that his religious observances were 'unreal and unorthodox'. Still, when the mahant obstinately refused to vacate, Curzon backed down. As the British found themselves, Curzon wrote in 1904, involved in 'so many sources of somewhat sharp disagreement with the native community in Bengal (arising out of our Universities Bill, the Official Secrets Act, and the suggested partition of Bengal), it did not seem to be worthwhile to add another to their number, or to provide a possible handle for a religious agitation'.

Despite this setback, the ideas which informed the challenge to the Bodh Gaya mahant remained compelling. History, so the British insisted, should determine what Curzon called the 'proper conduct of worship', and hence the oldest, or original, form of religious devotion ascertained to have taken place in any structure possessed an overriding claim to it. Taken up in the late twentieth century by the Indians themselves, this colonial ideology now informs, not a challenge to the mahant of Bodh Gaya, but the insistent demand that later, Muslim, religious structures must give way to presumably earlier, Hindu, ones. Based in large part on British archaeological excavations dating back to Cunningham's time, these claims sustained the long assault on the sixteenth-century Babur mosque in Ajodhya, culminating in its final tragic demolition by crowds of Hindu activists in December 1992. Alleged to be set on the ancient site of the birthplace of Ram, it could not be allowed to stand. The colonial notions of India's enduring division into Hindu and Muslim, and of 'history' as a mode of validation for one's actions in the present, had borne bitter fruit.

As the British defined India's past, they sought always to make room in it for themselves. The massive six volume *Cambridge History of India* can be seen in particular as a complementary enterprise to the archaeological survey, as it sought to comprehend all of India's past in a single narrative that led inevitably to the Raj. As we have seen in chapter 3, in this historiography the past was always the present. The ancient empires, as Ronald Inden has indicated in discussing the work of the historian Vincent Smith, were seen as the product of an 'active male and Aryan rationality' that arrived by conquest and imposed its order on an inherently divided non-Aryan populace. Following in the footsteps of these imperial rulers, the British, in this view, could take pride in having erected a polity in India that 'was not only true to India's history, but even an improvement on it'. By contrast, in Smith's account, India's medieval history, with its petty warring kingdoms, was not just a story of decline, but 'a parable of the future, of what would happen in India if the British withdrew'.[38]

As they approached their own time, the British sought to define the Raj as itself truly Indian, while yet retaining a conception of themselves as Western, and the bearer of the values of 'civilization'. The history, the architecture, and the ritual of the Raj alike bore witness to this endeavour. The events of the Mutiny, for instance, in such monumental works as J.W. Kaye's three-volume *History of the Sepoy War* (1867) were cast in heroic form to create a 'mythic' triumph. For Kaye the British themselves, by their 'over-eager pursuit of Humanity and Civilization', what he calls the 'progress of Englishism', provoked the uprising; yet that same English 'self-assertion' alone made possible a victorious outcome. At the same time the monuments associated with the events of 1857 were organized in a sacral way, linking the Residency at Lucknow with the well at Kanpur and the Ridge at Delhi. Marked with British blood, these sites defined a landscape that for the British indelibly connected their Raj at once to an Indian past and to their successful mastery of an India stained by 'treachery' and 'savagery'.

The endeavour to mark out the distinctive character of the Raj took shape most visibly in the buildings the British themselves put up in India. As we have seen, during the era of Company rule most British building in India was fitted to the forms of European classicism. Such 'eternal' forms, with their origins in ancient Greece, asserted an aesthetic perfection that stood above the vagaries of time; while at the same time they proclaimed for all to see what were regarded as universal values of law, order, and proportion. The adoption of European classical forms did not, however, resolve the problem of representing Britain's empire as Indian. So long as a mercantile company controlled the government, and the Mughal emperor sat on his throne in Delhi, the British had but little choice other than to use a European, and largely classical, idiom in their imperial building. After the Mutiny, however, with the transfer of power to the Crown and the banishment of the Mughal ruler, the British began to construct for themselves a notion of empire in which they were not merely foreign

[38] Inden, *Imagining India*, chapter 5, especially pp. 180–88.

9 *The Madras Law Courts*, designed by J. W. Brassington and H. C. Irwin (1889–92). The structure, in the characteristic manner of the British Indo-Saracenic, joined together features, most notably arches and domes, from a variety of Indian styles, and incorporated as well arcaded verandas, colonnades, and a tower in the shape of a minaret containing a light to guide ships toward the nearby harbour. From *Indian Engineering*, 7 September 1895.

conquerors, like the Romans, but legitimate, almost indigenous rulers, linked directly to the Mughals and hence to India's own past. Part of this endeavour took the shape of the proclamation of Victoria as Empress of India. In architecture it involved the creation, from the late 1860s onward, of a new style, known as the 'Indo-Saracenic'.

As the British set out to incorporate Indic features into their architectural work, they were drawn especially to the forms, above all those of the arch and dome, that made up what they conceived of as the 'Saracenic' style. As they disdained the 'idolatrous' Hindu religion, so too did they disdain the architectural styles that, in their view, expressed its values in stone. Unlike the heavy, dark forms of post and lintel construction that informed Hindu temple architecture, the arch and dome were, as Lord Napier, governor of Madras, put it, 'the most beautiful, the most scientific, and the most economical' way of covering large spaces. Central to the appeal of that style, however, were its

157

political implications, for the Saracenic was the style associated with the Mughal Empire, whose power and majesty the British now wished to claim as their own. Indeed, Napier argued, the Government of India would 'do well to consider whether the Mussulman form might not be adopted generally as the official style of architecture'.

In the end, late-nineteenth-century British builders in India adopted Indian design elements in a highly eclectic fashion. (See fig. 9.) R. F. Chisholm, who inaugurated the new architecture with his 'Saracenic'-styled Revenue Board buildings in Madras (1870), in subsequent designs borrowed features from the architecture of Travancore, Bijapur, Ahmedabad, and elsewhere. Similarly, Major C. Mant's Mayo College, Ajmer (1875), mixed Rajput and Mughal forms in a striking design capped with an ornate clock tower. Nor did British builders confine themselves to Indian forms. Chisholm incorporated Byzantine elements in his Madras University Senate House; while, as William Emerson wrote of his design for Muir College, Allahabad, he had 'determined not to follow too closely Indian art, but to avail myself of an Egyptian phase of Moslem architecture, and work it up with the Indian Saracenic of Beejapore and the northwest, confining the whole in a western Gothic design'.[39]

The mingling of elements from across India ideally suited the British vision of their role as colonial rulers. By drawing together forms distinctly labelled 'Hindu' and 'Saracenic', the British proclaimed themselves the masters of India's culture, able to shape a harmony the Indians, divided by caste and community, could not themselves achieve. This eclecticism reflected also, and itself constituted, British notions of India's enduring 'difference'. As India's society was unchanging, traditional, in a word 'Oriental', the elements of its architecture were, at the deepest level, similar and interchangeable. For the colonial builder its forms represented, not an on-going tradition within which he worked, but rather colours on a palette from which he could pick and choose to create the image he desired: that of order imposed on a backward and divided society.

At no time was Indo-Saracenic design ever conceived of as an exercise in antiquarianism. Central to its conception was always a combination of 'European science' and 'native art', of 'traditional' forms and 'modern' functions. The buildings constructed in this style were meant to advance the novel objectives of the Raj, and they

[39] Metcalf, *Imperial Vision*, chapter 3.

included a wide array of public structures, from law courts and post offices, railway stations and banks, to colleges and museums. Indeed, Indo-Saracenic architecture expressed within itself the enduring tension between a British commitment to a 'civilizing' enterprise, with its vision of an India transformed, and an insistence, announced in the facades these structures presented to the public, that India remained of necessity a 'traditional' Oriental society.

James Fergusson, with his *History of Indian and Eastern Architecture* (1876), had begun the extended process of ordering, labelling, and classifying India's historic architecture. This sense of mastery culminated with Swinton Jacob's *Portfolio of Indian Architectural Details* (1890). Comprising six massive volumes, containing some 375 plates of detailed architectural drawings – of brackets and capitals, arches and plinths – from historic buildings across northern India, this portfolio of 'working drawings', so Jacob announced, would enable the architect to take full advantage of features 'so full of vigour, so graceful and so true in outline'. The volume announced as well that the British had now made India's architectural heritage their own. No longer would the builder have to 'copy piecemeal and wholesale' structures of the past; rather, having mastered 'the spirit which produced such works', he could 'select, reject, and alter the forms to suit the altered conditions'.

By 1900, then, alike in ethnography, archaeology, and architecture, the British had, or so they thought, ordered, and so mastered, at once India's past and its present. Informed by an ideology that announced India's enduring 'difference', yet uneasily insistent upon communicating the 'principle of progress' to India, they had fashioned for India a past linked to a vision of empire in which, as the viceroy, Lord Lytton, told the Imperial Assemblage in 1877, 'Providence' had called upon the British to 'replace and improve' the 'constantly recurrent' anarchy of its strife-torn predecessors. The ordered India which the British had created could not, however, wholly obscure the contradictions that underlay its divergent elements, nor could an insistence upon 'difference' forever keep at bay the challenges posed in the name of 'similarity', above all by the educated Indian.

CHAPTER 5

COPING WITH CONTRADICTION

Throughout, as the British put together an ideology for the Raj, they had to contend with the internal contradictions that bedevilled it, above all those between an insistence on India's difference, and a similarity they could never entirely repudiate. As time went on, these tensions grew ever more unmanageable. By the later decades of the nineteenth century an educated elite, organized in the Indian National Congress, asserted their equivalence to their rulers, and so claimed the rights they felt entitled to as British subjects. Medical researchers in the field of parasitology made discoveries at the same time which revealed that all bodies were inherently the same in their susceptibility to disease. The British did not readily embrace either the political or the medical parallels between themselves and the Indians. On the contrary, in the later years of the century, especially with the outbreak in the 1890s of famine and plague, India was ever more visibly imagined as a land set apart, a land of disease (or of 'dis-ease') and disorder. The legacy of the Mutiny in particular contributed to a growing fearfulness that could never wholly be quelled. There remained always a remembrance of a time, evoked in fiction and memoirs for half a century afterward, when all Englishmen, and especially English women, were at risk of dishonour and death.

This sense of vulnerability, of anxiety existing side-by-side with a self-proclaimed 'mastery' over an ordered India, found an imaginative centre in Calcutta. Once a 'city of palaces' in which the British had taken pride, Calcutta had by the end of the century become the 'city of dreadful night'. Seen as overrun with sewage, home to endemic disease, and given over to the despised babu, who controlled the Calcutta Corporation, the city nonetheless assumed for the British the shape of a glittering capital, illuminated by the commanding presence of such figures as the viceroy, Lord Curzon. Within it all the contradictions of the Raj converged.

To keep this ever more threatening India at bay the British devised a strategy built upon distancing and denial. The late nineteenth century marked the high point of the British retreat into the club and the hill station, and with it the insistence that, as Kipling wrote in 'Beyond the Pale', one must let 'the White go to the White and the Black to the Black'. Yet evasion could never be wholly successful, for much in India remained seductively attractive, while the contamination of India inevitably seeped into club and cantonment with servants and disease. Nor could the British forever ignore, and so dismiss, the demands of the educated for increased political participation. Increasingly, British fearfulness was propelled by political anxieties, by the challenge of a 'new' India, as well as by the enduring unease of an ideology that suppressed complicitous similarity. This chapter explores the British response to the crisis of the Raj in the late-Victorian and Edwardian era. It begins, in its first two sections, with a discussion of the cultural and psychological mechanisms the British used to cope with a land of both danger and desire. The last two sections, returning to politics, look first at the construction of constituencies meant to bulwark a vulnerable Raj, and then at a frontal assault, from within the ideals of British liberalism, upon the ideology of difference itself.

KIPLING'S INDIA: THE RAJ UNDER STRESS

In his Indian stories, as well as in his own early life, Rudyard Kipling made visible the psychic tensions that lay hidden beneath the seemingly placid surface of the late Victorian Raj. Born in Bombay in 1865, Kipling looked back upon his early years, speaking Hindustani in the care of his Indian *ayah*, as a time of 'light and colour and golden and purple fruits at the level of my shoulder'. This seductive India continued to attract him twenty years later as a young reporter, when he spent the stifling summer nights roaming the streets and bazaars of Lahore. Kipling subsequently recreated this idyllic past in the carefree Kim, the 'friend of all the world', conversant with everyone and at home everywhere. Yet this childhood fantasy of an India where racial boundaries did not matter could not be sustained into adult life. Then the powerful attraction of a sensual India had always to be held in check by the stern demands of imperial duty. In Kipling's story 'Without Benefit of Clergy', the hero, John Holden, was caught up in an illicit relationship, with his beloved Ameera, that provoked in him feelings of 'riotous exultation'. After participating in a ritual sacrifice meant to secure the life of his new-born son, he admitted that 'I never felt like this in my life.' Yet he could not give way to such feelings. At once, 'eager to get to the light and the company of his fellows', he decided, 'I'll go to the club and pull myself together.' Later, when his Indian son died, 'one mercy only was granted to Holden'. He rode to his office and 'found waiting him an unusually heavy mail that demanded concentrated attention and hard work'. For Kipling too the streets at night stood always in tension with the club, a sanctuary where work and duty were necessary to ward off 'riotous exultation'.

Such love affairs as Holden's embodied an enduring vision of India as temptress and seductress. For Kipling, whose wide popularity attests to the imaginative power of his writing, this was a central representational mode. In his stories Indian women were almost invariably defined by their sexuality – whether the prostitute Lalun, who by her intrigues shook the stability of the Raj, or the beautiful young Bisesa and Ameera, who drew British officers into doomed love affairs. The greater the erotic attraction, the more such sensuality was linked to danger and to death, and more generally to the heat and disease which for the British typified so much of India. In Kipling's 'Beyond the Pale', once the affair was discovered, Bisesa held out her arms to her lover in the moonlight to reveal both hands cut off at the wrists, while the Englishman Trejago was at the same time wounded by a thrust to the groin delivered by an unseen assailant. In 'Without Benefit of Clergy' Holden's infant son and his Ameera alike died of disease. The death of the latter was part of a vast cholera epidemic speading across India 'from all four quarters of the compass'. When finally the rains came to end the epidemic they left the lovers' house so dilapidated that it was torn down. In the end, Kipling concluded, in a parable of colonialism, the municipality made a 'road across, as they desire, from the burning-ghat to the city wall, so that no man may say where this house stood'.

The very streets where these Indians lived were at once mysterious and forbidding. Bisesa, for instance, lived at the end of a *gali*, behind a 'dead wall pierced by one grated window'. Nor was Kipling himself comfortable even in the palaces of Rajasthan, with their 'cramped and darkened rooms, narrow smoothwalled passages with recesses where a man might wait for his enemy unseen, the maze of ascending and descending stairs leading nowither, the ever present screen of marble tracery that may hide or reveal so much'. In these dark confines not even sexual identity was secure. Trejago went each evening to meet his Bisesa, between the 'sleeping cattle and the dead walls', clad in a *burqa*, 'which cloaks a man as well as a woman'. He threw off the burqa only after the attack, when he fled that quarter where 'each man's house is as guarded and unknowable as the grave'.

Similar themes informed the writing of many of Kipling's contemporaries. In Flora Annie Steel's novel of the Mutiny, *On The Face of the Waters* (1896), for instance, the hero Jim Douglas enjoyed with his mistress Zora, whom he had set up in a 'cool scented retreat' above a 'rabbit warren of dark cells crushed in on each other', an 'idyl' of some eight years only to watch her die, 'as so many secluded women do, of a slow decline'. Returning later to this 'peaceful garden', Douglas found it, and with it Indian sensuality, 'oppressive'. The Indian woman's 'eternal cult of purely physical passion', so Steel wrote, her 'eternal struggle for perfect purity and constancy, not of the soul, but the body', and her 'worship alike of sex and He who made it' was simply 'incomprehensible'. In such writings, which define the colonial encounter in terms of the possession of a feminine India by a masculine Britain, sexual imagery was used to represent not control, but fear of the loss of control. Cast as a seductive, sometimes castrating, female, India embodied the overwhelming of the rational by the sensual.

In this vision of a sensual India the English woman, was, as we have seen, made to play a distinctive role as the embodiment of the virtues of domesticity and moral purity. However much she might amuse herself, as in Kipling's 'Plain Tales from the Hills', with gossip and flirtation, the English woman of necessity existed as something approaching a sacralized figure. The crisis of the Mutiny, therefore, as it exposed Britain's vulnerability, not surprisingly generated a near obsessive fear of savage Indian men raping helpless English women. Even though the evidence available even at the time made it clear that no British women were sexually violated before being killed, tales of systematic rape, torture, and mutilation began to circulate among the British before the revolt had been suppressed. Even Harriet Tytler, who had been present at the seige of Delhi, conjured up a vision of 'so many poor women' who had had to face a 'worse death' than mere killing. These stories served at once to reassure the British of their right to rule India, and affirmed afresh the image of English women as virtuous and innocent. (See fig. 10.)

10 *Miss Wheeler Defending Herself Against the Sepoys at Cawnpore*, from Charles Ball, *History of the Indian Mutiny* (1858). When British women were depicted as acting heroically, as at the time of the famous Kanpur massacre in July 1857, commentators represented them as doing so in order to protect their moral purity from dishonour at the hands of licentious Indians. Miss Wheeler, daughter of the commanding general at Kanpur, was reported at the time to have thrown herself into a well after shooting a number of sepoys. In fact, her fate is not known.

British Indian fiction for half a century after 1857, in a way that had not been the case before, as Nancy Paxton and Jenny Sharpe have made clear, continued to retell tales of rape, and more importantly, of English women as martyrs for the empire, killed while resisting dishonour. In so doing these writings at once kept alive the memory of the Mutiny, and nourished enduring racial and sexual anxieties that, as we shall see, gained renewed power with each recurring crisis. Occasionally these works, as in the case of Steel's *On The Face of The Waters*, present English women as resourceful, even sensual; in this novel too the heroine, Kate Erlton, preserves her honour not by facing death, but by staging a mock abduction, in which, thrown across the horse's saddlebow, she pretends that her English rescuer Douglas, disguised as a marauding Afghan, is about to rape her. By thus undercutting the classic imagery of female self-sacrifice, Steel adopts a stance to some degree critical of the imagined Victorian role for women. Steel also acknowledges a sympathy with Indian customs. When Kate wrapped herself in a veil to avoid detection in the city, she reflected that, unlike in England, 'where a lonely woman might be challenged all the more for her loneliness', in 'this heathen land the down-dropped veil hedged even a poor grass-cutter's wife about with respect'. Subsequently, hiding from the mutineers in Delhi, Kate is portrayed as content in her seclusion, wearing Indian dress, even the gold bangles of Douglas's former mistress. Yet Steel never called into question the larger values that sustained the Raj. Despite her content-ment, Kate rejoined the British camp, and urged on the troops to 'revenge' the 'wrongs' done to English women. By the end of *On The Face of the Waters*, Kate and Jim Douglas, married, are settled in Scotland. Neither in the way they were represented, nor in their own lives, did English women in India pose any fundamental challenge to the dominant ideologies of race and gender.[1]

The fears triggered by the events of 1857 were not confined wholly to fantasies of the violation of innocent women. A writer like Kipling could imagine even, in the chilling tale of 'The Strange Ride of Morrowbie Jukes', the English placed at the mercy of their Indian subjects. In this story the English officer, Jukes, fell into a desolate sand crater inhabited by Indians, among them an English-speaking Brahmin and former government servant, who had survived a cholera epidemic. Treated with the 'most chilling indifference', this 'repre-sentative of the dominant race' lay 'helpless as a child' amidst his former subjects, who announced that 'we are now a Republic', and invited Jukes to partake of his 'fair share of roasted crow'. The story sharply marks out the contrast between, on the one side, the educated Gunga Dass, who spent his time, 'in a deliberate lazy way', torturing Jukes 'as a schoolboy would devote a rapturous half-hour to watching the agonies of an impaled beetle', and, on the other, the faithful servant Dunnoo, who looked after Jukes's dogs, and who came to his rescue by letting a rope down over the edge of the crater.

By the last decades of the century such fears had become focussed with a renewed intensity on the figure of the educated Bengali. At once

---

[1] Nancy Paxton, 'Mobilizing Chivalry: Rape in British Novels about the Indian Uprising of 1857', *Victorian Studies*, vol. 36 (1992), pp. 5–30; Jenny Sharpe, *Allegories of Empire: The Figure of Woman in the Colonial Text* (Minneapolis, 1993).

a political threat to the stability of the Raj, and a parody of the Englishman himself, the babu, no longer simply a stock figure of caricature, was, in the hands of men like Kipling, the object of a hatred informed by mockery and derision. Throughout the writings of his Indian years Kipling denounced the educated 'native' with bitter satire. In his sketches for the 'City of Dreadful Night', for instance, Kipling linked Calcutta's inadequate sanitation directly to its system of municipal self-government. 'In spite of that stink', he wrote, 'they allow, even encourage, natives to look after the place! The damp, drainage soaked soil is sick with the teeming life of a hundred years and the municipal board list is choked with the names of natives – men born in and and raised off this surfeited muck heap!'

Not only in Calcutta, but at the opposite end of the country, on the Northwest frontier, the hapless and ineffectual Bengali was made the butt of ridicule. In Kipling's story 'The Head of the District', when the respected deputy commissioner, Yardley-Orde, dies suddenly, the viceroy, determined to advance the principles of the 'New India', appoints as his successor Grish Chunder De, MA, a Bengali 'more English than the English', who is 'crammed with code and case law', but wholly incapable of rule. The tribesmen refuse to accept this 'fat, black eater of fish' as their ruler, and so rise in rebellion. Stammering that he had not yet taken official charge of the district, Chunder De contrived to 'fall sick' and fled, leaving his British assistants to quell the uprising. Facing the defeated hillmen, the assistant Tallantire assured them that next time the government would 'send you a *man*!' The hillmen were, of course, in Kipling's opinion, no more capable of self-rule than the Bengali. Though 'strong men', they remained captives of their own impulsiveness. They were, as Orde told them on his deathbed, 'children'; hence they, as much as the effeminate Bengali, required the ordering presence of the Raj.

One might argue that Kipling's visceral animosity toward the educated Bengali had deeper roots than simply the desire to sustain the British Raj. As Wurgaft and Nandy have alike pointed out, the so-called effeminacy of the Bengali, together with the attraction these men expressed for English learning, brought a man like Kipling, a writer and literary figure, face to face with a side of his own personality he could not openly avow in the hypermasculine society of late Victorian India. Only by a vigorous repudiation of everything connected with the babu and his culture could he effectively contain those elements he saw, and despised, within himself, and so retain a place amongst his Anglo-Indian peers. Oddly, and revealingly, years later, after he had left India for good, Kipling was able, in the character of Hurree Chunder Mookerjee, to craft a figure who mocked not just the educated Bengali but the colonial stereotype itself. For the 'hulking obese Babu' in *Kim*, so incongruous in the masculine arena of the Great Game, was one of its most skilled practitioners. His actions, as he took on the task of instructing Kim in the ways of espionage and led two Russian spies to their undoing across the trackless wastes of the Himalayas, stood always in ironic contrast to his derogatory description of himself as a 'very fearful' man.[2]

Connected to the insistent denial of any complicity in Bengali effeminacy was an equally strong repudiation of the homoerotic. As India presented the seductive image of the feminine to the Englishman, so too did it open up for him a field of homoerotic possibilities. They could never be acknowledged, but, as Sara Suleri has argued, homoeroticism, as much as the classical Orientalist imagery of rape, defined the sexual appeal of India for the British. In her view, indeed, the imperial dynamic was shaped more by a 'dialogue between competing male anxieties' than by the 'traditional metaphor of ravishment and possession'. However India's attraction made itself felt, the tensions it generated – between mastery and submission, denial and desire, an insistence upon difference and the perception of sameness – could not easily be reconciled. Kipling sought some resolution by insisting on the value of steady and unreflecting hard work. His hero was the district officer, a man such as Orde, riding hard in the saddle, or the bridge-builder Findlayson who subdued the raging Ganges. The 'still small voice of fact' could to some degree quell doubt and uncertainty, and carve out a space of order amidst the chaos of India.[3]

As anxiety mounted, the British turned for reassurance to a ringing show of self-confidence. After all, the turn of the century was the heyday of imperialism – of the partition of Africa and the Boer War – and European supremacy throughout the world, sustained by the theories of social darwinism and scientific racism, seemed assured. Curzon, especially, excelled as viceroy in giving voice to the ideals, and the ideology, of the Raj. As he so forcefully put it in his last speech

---

[2] Wurgaft, *The Imperial Imagination*, pp. 132, 142; Nandy, *The Intimate Enemy*, pp. 37-38, 69-70.
[3] Suleri, *The Rhetoric of English India*, especially pp. 16-17, 77.

before leaving India, in Bombay in November 1905, the purpose that sustained the empire was

to fight for the right, to abhor the imperfect, the unjust or the mean, to swerve neither to the right hand nor to the left, to care nothing for flattery or applause or odium or abuse ... but to remember that the Almighty has placed your hand on the greatest of his ploughs ... to drive the blade a little forward in your time, and to feel that somewhere among these millions you have left a little justice or happiness or prosperity, a sense of manliness or moral dignity, a spring of patriotism, a dawn of intellectual enlightenment, or a stirring of duty, where it did not before exist.

'That,' Curzon concluded, 'is enough, that is the Englishman's justification in India.'[4]

Such extravagant language could nevertheless not wholly obscure a defensive sense of unease. Curzon insisted, when he spoke at the London Guildhall in 1904, that the Indian Empire 'is not a moribund organism. It is still in its youth, and has in it the vitality of an unexhausted purpose.' 'Let no man', he concluded, 'admit the craven fear that those who have won India cannot hold it ... That is not the true reading of history. That is not my forecast of the future. To me the message is carved in granite, it is hewn out of the rock of doom – that our work is righteous and that it shall endure.' The impassioned character of these denials – protesting, one might say, too much – surely reveals a good deal more than the words themselves. A fearfulness had taken hold of the Indian government at its highest level.[5]

In similar fashion much British building in India during Curzon's time, and in the years following, shouted forth an overwhelming magnificence. By its vast size, with tesselated marble paving, soaring domes, and Renaissance styling, a building such as the Victoria Memorial in Calcutta sought to reassure the British, and indeed their newly powerful European rivals as well, that the British Empire still mattered. (See fig. 11.) To be sure, in Curzon's vision, the memorial was meant also to bind the educated Indian to the Raj, but, as his advisors warned him, in the absence of any genuine sharing of power, this was a hopeless task. The building's memorials in the end celebrated only

---

[4] Lord Curzon, Speech at the Byculla Club, Bombay, 16 November 1905, in Thomas Raleigh (ed.), *Curzon in India* p. 589.
[5] Lord Curzon, speech upon receiving the Freedom of the City of London in the Guildhall, 20 July 1904, *Speeches on India Delivered while in England in July–August 1904*, pp. 20–21.

11   Victoria Memorial, Calcutta, designed by William Emerson (1905–21).

Clive, Hastings, and other 'heroes' from whose exploits the British could convince themselves that their past in India had been 'glorious'.

The use of European classical forms, rather than the Indo-Saracenic styles characteristic of British building during the preceding fifty years, further indicated a loss of the self-confident mastery of India and its past that had shaped the designs of such men as R. F. Chisholm and Swinton Jacob. These builders, as we have seen, conceived of themselves as manipulating enduring elements of India's architectural heritage to shape a harmonious social order Indians themselves could not achieve. Although Indic elements were incorporated into the design of the buildings for the new capital at Delhi in the years after 1912, by the architects Edwin Lutyens and Herbert Baker, they were carefully subordinated to the forms of European classicism, while the buildings themselves were set within an overall urban layout informed by the dictates of *beaux-arts* formalism. Lutyens' reinterpretation of Indic forms in the viceroy's house was stunning in its imaginativeness. But the dominant features of the design were the immense size of the building, its huge dome, and its seemingly endless ranks of massive

12 Viceroy's House, New Delhi (now Rashtrapati Bhavan), designed by Edwin Lutyens (1913–31). Note the use, together with the European-styled colonnade, of such Indic forms as the horizontal overhanging chajja, clustered chattris (cupolas), and a dome and encircling railing modelled on the ancient Buddhist stupa at Sanchi.

columns. Together they announced to an increasingly anxious British public that their empire, its buildings around the world sharing familiar classical forms, was still one on which the sun never set. (See fig. 12.)

Despite the apparent security of the early-twentieth-century Raj – its self-assurance defiantly asserted, its strategies for governance fully elaborated, its authority sustained by the best science of the day – men like Kipling, and even Curzon, uneasily, perhaps at times unwittingly, revealed an inner core corroded by doubt, uncertainty, and a fearfulness that could not be wholly kept from view.

DIRT, DISEASE, AND DISTANCE

From the beginning the British conceived of India as a land of dirt, disease, and sudden death. While not perhaps quite a 'White Man's Grave', like the coast of West Africa, still India in the eighteenth century was viewed as a place where fortunes might be made quickly, but where the Englishman was not likely to enjoy a long and healthy life. The towering tombs of the Park Street cemetery bear silent witness to the suddenness of death among the 'Nabobs' of early Calcutta. Nor did medical theory offer much hope for ameliorating the effects of residence in India. From the time of the ancient Greeks onward, health was perceived to be linked widely to an array of topographical and environmental factors. The elevation of the ground, the condition of the soil, the humidity of the atmosphere, and above all the extent of marshes and wet ground, determined the occurrence of epidemic disease. This environmental theory of disease marked out India, with its unfamiliar plant and animal life, its excessive heat and numerous 'miasmatic' fluxes, as an exotic, and dangerous space. Of course, in climate, as in so much else, what the British called 'India' was in fact shaped by their experience of Bengal, the area they knew best. The furthest from the norms of northwestern Europe, marshy humid Bengal, with its presumably disease-generating 'miasmas', most fully realized for the British the ideal of a 'tropical' climate. Always, Bengal embodied the vision of India as a land of peril.

To be sure, England too, in the eighteenth century, and into the early industrial era, was a land of cities laden with filth, of poverty among the working classes, of lives cut short by diseases for which medical science had no cure. Britain was even subject to occasional waves of devastation, such as the great cholera epidemic of 1831, that struck suddenly and killed without warning. Nevertheless, although some few diseases, such as smallpox, were recognized as largely free of environmental influences, the great majority of what early Victorian medicine classified as 'fevers', from malaria and typhoid to cholera and hepatitis, were at once, by contrast with England, far more prevalent in India, where they ravaged the health of vulnerable and ill-adapted Europeans, and, more importantly, were perceived as the product of India's 'tropical' climate.

Hot climates brought with them not just discomfort and disease, but, in British thinking, an enduring degeneration of mind and body. Indians, so this medical theory insisted, having adapted to the tropical environment, were invariably lethargic, while Europeans, once transplanted from their native soil, lost their accustomed vigour, and gradually declined. In such climates too, as we have seen in our accounts of the writings of Dow and Orme, despotism and fatalism invariably triumphed over self-reliance. Each climatic region thus shaped the human 'constitution' most suited to it. Europeans took up residence in the tropics at their peril. Nevertheless, once committed to the rule of India, the British devised, as we will see, strategies thought to insure a greater degree of survival in its climate, while increasingly they sought to blame India's disease-ridden character not just on its climate but on Indian fatalism, inertia, and superstition. The environment comprehended the character of the people it had shaped, as well as the physical elements of humidity and topography. Climate made the Indian and the British 'constitutions' fundamentally different, but Britain's moral superiority, and medical knowledge, made it possible for the British to blunt the impact of Indian disease upon themselves, and even, so they believed, to instruct their Indian subjects in how better to preserve their own health. In place of 'medical doctrines which would disgrace an English farrier', as Macaulay put it in his Minute on Education, the British had the obligation, as the possessors of a higher civilization, to spread 'full and correct information respecting every experimental science'.

Though seen as a land of pestilence, India was not at the outset reviled as a land of filth and dirt. The English also lived amidst excrement and sewage; even the Thames sometimes stank so badly that the windows had to be shut in the Houses of Parliament. Until the 1840s, though observers might decry the state of its sanitation,

England was not set apart from India by its smell, or its drains. For the early-nineteenth-century Englishman, what made India pestilential was its climate, not the sewage in its streets. By the middle decades of the century, however, as Edwin Chadwick's sanitary movement took hold with the coming of the Victorian administrative state, filth, and the epidemic diseases linked to it, were increasingly brought under control in Britain. Despite much popular resistance to such government interference, in 1848 the first Public Health Act began the process of cleaning the cities and rivers of Britain, providing safe drinking water, and establishing compulsory vaccination. Similar measures, only fitfully enacted and rarely enforced, were less successful in India, so that as time went on the difference between Britain and India grew ever more palpable. In a process similar to that which brought the English working classes into the constitution after 1867, and so definitively marked off the British from colonial peoples politically, by the 1890s, apart from a few exceptional areas such as Glasgow, Britain was set apart from its Indian dependency as decisively in its health and sanitation. Calcutta, one might say, became filthy only as London became clean.

India's disease and dirt thus became markers of its enduring 'difference', and so helped sustain the larger ideology that undergirded the Raj. At the same time, this notion of India as a land of disease became inextricably bound up with the parallel notion of India as a sensual society lacking proper self-control. The 'tropics', that is, gendered feminine, were the kind of place, subject at once to indolence and passion, where disease and sexuality alike flourished. Indeed, the two complemented each other. As the one represented India as an alluring land of desire, the other revealed the horrifying attraction of disease, and ultimately of death. Connected to this was the obsessive yet ineffectual British concern with Indian sanitation. From Dr Bonavia's hapless endeavour in the 1860s to put an end to public defecation among the citizens of Lucknow to the fierce denunciations, continued up to the present, of 'filthy drains' and 'stagnant cesspools', India's sanitary shortcomings distinguished it as a land of squalor and of indulgence, of bodies that were out of control.[6]

This sinister India took shape above all in the menacing figure of

[6] Veena Talwar Oldenburg, *The Making of Colonial Lucknow, 1856–1877* (Princeton, 1984), pp. 96–144; also see V.S. Naipaul, *An Area of Darkness* (London, 1964), for classic statements on dirt and disease in India.

cholera. By the mid-nineteenth century, this disease had become a symbol for much that the West feared about a society so different from its own. In part this was simply because the major nineteenth-century cholera epidemics, beginning with that of 1817–21, had spread across the globe from India, where the disease had its homeland in the 'miasmatic' paradise of the lower Ganges basin. It was as visibly Indian as it was threatening. Furthermore cholera, to some degree like smallpox, was intimately bound up with Hindu 'superstition'. Hinduism gave rise, especially at the village level, to disease goddesses, and even human 'avatars', who represented and warded off the disease for their devotees. In the British view the existence of such goddesses, 'disgusting' examples of Hindu fatalism, stood in stark contrast with European rationality and the presumed scientific control of disease.[7]

Especially disturbing to the British was the link between pilgrimage, both Hindu and Muslim, and the spread of disease. Belief in such a connection was not without foundation, for pilgrimage brought large bodies of people together in close proximity, but in the British imagination these gatherings assumed terrifying proportions. The Jagganath temple at Puri, for instance, with its car festival in which devotees were said to be crushed under the wheels, represented for evangelical Englishmen the ultimate horror of Hinduism. 'Probably no spot on earth', as one missionary wrote in 1828, 'represents, within so small a compass, such complicated scenes of misery, cruelty, and vice, as are presented to view round the temple of Juggernaut.' At the same time its concentrated masses of worshippers made this city a central point for the spread of epidemic cholera. Hence it is not surprising that, in Western eyes, as David Arnold has written, Puri epitomized all that was obscene, degrading, and epidemiologically dangerous about Hindu India. Frequently, indeed, moral and medical condemnation was mixed together. In a report of 1868 Dr. David Smith, the Bengal sanitary commissioner, contrasted the pilgrims' view of Puri as a holy city where they would be freed of their worldly sins, with the sanitarian's view of it as anything but 'heaven on earth', containing in its many tanks 'the waters of death and not those of immortality'. The image of the god, Smith wrote, 'terrible in its innate

[7] David Arnold, 'Cholera and Colonialism in British India', *Past & Present*, no. 113 (1986), p. 132.

hideousness', was 'yet more terrible in its connection with all the surrounding circumstances' of disease and filth.[8]

The link between Indian religion and disease was further reaffirmed at an international sanitary conference held at Constantinople in 1866. The European powers here sought to cordon off India, and pointed an accusing finger at both Hindu pilgrimages and the Muslim pilgrimage to Mecca. Such pilgrimages they declared to be 'the most powerful of all the causes which conduce to the development and propagation of cholera epidemics'. What lay behind such intense anxiety was nothing less than fear of Europe's vulnerability. 'The squalid pilgrim army of Jagannath', as W. W. Hunter wrote apprehensively in his history of Orissa (1872), 'with its rags and hair and skin freighted with vermin and impregnated with infection, may any year slay thousands of the most talented and beautiful of our age in Vienna, London, or Washington.'[9]

By the later decades of the nineteenth century, the discoveries of parasitology began to call into question the environmentalist explanation of not just cholera but all so-called tropical diseases. Committed to the 'Orientalist' view that Indians were fundamentally different from Europeans, the senior British medical establishment, as David Arnold has argued, clung tenaciously to a climatic, and with it a racial, determinism. India had to be as distinct epidemiologically as it was racially and culturally; India's diseases had somehow to be connected to the soil and people of the land. Nevertheless, by the 1890s researchers in the Indian Medical Service, with Patrick Manson in China, had elaborated in convincing detail what has become known as the 'germ' or 'contagionist' theory of India's most deadly ailments, among them malaria, plague and cholera. Although, as Douglas Haynes has shown, much of this research was driven by narrowly professional motives, as medical officers in the colonial world sought to advance their careers at home by contributing to the advance of a universal medical science, still the new bacteriological explanation of disease inevitably challenged the whole ideology of 'difference'. From the 'contagionist' point of view all bodies were the same, and all equally susceptible to the attack of disease-carrying fleas, mosquitoes, or other vectors. A

---

[8] Ibid., pp. 138–41.
[9] W.W. Hunter, *Orissa*, vol. 1 (London, 1872), pp. 166–67. The Indian government objected to the quarantine policy on political and economic grounds. See Mark Harrison, 'Quarantine, Pilgrimage, and Colonial Trade: India 1866–1900', *Indian Economic and Social History Review*, vol. 29 (1992), pp. 117–44.

universalistic science by its very nature had no room, except in a few special situations such as sickle cell disease among Africans, for racial immunities or any sort of special vulnerability.[10]

India, and with it the 'tropics' more generally, nevertheless remained a place set apart, and one no less threatening. The humid marshes of Bengal, and the open drains of Calcutta, might no longer be the source of pestilential 'miasmas', but they were still the primary breeding grounds of the organisms that transmitted disease. It was in India, and similar hot climates, that malaria, cholera, and other such fearful diseases were most often to be found. The discoveries of the end of the century, far from putting an end to the notion of the 'tropics', helped give it an institutional base with the founding in 1899 of the London School of Tropical Medicine. Notions of European superiority also remained firmly set in place. Not only had European modes of scientific inquiry made possible the great advances of the 1890s, but Europeans alone, as the officers of the Indian Medical Service, possessed the knowledge that permitted diagnosis, treatment, and eventual eradication of disease.

The result was a sharpening of the tension which since the 1830s had bedevilled the British as they contemplated Indian disease. On the one hand, the ideology of difference, grounded in environmentalism, combined with a lack of knowledge of the causes of disease, had justified a largely non-interventionist medical strategy. On the other hand, enthusiasm for what was seen as superior Western science had from Macaulay's time driven an interventionism which had taken shape most visibly in the appointment after 1864 of sanitary officers for the various provinces. But lack of funds and fear of popular antagonism, especially where illness was so closely tied to religion, had checked government action except in areas of substantial European settlement such as the presidency cities. The new medical knowledge of the end of the century prompted a renewed interventionism. Above all, drastic measures of quarantine were taken in the plague epidemic of the late 1890s, and measures for cholera inoculation and smallpox vaccination were slowly introduced over the subsequent decades. But funds remained limited, and public suspicion of the government and its

---

[10] For British tropical medicine during this period, see Douglas Haynes, 'From the Periphery to the Center: Patrick Manson and the Development of Tropical Medicine as a Medical Specialty in Britain, 1870–1900' (University of California, Berkeley, Ph.D. Dissertation, 1992).

motives did not easily dissipate. Most dramatic, of course, was the assassination of the plague commissioner W. C. Rand in 1897, as a result of the insensitive policy of search and quarantine carried out by military personnel in Poona.

Hence ideas of difference, and of separation, among the British in India did not vanish with the coming of a more universalistic medical theory. One might argue that at best a shift in emphasis occurred. One now sought to avoid not 'miasmatic' fluxes, but Indian bodies, the filthy carriers of contagious disease. The last decades of the nineteenth century, and the first two decades of the twentieth, thus saw the fullest elaboration of what may be called an ideology of 'distance', built upon a still enduring sense of difference. The security provided by this distancing was of course always more apparent than real, for the British had to drink Indian water, eat food grown in India, and breathe Indian air, and they always admitted Indian servants to their homes. Hence the strategy of 'distance' itself reinforced precisely the uneasy sense of vulnerability it was meant to combat. The forms this 'distance' took can perhaps best be imagined as a set of nested boxes, each walled off from the larger Indian world outside. The three most important were the bungalow residence, the civil lines (or cantonment), and the hill station.

The bungalow as a building style for the British in India dated back to the late-eighteenth century. Derived from the thatched roof Bengali hut (hence the name), but now constructed of masonry and elaborated to include a high ceiling, several rooms, and a verandah, the bungalow spread rapidly throughout the interior of British India. The style served a number of purposes. (See fig. 13.) Among them was protection from the hot climate, for the enclosed inner rooms and high ceiling kept the outside glare and heat at bay while allowing hot air to rise well above the heads of the occupants. The roofed verandah, sometimes surrounding the whole building, provided further protection for the interior, while affording a pleasant site for relaxation or work during the cool of the morning and evening. Its siting in a spacious compound, away from the reflected heat of other buildings, further enhanced the comfort of the structure. The bungalow, however, with its compound, also secured the important objective of keeping its English inhabitants at a safe distance from the surrounding noise, dust, and disease of India. Indeed the size of the compound, together with its wall, gate, guard, and long entry drive, served to

13 Bungalow, Allahabad (1866). Note the expansive thatched roof, encircling verandah, and placement in the centre of a large compound with curving entry way.

impress Indians with the power and authority of the British, while at the same time affording a way of regulating entry. Indians were almost never allowed beyond the verandah, where much business was transacted, and they were at all times at the mercy of uniformed *chaukidars* and *chaprassis* who protected the British residents from unwelcome visitors (and themselves often profited in the doing).[11]

In the endeavour to make the bungalow an island of Englishness, secure from a noxious India, the English woman, or memsahib, played a critical role. Not just a decorative figure meant to signify purity and domesticity, the memsahib had actively to enforce within the house, and its surrounding compound, the ideals of cleanliness, order, and industry. She had, that is, within the British Indian household, to take on the role her husband played outside: that of a masculine assertion of ordering rationality in the face of a feminized India where disease

[11] Anthony King, *The Bungalow: The Production of a Global Culture* (London, 1984).

and disorder raged unchecked. The home might be, as in England, a female refuge, and a place where the man could find emotional sustenance, but it was also the front line of a battlefield whose commanding officer was its British mistress. The task of keeping India at bay was made doubly difficult by the universal reliance upon Indian domestic servants, for their presence breached the barriers the bungalow compound was meant to throw up. Hence the battle against dirt, disease, and depravity had to be fought within the home as well as outside. Numerous household guides warned the Anglo-Indian housewife that she must ever be on the alert, and must exercise a careful surveillance over the habits and customs of her staff. As Flora Annie Steel wrote in *The Complete Indian Housekeeper* (1904), 'We do not wish to advocate an unholy haughtiness; but an Indian household can no more be governed peacefully, without dignity and prestige, than an Indian Empire.' Servants were meant, above all, to live within the bungalow compound, where they could be kept apart, along with its British residents, from the dirt and squalor of the 'native' city. The menace posed by the English woman's continuing intimate association with male servants was contained by desexualizing these men. Always portrayed as children, they ceased to be threatening, and so could safely be chastised, and guided, by a benevolent maternalism.

From the middle decades of the nineteenth century British bungalows in each locality (or 'station') were commonly grouped together in a spacious quarter known as the 'Civil Lines', or, where the military predominated, a cantonment. Such grouping set the British residential area sharply apart from the congested bazaar or 'native' city. Segregated residential areas could be found in some of the earliest British settlements in India, most notably in Madras, where from the late eighteenth century English garden villas encompassed a vast suburban tract set apart from the 'Black Town' of Indian trade and residence near the port. But until the mid-nineteenth century European residential areas were rarely planned in a coherent fashion, and segregation did not exist everywhere. Before the Mutiny, for instance, though the ridge to the north was being developed as a European residential area, the British inhabitants of Delhi mostly lived inside the walled city.

The Mutiny, however, initiated as it was by the massacre of all Delhi's English residents, so frightened the British that in the years immediately afterward the major cities of northern India were laid out anew with juxtaposed, but separate, British and Indian sectors. Considerations of military security, not surprisingly, dictated much of this planning enterprise. In the city of Allahabad, for instance, after 1858 the capital of the North-Western Provinces, the Civil Lines, laid out in 1858, were placed to the north of the old city and separated from it by the main line of the Calcutta–Delhi railway, which was constructed at the same time. Access from one part of the city to the other existed only at a handful of manned level crossings. (The Grand Trunk Road by contrast, the main artery of northern India before the coming of the railway, went through the heart of the old city.) Lines of railway similarly demarcated British and Indian areas in other major cities such Lucknow, while in Delhi the line was driven through the heart of the old city to break up its congested mass. In Lahore the station itself was designed as a fort in which the European population could take refuge in case of insurrection. To further reassure a fearful British populace, in larger cities, Lucknow and Allahabad among them, military cantonments were placed adjacent to the civilian residential areas.

The contrast in appearance between city and civil station in a town such as Allahabad could not be more striking. In 1868, as J. B. Harrison has written, the old city had two or three main streets of fair width, but from these a labyrinth of ever smaller lanes led off into the interior of the various *muhallas* (neighbourhoods), many of which still had gates to seal off the whole block at night. The houses, mixed together with shops and warehouses, looked inward, and with space limited grew slowly upward. The civil station by contrast was a gridiron of broad metalled roads, with newly planted avenues of trees framing bungalows which stood in lush 2, 3, and even 10 acre compounds. The main avenue, Canning Road, encircled the cathedral, and, after passing through the European shopping area, terminated at the Government House. Even 100 years later, in the 1960s, apart from the growth of suburbs and the dilapidation of the old British bungalows, little had changed – the contrast was as marked as before.[12]

Considerations of security may have determined much of the layout of these British urban settlements, but sanitary fears were no less prominent. Initially segregation on sanitary grounds was a matter of concern primarily for the military. Among British soldiers in India the

---

[12] J.B. Harrison, 'Allahabad: A Sanitary History', in Kenneth Ballhatchet and J.B. Harrison (eds.), *The City in South Asia* (London, 1980), p. 176; Anthony King, *Colonial Urban Development* (London, 1976), especially chapters 5 and 8.

death rate from disease, even during 1857, as in the Crimea a few years before, was far higher than on the battlefield. Overall, during the half-century preceding the Mutiny, the mortality rate among the British military in India was 70 per 1,000, as compared with 17 per 1,000 at home. It was of course impossible to separate British from Indian troops posted to the same station, and every cantonment employed a large number of Indian servants as well. The cantonment bazaar, with its prostitutes whom the military authorities sought vainly to register and inspect, was a further source of potential infection. Nevertheless, especially after the 1863 report of the Royal Commission on the Health of the Army, which pointed to the connection between health and sanitation, the government sought to isolate the troops, and with them the civilian British population, so far as possible from areas of dense urban settlement. After all, as the commission insisted, 'the habits of the natives are such that, unless they are closely watched, they cover the whole neighbouring surface with filth', or what one medical officer called a 'daily offering of impurity exposed on the surface of the earth'.[13]

Although cantonments could not be wholly secluded, still they were commonly protected by a wide band of open land, ideally 1 to 2 miles in depth, as a *cordon sanitaire*. Irrigation and cultivation were prohibited in this area, and Indian villages were even, as in Allahabad, forcibly uprooted from within this tract in order 'to preserve the health and life of the remaining and more important section of the community'. In similar fashion resources were disproportionately lavished on the European residential areas at the expense of the Indian. As the sanitary commissioner wrote so early as 1868, while the Allahabad civil station, 'inhabited by the European community, has been covered in all directions with very good roads, and its drainage has been carefully attended to', many of the roads in the city were of dirt, badly drained, and 'almost impassable in the rains'. Respectable British women, especially, avoided at all cost the narrow dark streets, evil-smelling courtyards, and polluted open drains of the 'native' city.[14]

Short of leaving India altogether (which the British had no intention of doing), the most effective way of securing a suitable distance from a hot disease-ridden land was to escape to the hills. There, in the cool heights of the Nilgiris and Himalayas, the British constructed an

[13] Harrison, 'Allahabad', pp. 173, 178.   [14] Ibid., 177–78.

arcadian idyll where the fears and anxieties of colonial rule could be kept at bay in a landscape of exceptional beauty. The British first began to explore the hills in the 1820s, and the three major resorts of Ootacamund, Darjeeling and Simla were established by the mid-1830s. Until mid-century, however, the hills were used mainly as convalescent retreats for British troops, with only occasional and irregular visits by civil officials. After 1865, when John Lawrence made Simla the regular summer capital of British India, and railroads facilitated access, the hill station loomed ever larger in the British imagination. The ideology of 'difference' can be visibly read in the landscape in the opposition of 'plains' and 'hills'.

The presumed health benefits of residence in the hills did not depend upon either of the competing theories of tropical disease, nor were they linked to any particular diseases. Almost by definition the hills were seen as providing protection against diseases thought to be caused by 'miasmatic' fevers. In similar fashion, when contagionist theories came into vogue, the thin populations of the hill areas, and the scarcity of breeding mosquitoes at high elevations, were shown to be decisive in reducing infection from diseases such as cholera and malaria. Cholera outbreaks did, however, take place in the hills, and of course malaria could be brought there by travellers passing through the highly malarious Tarai foothills on the way. In the end the health benefits of hill residence were largely defined by the logic of social distance. Those who derived most benefit from the hills, as several medical officers put it, were those 'who labour under no organic disease, but suffer from general debility, the result of a residence in the low country; these cases rally wonderfully and rapidly'.

Behind the enthusiasm for the hills lay the ever-present fear of 'degeneracy'. Too long a continued residence in the hot Indian climate would inevitably, so the British were convinced, lead to an enfeeblement announced by languor, irritability, and depression. Such maladies were often described by vague medical terms such as 'neurasthenia', and their symptoms were not always easily distinguished from other tropical ailments. The British sought to counter such degeneration above all by avoiding life-long residence in India. Whenever finances permitted, children were sent to England for schooling and the colonial British themselves returned 'home' for retirement. But the hills too could help restore 'Saxon energy'. The prescription for a 'change of climate' in such cases involved nothing less than the flight of a vulnerable English body to a world that was secure and comforting from one perceived as oppressive and threatening. For nearly eighty years, from the 1860s until the early 1940s, following the senior officers of government, British women and children journeyed regularly to the hills each summer, while their husbands soldiered on below, ever on the lookout for an excuse that would bring them for a short time at least to the cool heights. Missionaries, and even Indian princes, following the lead of the government, created hill stations of their own, in such places as Mussoorie and Kodaikanal, Murree and Mt Abu. Schools too flourished in these settlements, where they drew a clientele of mixed race Eurasians and less affluent Europeans unable or unwilling to send their children to boarding schools in England.

The British made of the hills not only a sanctuary from India, but an idyllic England defined as India's exact opposite. Imbued with an attraction for the 'picturesque', derived from late-eighteenth-century aesthetic sensibility, the British sought to create in India's mountains a vision of flowers and gardens, lakes and crags, nourished in such places as the Lake District and the Scottish Highlands. Outside the rolling hills of the Nilgiris this was not an easy task. The Himalayas, soaring dramatically to the eternal snows, bore no resemblance to British landscapes, and were indeed most commonly described, in accordance with the conventions of contemporary aesthetics, as 'sublime'; not just wild and untamed, they were, even more than the vistas found in the Alps, awe-inspiring, even overwhelming in their gigantic scale. In the late eighteenth and early nineteenth centuries, in the days of William Hodges and the Daniells, the Indian 'picturesque' was sought, not in the mountains, but in reassuringly domestic vistas along the banks of the Ganges, in peaceful pastoral landscapes, and among the ruined monuments scattered across the plains.

As the British moved into the hills they adopted various strategies to fit these mountains into the descriptive conventions of the picturesque. One was simply to reduce them in size by referring to them as 'hills' rather than the mountains they so obviously were. Another, in writing and illustration, was to focus upon the more tractable Nilgiris, which because of their accessibility had gained an early and enthusiastic recognition. Visitors from Bentinck and Macaulay to Lytton in the 1870s waxed rhapsodic over the beauty of the area around Ootacamund. 'The afternoon was rainy and the road muddy', Lytton wrote;

'but such beautiful *English* rain, such delicious *English* mud. Imagine Hertfordshire lanes, Devonshire downs, Westmoreland lakes, Scotch trout-streams, and Lusitanian views!'[15]

Taming or 'domesticating' the Himalayas was a lengthy process, and took shape primarily within the hill towns themselves. The English dwelling in the hills, in sharp contrast to the regimented bungalow of the plains, was designed on the model of the English country cottage, or, more grandly, that of the decorated Swiss chalet. Each was meant to express the personality of its owner, and, like an English country house, each was given a distinctive name that denoted its picturesque site or nostalgia for an England left behind. Each too was surrounded by imported English flowers, with English fruits and vegetables grown in nearby gardens. A bandstand, Gothic church, and Mall, its buildings often constructed in Elizabethan half-timbered style, completed the illusion, even though set amongst looming peaks and precipitous gorges, of an English country town. The hill station arcadia was, for the inhabitants of 'Woodacre' or 'Myrtle Cottage', a repudiation at once of a feared India and a disdained urban industrial England.

Not only the landscape but the peoples of the hills were shaped to fit the requirements of the new colonial order. As Dane Kennedy has pointed out, although the Nilgiri Todas, the Paharis of the Simla hills, and the Lepchas of Darjeeling, separated each from the other by a thousand miles, had almost nothing in common, the British fashioned them all into simple people, formed by such qualities as gentleness, openness, and innocence. In the British view these mountain peoples, 'noble guardians of edenic sanctuaries', conveniently lacked almost all the vices that marked the Indians of the plains. Less indolent, less enmeshed in caste and 'degrading superstitions', they had even almost escaped India's pervasive sensuality. As one officer wrote, 'I have seen some beautiful and sinless little hill girls of grace and air so innocent, so pure, so cherub-like, that it seemed impossible that ... they should have within them the seeds of lasciviousness and guilt.' These hill peoples contrasted sharply not only with the residents of the plains but with those other hill dwellers, such as the Gurkhas and the Pathans, whom the British had fashioned into 'martial races'. Whereas the fierce Pathan was meant to test the manly qualities of the British officer, the

[15] Lady Betty Balfour, *The History of Lord Lytton's Indian Administration* (London, 1899), p. 220.

gentle Pahari was meant to guard his women and children. Modest, harmless, and submissive, the hill peoples were presumed to harbour no surprises and pose no threats to the British Raj. As such they were the ideal complement to the ideal of separation that lay at the heart of the opposition of hills and plains.[16]

CREATING CONSTITUENCIES

Throughout the years of their rule over India the British sought always, like imperial rulers everywhere, to mobilize supporters from among their subjects. The process of defining and labelling the peoples of India, discussed in chapter 4, had as one of its major objectives the identification of groups who might be shaped to the service of the Raj. After 1858, anxious and apprehensive, the British redoubled their efforts to mobilize support from within India, and so counter the challenge posed by the rebels of 1857. By the later decades of the century, as they were thrown on the defensive by the demands of the fledgling Indian National Congress, the British turned, with increasing desperation, to the devising of a political ideology that would at once accommodate Indian participation in a public arena, and yet secure power firmly in British hands. This process of definition was not an easy task, for it involved the extension to India of the Victorian liberal ideals of public discourse and representative government, and yet sought to confine them within the ideology of 'difference'. It was never possible to reconcile educated Indians to the assumptions that underlay this ideology, nor to stay the growth of nationalism. Nevertheless, like the demarcation of spaces meant to separate the British from the Indian people, the creation among those people of pliable 'constituencies' helped to contain, though it could never eradicate, a growing sense among the British of vulnerability and unease.

To secure the cooperation of their Indian subjects the British made use of an array of devices, from the membership of boards and councils to the award of titles and honours. Some, above all the concepts of election and representation, were drawn from British experience, informed by the ideas of liberalism; others, especially the imperial durbar, had Indian roots. All, however, were transformed as the British endeavoured to fit them to what they conceived of as the

---

[16] Dane Kennedy, 'Guardians of Edenic Sanctuaries: Paharis, Lepchas, and Todas in the British Mind,' *South Asia*, ns vol. 14, no. 2 (1991), pp. 57–77.

distinctive character of Indian society. Most importantly, when election was selected as the method of representation, constituencies were almost never defined, as they were for the most part in Britain after 1832, on the basis of territory, in which all the electors of a certain area jointly elected their representatives. In India, as we have seen, the British insisted that its society consisted of a large number of particularistic 'communities' held in place by the structure of the imperial state. As people existed in India only in and through these groupings, each of which was presumed to have enduring and essential characteristics of its own, representation inevitably took the form of drawing the more important of these 'communities' into the structure of the colonial order. As David Gilmartin has written, to be a Muslim for electoral purposes involved no particular statement of principle or belief. 'Instead, "objective" census considerations, by far the most important of which was descent, determined who would count as a Muslim.' The classificatory system of the Raj was thus transformed into a political system.[17]

Whether representation was accomplished by nomination or election, the objective was to secure the participation of those whom the British considered the 'natural leaders' of each group. These were men whom the British regarded as having traditional status, usually local, personal, and inherited, that set them apart from upstarts and self-made men. By its very nature the use of such a representational strategy ignored the differing interests and the rivalries among those whom the British had bundled together in a single 'community', and denied representation altogether to other groups. The urban society of Surat, for instance, in the view of nineteenth-century British administrators, as described by Douglas Haynes, comprised four communities defined by religious belief: the Hindu-Jains (treated as a single entity), the Parsis, the Muslims, and the Daudi Bohras. These communities collectively had at their head some dozen local families who had gained recognition as 'natural leaders' from the British. Other important local leaders, among them the heads of occupational *mahajans* and caste *panchayats*, together with all petty traders and artisans, were excluded from any direct access to the British authorities. Such exclu-

---

[17] Anil Seal, 'Imperialism and Nationalism in India', in J. Gallagher, G. Johnson and Anil Seal (eds.), *Locality, Province and Nation: Essays on Indian Politics, 1870–1940* (Cambridge, 1973), especially pp. 6–15; David Gilmartin, 'Democracy, Nationalism and the Public: A Speculation on Colonial Muslim Politics', *South Asia*, ns vol. 14 (June 1991), pp. 123–25.

sions were not accidental, but rather expressed an underlying philosophy that sought at once to bring together and to keep separate India's peoples.[18]

These various 'communities' participated with the imperial rulers in a distinctively colonial public arena. In Europe, according to Jurgen Habermas's influential formulation, 'public opinion' and the 'public sphere' functioned within an intermediary realm between the 'state' and the 'people', and so provided a locus of legitimacy and authority independent of, and exercising surveillance over, the state. An expanding print media, with public meetings and voluntary associations, gave expression to this autonomous public discourse. In colonial India, to be sure, a fledgling 'native' press and a certain number of voluntary associations did come into being over time. But they remained severely limited in their scope and responsibility. For the most part the state itself at once created and defined the 'public'. The growth of electoral representation, above all, as we have seen, did not emerge, as in England, in the context of a developing public sphere, but rather as a mechanism by which the state could encompass more effectively a society composed of a number of particularistic local communities. More generally, by creating channels through which the Indian 'public' could make itself heard, the state set itself up as the sole arbiter of which public discourse was legitimate, and which illegitimate, and so delimited the 'public' from the 'private' in India.[19]

In the British view, although the various communities themselves were included as actors in the public arena, most of what their individual members did was defined as 'private', or as the internal affair of the group, and so outside the realm of the 'public'. These 'private' matters included not just marriage and family life, but the practice of religion. Even though religious belief might define membership in a community, unlike England where church and state were joined, in India the British endeavoured to confine religious observance to a distinct 'private' sphere which Indians were meant to manage on their own (although the British intruded into it at every turn through the actions of their law codes and courts). By their very nature, so the British implied, Indians were incapable of constructing

[18] Douglas E. Haynes, *Rhetoric and Ritual in Colonial India* (Berkeley, 1991), pp. 101–11.
[19] For a broader discussion of these issues, see Sandria Freitag, 'Introduction' and 'The Changing Nature of "the Public" in British India', *South Asia*, ns vol. 14, no. 1 (June 1991), pp. 1–13, 65–90.

the universalistic 'public' sphere characteristic of bourgeois Europe. A people dominated by passion and emotion, they lacked the rational sensibility that alone made such civic discourse possible. Curzon made such views explicit when he wrote that Indian political activity was marked by an 'utter want of proportion, moderation or sanity'. Indeed, he further insisted, as he rather provocatively told Calcutta University graduates in 1905, 'the highest ideal of truth is to a large extent a Western conception'.[20] That there might be a contradiction between such assertions and the incorporation of Indians in the political order went unperceived.

Disabled by their fundamentally different character, Indians had by themselves no way of transcending the particularistic interests of their individual communities. No one, that is, could claim to represent any 'people' other than those constituting their own community. In a manner reminiscent of the unreformed eighteenth-century English constitution, with its narrow constituencies and ideas of 'virtual' representation, there existed no conception of a larger 'public' deserving of representation apart from the classificatory system of the Raj. The colonial state itself could alone overcome particular ties to create a rationalized whole concerned with 'general' interests. By definition, therefore, no activity undertaken by self-appointed leaders, or self-defined communities, could be legitimate. The rhetorical claims of the Indian National Congress to represent the 'people' of India were on these grounds from its very foundation dismissed as preposterous by most British officials. As John Strachey put it in his authoritative *India*, there is not, and never was, an India possessing 'any sort of unity, physical, political, social, or religious; no Indian nation, no "people of India", of which we hear so much'.[21]

As there could be no self-defined leaders in the public arena of the colonial world, so too was the expression of opinion in this arena to be confined to the institutions established for it. Above all, the 'public' arena did not extend to the streets and bazaars of India. As in eighteenth-century Britain, where the government sought to curb popular demonstrations such as those of John Wilkes, the streets were an especially feared site of disorder. The government could not, without intruding on the presumably 'private' sphere of religion, deny Indians the right to organize the ceremonial processions connected with religious observance. But these were not, so the British insisted,

[20] Raleigh, *Curzon in India*, p. 491.   [21] Strachey, *India*, p. 5.

occasions where public opinion could properly find expression. From the time of the 1893 cow protection movement onward, all unauthorized public activities were presumed to be 'unlawful', if not 'seditious'.

To contain the potential for disorder, the British insisted always that ceremonial observances be confined to that which could be regarded as sanctioned by 'tradition'. As an official wrote at the time of the 1911 Ramlila festival, the government had to 'enforce the principle that innovations must be prevented'. Current usage was thus frozen as time-honoured 'custom', and validated as 'history'. Any complainant, as Katherine Prior describes the process, had to prove that 'he had precedent on his side, that what he and his co-religionists claimed as their rights now was justified by the practices of their ancestors ten, twenty or even more years ago'. Inevitably, of course, as time went on, the British found it ever more difficult to insist upon a vision of permissible activity so much at odds with their ideals of religious freedom, or to deny legitimacy to leaders thrown up in the tumult of political agitation. Nevertheless even so late as the Kanpur mosque incident of 1913, when the siting of a road and the relocation of a bathing place provoked widespread protests, the government adamantly insisted that, because the protestors had expressed their grievances through open public activities, instead of through the 'natural leaders of the Muhammedan community', their actions were illegitimate. The 'great danger', as a Punjab administrator wrote a year later, 'lies in the mob throwing its leaders overboard'.[22]

Over time Indians at once assimilated and turned to their own advantage these British categories. Because domestic life and religious observance were defined as 'private', and hence outside the public sphere, they could be constructed as a space 'safe' from British interference. In the home especially, notions of domesticity, defined by proper female behaviour, could be nurtured to express an idealized 'Indian' personality distinguished from the anglicized world outside. Even though these ideals were often derived from Victorian notions of women's role, Bengali men especially found in them a satisfactory resolution of the tensions generated by the colonial encounter. Simi-

[22] Sandria Freitag, *Collective Action and Community: Public Arenas and the Emergence of Communalism in North India* (Berkeley, 1989), chapter 2, especially pp. 62–75; Katherine Prior, 'Making History: The State's Intervention in Urban Religious Disputes in the North-Western Provinces in the Early Nineteenth Century', *Modern Asian Studies*, vol. 27, part 1 (February 1993), pp. 179–203.

larly, in large part because the natural development and adjustment of religious observance was constrained by the British insistence on the freezing of past practice, contentious religious display offered an arena in which new political figures, and new ideologies could find a footing, and from which they could challenge established institutions and the dominance of old elites. In the end, ironically, the British endeavour to stifle religious innovation had the effect of only promoting it.

Repudiating alike the urban 'mob' and Congress's claims to represent an India-wide constituency, the British sought out communities perceived as stable and unthreatening, securely under the control of 'natural leaders'. Similarly, in their view, the appropriate arenas for public discourse were the institutions established by the government for that purpose. These existed at various levels, and grew both in number and in power as the British widened the circle of those incorporated into the political system of the Raj. The Councils Act of 1861 first announced the principle that Indians ought to be members of India's highest legislative body, and with it of provincial legislative councils as they in turn were established in the subsequent two to three decades. Municipalities meanwhile had been founded in some cities in the 1850s and 1860s, but they remained under the control of the district collector until Ripon's local self-government acts of 1882 set Indian controlled district and municipal boards in place across British India. The Councils Acts of 1892 and 1909, as we shall see in the next chapter, further extended Indian membership in the provincial and imperial legislative bodies, and recognized election as the normal and appropriate means of securing Indian representatives. Neither the composition nor the powers of these various bodies, before 1919, challenged British control of the levers of government.

Side-by-side with the growth of Indian membership in the institutions of government went the elaboration of honours and titles, and the regular enactment of ritual observances at all levels, from that of the district collector to that of the viceroy and king-emperor. Such ritual played a central role in the integration of Indian elites into the imperial order, especially those, like the princes, who as rulers of quasi-independent states had no recognized position in the institutional structures of British India. Though based upon Mughal, rather than British, precedents, these rituals were under the British radically transformed. As Bernard Cohn has shown for the imperial durbar and Douglas Haynes for civic ritual in Surat, in place of the affirmation of personal ties of patron and client, defined by the exchange of offerings and honours, colonial rituals became a 'vehicle for rendering deference to the imperial overlords and for demonstrating that the notables shared a common ethical ground with their rulers'. Participation in even the least consequential civic ceremony enabled local notables at once to lay claim to a high status as public leaders and to acknowledge the authority of the Raj which sustained them.[23]

In principle any group, so long as it was sufficiently influential, might be incorporated into the imperial order. Even the English-educated 'Indians' were often included, for, although, as the British saw it, they 'represented no one but themselves', they were still after all an important constituency. From the British point of view, however, by far the most attractive participants were India's ruling princes and landlords. These men comprised the overwhelming proportion of those invited to the great imperial durbars, and, when residents of the British Indian provinces, and so eligible for membership, they were disproportionately represented on the various legislative councils. They secured in addition various special privileges, from guarantees of their thrones to assistance in paying off their debts. Much of this was a matter of straightforward political expediency, a reward for the support which the princes, 'breakwaters to the storm which would otherwise have swept over us in one great wave', as Canning put it, had given the British during 1857. But even those who joined the revolt, as we have seen in chapter 2 above, impressed the British with their ability to command the loyalty of their followers and tenants; hence these men also deserved recognition and reward. More than mere allies of a vulnerable Raj, India's landlords and princes had now become an 'ancient, indigenous, and cherished' elite, whose superiority was a 'necessary element' in the country's social constitution.

Although the British after 1858 encouraged India's landlords to be like the English gentry, that is, to patronize agricultural improvement, modern education, and such philanthropies as famine relief, and awarded them the powers of honorary magistrates in their districts, the landlords had little interest in such activities beyond a conspicuous

---

[23] Haynes, *Rhetoric and Ritual*, pp. 126–137; Bernard Cohn, 'Representing Authority in Victorian India', in Hobsbawm and Ranger, *The Invention of Tradition*, especially pp. 168–74.

show for the benefit of their rulers, and the British, though often frustrated by their indifference, did not care to push them. India's gentry was instead being fitted for another role altogether: that of leaders of a caste-bound society, 'equally incapable of development and impervious to decay'. The 'visible and outward embodiment of Hindu secular power', the ksatriya raja, even when stripped of his kingly powers, retained, in this view, along with the Brahmin priest, his 'old world claim and grasp upon the reverence of Hindus'. As Harcourt Butler, author of two influential pamphlets on 'Oudh Policy', and subsequently lieutenant-governor of the United Provinces, put it in 1907, though the raja may be

over-bearing, often cruel [his people] live at his gate, where his horses and cattle and elephants are stalled, and there is a strong bond of common humanity between them. It is the old idea, 'You shall be my people and I will be your God.' Their lives are dull; their outlook is tinged with the deepest pessimism; when the day's work is over they long to huddle together under the blanket of common humanity. This feeling comes to all ... It is in the eastern air.[24]

Butler's vision of a contented peasantry under their 'old world' raja did not go wholly unchallenged. A number of officials protested the denial of class antagonism in the countryside, and insisted that India's gentry, uninterested in agricultural improvement, and stripped of their former powers as rajas, no longer played any useful role in society. Britain's duty, as men like H.C. Irwin passionately argued from his post in Oudh, was to 'uphold the cause of the poor and of him that hath no helper'. But such protests had little impact on the settled 'aristocratic' policy, and in any case the dissidents made no attempt to counter the underlying ideology of Indian 'difference'. For men like Irwin the peasantry served only to remind the British of their imperial responsibilities. Children in need of succour, they were not expected to initiate change in rural society.[25]

As part of the larger colonial project of ordering the whole of India's society, its princes and landlords, like its castes and tribes, were set into a 'scientifically' structured hierarchy. As 'natural leaders', situated at the top of society, however, these men were the beneficiaries of an

[24] Cited in Metcalf, *Landlords*, pp. 191–99, and chapter 11; see also P.D. Reeves, *Landlords and Government in Uttar Pradesh* (Bombay, 1991).
[25] H.C. Irwin, *The Garden of India* (London, 1880), pp. 184–95; see also C.W. McMinn, 'Introduction to the Oudh Gazetteer' (1873) (proof copy in the India Office Library).

exceptionally precise and careful exercise in marking out their rank and status. Only after they had been properly ranked and labelled, and so frozen into place, so the British believed, could they exercise their 'traditional' authority. Yet, obsessed with a desire to tidy up all ambiguities, the British inevitably constructed constituencies among the landed and princely elite whose coherence, far from being 'natural', was highly artificial. Sustained by administrative fiat, these men had little in common with their forebears under the Mughals, and resembled even less the English landed gentry.

The treatment of one major group of landlords, the Oudh taluqdars, may usefully illustrate the larger processes at work. For these men the process of definition began with the restoration of their estates, and the award of sanads, after the Mutiny. By contrast with the days of the Nawabs, when the title 'taluqdar' was applied loosely to those who had succeeded in the struggle for power in the countryside, and so could claim the right to engage for the revenue of an agglomeration of villages, the British set an arbitrary minimum limit of a revenue assessment of Rs. 5,000. They then at once proceeded to introduce an array of exceptions. Sole proprietors, for instance, and those whose estates succeeded by primogeniture, were sometimes given sanads even when their assessments fell below the minimum, while cosharers in larger undivided properties were often turned away. The British also gave the lands and status of taluqdar to favourites of their own who had had no previous connection with Oudh, including Sikhs, Europeans, and a Bengali babu. The process of definition was brought to a close by the enactment of Act I of 1869. This act promulgated a list of some 276 individuals entitled to the status of 'taluqdar'. Thereafter a taluqdar was a person whose name appeared on this list, or an heir of such a person; and no one else. No amount of opulence could henceforth gain a newcomer admission, nor would penury, so long as even a tiny amount of land remained, lead to the removal of a member's name from the list.

A similar obsession with order and tidiness shaped British relationships with India's ruling princes. Here too the award of adoption sanads after the Mutiny was but the first step in a minute process of ordering and ranking that took shape in such documents as the *alqabnamah* register. This list, first compiled in 1865, provided for every prince not just his name, titles, and state, but the form of address to be used in Persian and in English, the number of gun salutes to which he was entitled, the official of the Indian government with whom he was allowed to correspond directly, and even such details as the colour of the crest to be used on paper employed for correspondence with him. The 1889 edition of this list covered some forty-four pages of small print. Yet even so, consistency remained elusive. Despite an effort to link a salute of ten guns, and the address of 'His Highness', with the right to correspond directly with the viceroy, exceptions could not be eliminated. The Maharaja of Darbhanga, for instance, a large landlord in Bihar, possessed the right to direct correspondence with the viceroy even though his name did not appear at all in the alqabnamah.

These untiring efforts to achieve order encompassed the award of titles as well. Although the British had awarded titles to their Indian subjects since at least the 1820s, their own ambiguous status as rulers, as Bernard Cohn has pointed out, made it difficult for the governor-general to act as a 'fountain of honour'. After 1858, with the establishment of Crown rule, the British set out to regularize the award of honours. In 1861, as we have seen, they established the Star of India as the first Indian order of knighthood. Its organization and mode of address, placing the holder among the knights of Britain, made membership in this order attractive. It was, however, together with the companion Order of the Indian Empire, instituted in 1877, the only European-style honour most Indians could expect to receive; membership in other British orders, and in the hereditary English peerage, was accorded to only a handful of Indians, and as a matter of policy was officially discouraged. At the same time the government determined to devise uniform criteria for the award of Indian titles. Above all, in keeping with the overriding importance accorded to religious affiliation, they announced that 'titles to be conferred on the Mahomedan subjects of the British Empire in India will be ordinarily those of Khan Bahadoor and Nawab', while Hindus should receive those of 'Raee, Rajah Bahadoor, and Maharajah Bahadoor'. In addition, titles of the 'higher grade', above all *maharaja*, were to be 'reserved for the sovereigns of feudatory and dependent states except in cases of extraordinary merit'.[26]

In practice, however, when awards were to be made, the artificiality of these distinctions became apparent. The Bombay government in 1870, for instance, conferred the 'Mahomedan title' of Khan Bahadur

[26] See NAI Home Public, 15 January 1858, no. 9–10.

on a Parsi over the objection of the Indian government, who protested the grant as 'somewhat incongruous'. The foreign department, on similar grounds, opposed the award in the following year of the 'Hindu' title of 'raja' to two Muslim taluqdars. The chief commissioner insisted that such awards were nevertheless a 'very common custom' in Oudh. 'If the British Government give *Native* titles', he argued, 'it hardly seems incongruous ... to bestow such titles according to established native custom.' While admitting that it did 'appear a strange practice certainly', he acknowledged that the taluqdars 'themselves prefer the title of Raja to that of Nawab'. Consistency in the style of honours was a British, not an Indian, obsession.

The award of titles also raised the awkward question of whether such awards were meant simply to recognize, and honour, the established eminence of the 'natural' leaders of Indian society, or whether they should be held out to all as a way to encourage a spirit of liberal reform. When the Punjab government proposed, for instance, that the title of Khan Bahadur be bestowed upon a sub-assistant surgeon who, they claimed, had 'done more than anyone else to overcome the prejudices of the natives of the Punjab to European medical science' both by his practice and by translating and publishing medical works, some of the local officials, like the Amballa commissioner, applauded the decision on the ground that titles were 'cheap incentives to exertion and to the adoption of a higher tone of morality'; others by contrast insisted that such awards should be 'confined to persons of a certain social rank and eminence'. For the most part, only lesser titles, such as Rao Saheb and Rai Bahadur, were awarded to those distinguished chiefly for civic, educational, and philanthropic activities. Overall, titles were meant to solidify loyalty more than to trigger social change.[27]

The imperial durbar, as the arena where titles were awarded and homage offered, gave a visible, institutional shape to the late-nineteenth-century ideology of 'difference'. While the other institutions which defined India's 'public' space, such as the legislative councils, were drawn from English precedents, and so carried with them, at least implicitly, and for Indians often explicitly, expectations of liberal reform, the durbar sought to define Britain's relations with its subjects in Indian terms. Presiding over the durbar, surrounded by

---

[27] For controversy over titles, see correspondence in NAI For. Pol. A files of October 1870, no. 110–12; May 1871, no. 83–92; and March 1872, no. 252–58.

his loyal subjects, the viceroy easily imagined himself as the successor of the Mughal emperor Akbar, ordering a harmonious world where nothing ever changed.

The 'durbar' model especially suited India's ruling princes, for as the sovereigns of states linked to the Indian political order only through the exercise of British 'paramountcy', they possessed no way of participating in the European-style public arena of courts and councils. Further, this 'Indian' strategy of rule complemented the fantasies of medievalism discussed in chapter 3. The viceroy could be Henry II, as well as Akbar; and, as we have seen, Lytton designed the Imperial Assemblage of 1877 to represent a medieval vision of the monarch surrounded by his loyal feudatories. Butler's fantasy, of the raja with his people and cattle at his gate, carried overtones too of the medieval baron and his serfs.

Yet medievalism was not a wholly satisfactory mode for representing Britain's relations with India's princes. As men like Salisbury pointed out even in 1877, medievalism could be conceived of as a stage on the road to modernity; and as such it inevitably called into question the idea of India's enduring difference. Hence medieval, and feudal, terminology gave way over time to a more explicitly 'Indian' representational mode. The tension between the two, and the endeavour to reconcile them, can be seen clearly in a work such as Charles Tupper's *Our Indian Protectorate* (1893). For Tupper the Indian Empire derived 'from its Oriental surroundings' many of its 'most important principles of life and growth', so that 'we are the heirs of the Moghals'. Yet at the same time there were 'many tendencies making for feudalism in the India of our predecessors', and 'our protection has been sought in India as vassals sought the protection of their lord'. Hence the Indian protectorate took on the shape of a 'feudal system', but one which 'rests on ideas which are fundamentally indigenous'. Indeed the British had not only established a 'reconstituted Delhi Empire, greatly improved and strengthened', for their Raj was 'much more largely moulded on modern ideas of political morality', but, in this way as so many others, Britain's empire resembled that of the ancient Romans, who had 'reverenced law' as they adapted their institutions to local custom and tradition.

In his Coronation durbar of 1902 Lord Curzon explicitly rejected a 'medieval' in favour of an 'Indian' mode of representation for British rule in India. Lytton, he pointed out, had designated his durbar an

'Imperial Assemblage' to emphasize its novelty. He himself had decided, however, to revert to 'the older and more familiar form, because the Mogul and other sovereigns invariably held durbars to celebrate their accession'. The ritual of the durbar was, Curzon insisted, 'something familiar and even sacred' in 'the East'; hence it was altogether appropriate, as the British now sought 'to step into the shoes of the Great Moghul', for them to adopt 'some at least of the time honoured features of Indian durbars'. Curzon was especially careful, even though his ceremony took place on the same ground as Lytton's, to distinguish it from its predecessor. Insisting that there was nothing 'suggestive of the East' in the banners and shields of Lytton's Assemblage, Curzon had a 'Saracenic dome' set above the dais of his amphitheatre, while 'small kiosques and ornaments borrowed from the Mogul architecture' embellished the structure. As he proudly proclaimed, the entire arena was 'built and decorated exclusively in the Mogul, or Indo-Saracenic style'.

These architectural forms, with their illusion of an enduring Mughal order, provided an appropriate stage on which Curzon enacted the rituals he constructed to mark out his durbar as 'Indian'. As we have seen, as rulers the British had radically changed the meaning of Mughal ritual, and Curzon made no attempt to recover its original intent. He refused, for instance, to sanction an exchange of presents. He disdained as well anything that might suggest an equivalence between the Indian princes and the English aristocracy, such as the creation of an Indian peerage or the award of coats of arms of the sort Lytton had devised. But Curzon was anxious to secure the active participation of the leading princes in the ceremony. He did this by having each prince in turn mount the dais and offer a message of congratulations to the king-emperor. In place of the presentation of nazrs, Curzon simply shook hands with each ruling chief as he passed by. Some such interchange of 'homage and courtesy', so Curzon insisted, despite the obviously European inspiration of so much of it, had 'been an immemorial feature of Indian Accession Durbars'.[28]

Curzon did not wrap the Raj in Indian ritual as a way to elaborate a theory of indirect rule, such as Lord Lugard was simultaneously devising in Africa. Rather the durbar was meant above all to manifest the power and majesty of the British Raj. Never before, Curzon

[28] For durbar arrangements, see Curzon Minute of 11 May 1902 in NAI For. Secret-I, September 1902, no. 1–3.

exulted, had there been a gathering of the 'Asiatic feudatories of the British Crown' from such a 'sweep of territory', extending over 'fifty-five degrees of longitude' from Aden to Burma. By bringing together this vast array of peoples Curzon hoped to give India's ruling elite a sense of 'common participation in a great political system and of fellow citizenship of the British Empire'.

Yet the British had no coherent place for the princes in their imperial ideology. The durbar ideal implied that they were to form a constituency frozen in time and space, integrated into the larger imperial system only through ritual acts of subordination. Carefully kept apart from each other, each meant to enact in his own state alone the role of 'natural' leader, the princes possessed no common institutions until the formation of the Chamber of Princes in 1918. Whether turned to political advantage, as the British sought to use princely influence for imperial purposes, or simply displayed for all to see, these 'traditional' rulerships served the purpose of announcing India's enduring 'difference'. The states, as Curzon said in 1902, 'keep alive the traditions and customs, they sustain the virility, and they save from extinction the picturesqueness of ancient and noble races'.

Yet the British were never content to leave the princes to exercise their loudly trumpeted 'traditional' authority as they saw fit. The prince was meant to be, as Curzon told Maharaja Ganga Singh of Bikaner, 'at the same time a Liberal and a Conservative', to 'combine the merits of the East and West in a single blend'. Trained and educated in Western ways, but ruling their states 'upon Native lines', they were to be not 'relics' but rulers; not puppets, but 'living factors in the administration'. The Mayo College, where an elaborate Indo-Saracenic facade enclosed rooms in which young princes were to study English, history, and geography, perhaps most vividly represented Britain's inconsistent visions of princely India.[29]

Baffled by these contradictory demands, unable to wage war or extend their territories, yet secure on their thrones, the princes had little incentive to govern their states in any particular way, or indeed at all. Even the British Residents assigned to their courts had but limited space in which to direct their activities. Nicholas Dirks has described the princely rulership as that of a 'theatre state'. What the British

---

[29] Curzon of Kedleston, *Speeches by H.E. the Lord Curzon of Kedleston*, vol. 3 (in Curzon Papers, IOR MS Eur. F. 111/559), pp. 60–67; Curzon of Kedleston, *Speeches on India Delivered while in England in July–August 1904*, pp. 14–15.

wanted, he says, was 'a fiction' that pretended to be the preservation of the old regime. What they got was a diverse and unpredictable array of behaviour, which they could rarely control as they wished, from the 'model' prince of Bikaner to the ruler of Pudukkottai who, after being carefully educated as a minor, married an Australian woman and abandoned his state altogether. The British had hollowed out the crown of princely sovereignty. But that the crown was hollow mattered less than that it existed.[30]

THE CLAIMS OF EQUALITY

The ideology of liberalism, with its optimistic assumption that India could be transformed on a European model, did not wholly disappear during the later decades of the nineteenth century. Many of its claims still remained embedded in the larger currents of imperial thought and practice, for they expressed cherished British values. The idea of equality, for instance, despite the ideology of difference, could not be explicitly repudiated. In the 1858 Proclamation introducing Crown rule, the queen solemnly pledged her government not only to an 'equal and impartial' legal system, but assured her Indian subjects of equal access to employment in the government of their country. Western education, above all, though its products might be derided and caricatured as babus, could not be denied a place in the late Victorian Raj. By its very nature the patronage of Western education implied that the transformation of India was not only possible, but an appropriate and desirable objective for the British in India. Insofar as they saw it as their task to introduce 'civilization', defined in British terms as 'progress' or 'improvement' – and much of their justification for empire after all hinged upon such claims – the British could not rest content with the notion of themselves as Mughal emperors surrounded by loyal feudatories. They had at once to create, and to nurture, a constituency of Indians committed to the transformation of their own society.

For the most part, as we have seen in chapter 2, the British endeavoured to contain the contradictions within their imperial ideology by insisting that Indians, like children, required a long process of tutelage

---

[30] Nicholas B. Dirks, *The Hollow Crown: Ethnohistory of an Indian Kingdom* (Cambridge, 1987), chapter 13; for a full discussion of the princes, see Ramusack volume forthcoming in this series.

before they could participate in the governance of their country. The tasks of the schoolmaster could, of course, be so broadly defined, and the level of competence for the pupil set so high, as to leave little scope for change. It was not difficult to find reasons why any proposed reform was premature, or unsuited to India. Still, there were dissidents committed to the ideals of liberalism, who endeavoured to find ways forward, and who from time to time gained an ascendancy within the Indian government. On such occasions, above all during the viceroyalty of Lord Ripon (1880–4), the British were forced to confront the contradictory assumptions that underlay the Raj. Late Victorian liberals were, however, at all times cautious in their commitment to reform. Indians, in their view, were still hardly more than toddlers, learning how to walk, while liberals incorporated unquestioningly into their ideology many of the caste and communal categories that had been devised to master Indian society. The exuberant enthusiasms of the Macaulay era, when the concession of political power to Indians was only a visionary dream, had long vanished. As conservative imperialists could not repudiate the idea of 'progress', so too did liberal imperialists inevitably embed notions of India's 'difference' in their thinking.

Liberal ideology first took institutional shape in Indian local government. During the 1860s and 1870s municipalities with elected members were conceded to most major Indian cities, though only in Calcutta and Bombay did elected Indians control the corporation. These reforms were, however, the product of fiscal as much as of political calculation. Local bodies could raise local taxes, and so increase government revenue while diffusing popular animosity. They also aided the British as they sought to integrate local constituencies more tightly into the Raj. As Anil Seal has written, these boards 'enabled the government to associate interests in the localities more widely, and balance them more finely, than had the old rule of thumb methods of the Collector'. In most municipalities seats were apportioned among precisely defined trading and religious communities.[31]

As a Liberal appointed to the viceroyalty by Gladstone, Ripon introduced for the first time into Indian local government the objective of training Indians for self-rule. He was prepared even to sacrifice administrative efficiency for this purpose. As he put it in the 1882

---

[31] Anil Seal, 'Imperialism and Nationalism', pp. 12–13; Hugh Tinker, *The Foundations of Local Self-Government in India, Pakistan and Burma* (New York, 1968), chapter 2.

COPING WITH CONTRADICTION

Resolution which proposed the establishment of municipal and district boards throughout India, 'It is not primarily with a view to improvement in administration that this measure is put forward and supported. It is chiefly designed as an instrument of political and popular education.' Introducing the new reforms into the Bombay legislature, J. B. Peile echoed the same liberal sentiments: 'It may not seem a very lofty employment to teach the people ... of country towns how to manage local conservancy, primary schools and dispensaries, but it is the underlying growth of social organization which is really important, and I think it is not unworthy of the best abilities and the highest ambition to build up in one's people with unpretentiousness and patient assiduity, the first foundations of a national spirit.' In this way, with proper guidance, India could be prompted slowly along the same path of development which Britain had taken.[32]

Much in the constitution of these boards continued earlier practice. Above all, Ripon made no attempt to challenge the notion of India as a society of diverse interests, each entitled to representation. 'I am inclined to think', he wrote, 'that election by caste or occupation would in many cases be more consonant with the feelings of the people.' Hence Ripon's local self-government reforms inaugurated a vast proliferation of communal electorates, and laid the groundwork for much that was to follow at the provincial and national levels. The ideology of municipal reform too was permeated with a condescending paternalism. 'You have to prove', the district collector told the Surat council in 1894, 'that you can, like the men of the West, lay down a thoughtful policy and follow it with resolution ... The habit of sacrificing present advantages for the attainment of a distant object or for the benefit of generations yet unborn is the essence of national greatness.' Nevertheless, the new municipal and district boards announced a reaffirmation of liberal ideals, and opened up new opportunities, which they were not slow to take advantage of, for what Ripon in 1882 called the 'intelligent class of public-spirited men' rapidly growing up with the spread of education. In 1892 the Councils Act made these local boards electoral colleges for the provincial legislative councils, and so further extended the arena in which the English-educated could enact their role of representatives of an Indian public.[33]

---

[32] Haynes, *Rhetoric and Ritual*, p. 105; Tinker, *Foundations*, chapter 3.
[33] For developments in Surat, see Haynes, *Rhetoric and Ritual*, pp. 115–21.

Ripon's reforms obviously called into question the idealization of 'efficiency' that sustained the civil service, and they posed a challenge as well to the idea that India should only be accorded representation through its proper 'natural' leaders. Not surprisingly, as a result, the measures evoked widespread and intense hostility. This was most marked in Bengal, where the Calcutta Corporation possessed an elected Indian majority, with two-thirds of the members chosen, not on the basis of community, but by the ratepayers of some twenty-five territorial wards. For the British this institution, dominated by educated Bengali Hindus, foreshadowed precisely the horrors they had long feared. In it indeed they could see embodied the 'idea of a Bengali Parliament'. As the Bengal lieutenant-governor disparagingly put it in 1898, the Calcutta Corporation 'gives the fullest expression to the demoralizing doctrine that practical considerations are to be subordinated to the supposed educational influences of Local Self-Government'. Nor was animosity confined to Bengal. In the North-Western Provinces the lieutenant-governor, Auckland Colvin, complained of the rise of 'new men' through municipal elections, at the expense of Muslims and the majority of conservative Hindus; such innovations were, he said, but a further illustration of the 'levelling' of Indian society brought about by British rule.

Curzon as viceroy fully shared these sentiments. For him, as for so many British officials, Calcutta, at once the 'city of dreadful night' and the capital of British India, played a powerful imaginative role as the exemplar of the ill effects of Ripon-style liberalism. The city's sanitary shortcomings, its governance by a large deliberative body 'apt to diffuse [its] force in vague and vapid talk', and the control of that body by the 'minute minority' of the so-called 'Baboo Party', were all, in his view, inextricably linked together. Hence as viceroy he determined at one blow to 'cut the Baboo down to size', and to restore 'efficiency' to Calcutta's local government, by drastically reducing the electoral element in the corporation. 'Were I Lieutenant-Governor of Bengal', he arrogantly told the secretary of state, 'I would undertake to bring about a revolution in the sanitation and hygiene of the city in five years.'[34]

With twenty years' experience of the Ripon reforms behind them, men like Curzon repudiated election above all because it secured the

[34] Chris Furedy, 'Lord Curzon and the Reform of the Calcutta Corporation, 1899', *South Asia*, ns, vol. 1 (1978), pp. 75–89.

'wrong' kind of representative. As H. H. Risley put it, in a telling fishing metaphor, 'it selects those who rise to the surface – the men who talk and canvass and agitate – but it does not reach the silent depths of the stream. It does not give us . . . the genuine, representative Hindus, the men we really want.' In a rehearsal for the subsequent partition of Bengal, Curzon forced through his reform of the Calcutta Corporation over bitter opposition. Yet he could not eradicate the electoral principle, which, even though hedged round by communal constituencies, took on even greater importance in Indian politics with the enactment of the Morley–Minto reforms in 1909.

English-educated Indians not surprisingly learned to manipulate the system of local government to their advantage. Not only were they able to secure their own election to municipal councils, but they successfully laid claim to the ideology that underlay the Ripon reforms. They declared themselves committed to the 'common good' and to 'progress'; they insisted that they, not the aristocratic notables tied to parochial constituencies, represented the larger urban 'public'; indeed, as Haynes has pointed out, they adopted as their own the moral hierarchy embodied in the evolutionary conception of history, and so argued that as their political ideas were more advanced than those of the feudal 'notables', they were more worthy of Britain's trust. Masters of the liberal idiom of civic reform, educated Indians made it difficult for the British to repudiate them without repudiating the ideals of 'progress' as well. By the early years of the twentieth century the British found that they could no longer deny these new politicians an important collaborative role in the empire.[35]

By far the most momentous clash of ideologies in British India was that which took place in 1882–3 over the Ilbert Bill. At stake in this piece of legislation, which sought to empower Indians acting as magistrates in the countryside to try European British subjects, were contending views of the nature of the Raj that cut to the core of the British justification for their presence in India. In the course of this controversy, which grew ever more embittered until its final ambiguous resolution, the British were forced as never before to choose between fundamental principles of imperial governance. On the one side were ideals dear to the hearts of liberals: equality before the law, and the transformative power of education. Indians and Britons, supporters of the bill insisted, must, when similarly qualified, be accorded equal

[35] Haynes, *Rhetoric and Ritual*, chapter 8, especially pp. 152–53, 165.

treatment. On the other side stood the bill's opponents, who insisted on the essential difference of race, and argued for a legal system that would accommodate that difference. One was a vision of eventual 'sameness', the other of enduring 'difference'. Between these views – of an empire founded on equity, and one avowedly grounded in force – the alternatives were starkly posed. Hence it is worth examining the Ilbert Bill debate with some care.

From the days of the Company, Europeans in India had been accorded preferential treatment in the courts. Above all they possessed the right, confirmed by the 1861 code of criminal procedure, to a jury trial in the High Courts located in the presidency cities of Calcutta, Bombay, and Madras. Because of the delay and expense involved in bringing European defendants and Indian plaintiffs distances of up to a thousand miles for trial, in 1872 the government accorded district magistrates limited powers of imprisonment and fine over European British subjects. The question at once arose as to whether Indians were entitled to possess these powers. As we have seen, the Queen's Proclamation of 1858 authorized 'our subjects of whatever race or creed [to] be freely admitted to offices in our service, the duties of which they may be qualified by their education, ability, and integrity duly to discharge'. Under the authority of this pronouncement, informed as it was by mid-Victorian liberal idealism, scattered Indians, mostly Bengalis, had managed during subsequent years to pass the examination for entry into the covenanted service. Others, after 1878, gained entry to the so-called statutory civil service established by Lord Lytton as an alternative to the onerous journey to London and uncertain prospects of passing an examination confined by a maximum age limit initially of 25 years, then reduced to 21.

In 1872 there were only four Indians in the civil service, and all were relatively junior. Nevertheless, anticipating the eventual promotion of these men to higher positions, the government sought to amend the criminal procedure code so that Indian, as well as European, members of the service could try British subjects in the interior. The measure was, however, defeated in the imperial legislative council by the narrow margin of 7 votes to 5. The non-official British members of the council, with the law member James Fitzjames Stephen, contributed the deciding negative votes. The subject then lay dormant until 1882, when one of the Indian members of the service, Behari Lal Gupta, was due for promotion to the post of sessions judge in upper Bengal.

Thirty-two other Indians, though none were so senior in rank, had by that time also secured appointments in the service. The question of the exclusion of Indians from jurisdiction over Europeans could therefore no longer be evaded. Indeed, the anomaly was the more intensely felt in Gupta's case for his promotion would deprive him not only of powers enjoyed by his English deputy, but powers which he had himself exercised in his previous post in Calcutta, for Indian judges in the presidency cities, by contrast with the interior districts, had long possessed the right to try Englishmen. Hence the proposed bill, brought forward by C.P. Ilbert, the law member, sought to remove from the statute book all judicial disqualifications based on race.

Supporters of the bill, who included most of the senior officials of the Indian government, above all Lord Ripon himself, argued simply that equity and fairness demanded the removal of all 'invidious distinctions' in the law. As Ilbert put it:

with the removal of these disqualifications would disappear the arguments resting on privilege – arguments which are as unsound as they are invidious. The theory that an Englishman is entitled to the privilege of being tried exclusively by Englishmen, has to the best of my knowledge, been manufactured expressly for consumption in the Indian market. Imagine its being suggested to a Parisian magistrate on behalf of an English pick-pocket!

Ilbert's 'Parisian' analogy nevertheless revealed assumptions far beyond the mere removal of administrative anomalies. It implied that India, and Indians, were in some fundamental sense equivalent in status to England and the English, and that the law should express this equivalence. Britain's claim to rule India, in this view, rested upon a perceived reputation for fairness, and this in turn required uniform application of the law in all cases. It was precisely this equivalence that opponents of the bill contested.[36]

Insistence upon legal uniformity was a fundamental element of the liberal programme. From the 1830s onward, as we have seen in chapter 2, a fierce Benthamite assertion of the importance of uniformity had informed the process of Indian legal codification. Indeed, the first attempt to roll back the legal privileges of Europeans in India had taken place as far back as 1836, when Macaulay as law member had introduced legislation that would subject British residents in the country to the regular Company courts, with an appeal to the Sadr

[36] Memo by Ilbert of 4 September 1882, NAI Home Judl., September 1882, no. 219–39.

Diwani Adalat, rather than, as before, placing them under a separate jurisdiction with a right of appeal to Crown courts. This so-called 'Black Act' had evoked a fierce opposition among the British in India, but Macaulay, anticipating Ilbert's 'Parisian' analogy, argued that it would be ludicrous to expect an Englishman trading in France to be allowed to settle his contractual differences according to English law. John Stuart Mill likewise insisted in his Minute on the 'Black Act' that legal distinctions maintained on racial grounds would 'destroy the prestige of superior moral worth and justice in dealings which now attaches to the British name in India'. In the minds of liberals, equity and justice alone gave expression to Britain's superiority.

Opponents of the Ilbert Bill believed themselves to be moved not by unthinking racial prejudice, but by principle. They drew upon a theory of India's 'difference' whose origins could be traced back to Warren Hastings's elaboration of codes of Hindu and of Muslim personal law. The most outspoken advocate of this view was James Fitzjames Stephen. Though nominally a Liberal, and a utilitarian, Stephen insisted that India, in its social organization, was fundamentally different from Europe. Hence it was absurd to try to enforce European legal principles in India. As he told the legislative council in opposing the 1872 reform:

In countries situated as most European countries are, it is no doubt desirable that there should be no personal laws; but in India it is otherwise. Personal, as opposed to territorial laws, prevail here on all sorts of subjects ... I think there is no country in the world, and no race of men in the world, from whom a claim for absolute identity of law for persons of all races and habits comes with as bad a grace as from the Natives of this country, filled as it is with every distinction which race, caste, and religion can create, and passionately tenacious as are its inhabitants of such distinctions.

As the system of administering justice in India inevitably must differ 'in its characteristic features' from the English system, there could be, so Stephen argued, no reason why the English residents of India should be obliged to surrender privileges to which they attached 'the highest possible importance'.[37]

Stephen's critics countered with a vision of the Raj as a government committed to the steady 'whittling away' of all such privileges. The history of Anglo-Indian legislation, as W. W. Hunter described it, was

[37] Speech of 16 April 1872, *India. Proceedings of the Imperial Legislative Council,* pp. 398–99.

'the history of the absorption of these personal laws peculiar to classes into a common system of law applicable to all'. The curtailment of 'class distinctions' proposed by the Ilbert Bill was thus 'no isolated act', but 'one of a long series of measures absolutely inevitable in moulding the laws of the various races ... into a common body of law applicable to them all'. In contrast to Stephen's perpetuation of difference, for Hunter India's legal system would in time become like England's. This 'whittling away' of class privilege could take place, so Hunter argued, because the Indian members of the ICS were themselves becoming more and more like its British members. They had had, he reminded his fellow legislators, to 'overcome the inertia of climate and the prejudices of their race to partially re-educate themselves on a foreign model', and they had had to succeed in an examination framed to suit the British, not the Indian, educational system. 'Many of the Native Civilians thus selected', he concluded rather extravagantly, 'are more English in thought and feeling than Englishmen themselves.' Lyall argued in similar fashion that their education and training had made the Indian members of the civil service comparable in ability to Europeans, and hence 'as a class capable of exercising impartially the judicial powers' regularly exercised by their British colleagues.[38]

But matters could not be so easily resolved. Both Stephen's insistence upon 'difference' and Hunter's promise of 'sameness' raised troubling questions about the nature, even the existence, of the Raj itself. To be sure, men like Ilbert sought only the removal of 'anomalies' in the interests of 'equity'. Nevertheless, insofar as they justified ruling India by an ideology based upon legality and equity, they made the practice of that governance increasingly difficult. It was, that is, no easy matter at once to treat Indians and Europeans equally, and then to claim the right to rule a conquered India. The opponents of the Ilbert Bill lost no time in bringing this contradiction before the public. In a letter to *The Times* of 1 March 1883, Stephen pointed out that, 'If the Government of India have decided on removing all anomalies from India, they ought to remove themselves and their countrymen.' Echoing Stephen, the Tory, Ellis Ashmead-Bartlett, developed the same theme more fully in the House of Commons:

[38] Speech of 9 March 1883, *India. Proceedings of the Imperial Legislative Council*, pp. 188–97.

Once begin to base your Indian legislation and policy on the removal of anomalies, and you enter upon a course fatal to your dominion in India, fatal to the prosperity and wealth of these kingdoms. The removal of anomalies indeed! . . . if this be your principle the greatest anomaly of all is the presence of Englishmen in India at all. Will the right hon. Gentleman [Gladstone] and his Viceroy prepare to drive his countrymen, bag and baggage, out of the country they have rescued from war, from tyranny, and cruel devastation? . . . This bill does not extinguish anomalies. It only brings them out in clearer relief.[39]

Men like Hunter and Lyall, with the other members of the Indian civil service who conceived of themselves as liberals, preferred to avert their faces from these larger questions. Confronted by increasingly clamorous Indian political demands, they could not so easily join Macaulay in celebrating a transformed India, and with it the end of the Raj. Most of those consulted by Ripon about the Ilbert reforms were reluctant to concede more than a limited award of judicial authority to selected Indian members of the service. They especially disliked, as Lyall put it, having India 'stirred up by all these controversies', for 'government will not hereafter be so simple a matter as it has been hitherto'. They insisted too, in terms of expediency, that incorporating Indians into the government of their country would help secure the loyalty of these men, and so strengthen the hold of the Raj. Almost none among them had any sympathy for what Lyall called the 'sham democracy of the crude Bengalee who had no strength behind his words'. Yet, for all this, they refused to disavow the ideals of liberalism. Some two generations after Macaulay, the claims of those whom the British had themselves brought into being had now to be acknowledged. Hunter insisted, in two successive letters to *The Times*, that Britain could not repudiate the principles embodied in the Ilbert Bill, for that would be to draw back from a 'long series of pledges', above all that of the Queen's Proclamation, deliberately given to the Indian people. Guarantees, once made, had to be fulfilled. The empire had to stand, or fall, on principles of equity. No other base was conceivable.[40]

Similar sentiments informed the views of men like Hunter and Lyall towards education. It lay at the heart of Britain's mission in India, and so could not be repudiated, despite their own deep ambivalence. As a young man in 1859 Lyall had pondered the paradoxes implicit in the

[39] *Hansard's Parliamentary Debates*, 22 August 1883, col. 1678.
[40] *The Times*, 2 October and 10 December 1883; Durand, *Lyall*, pp. 165, 261, 278–83.

combination of education and empire. 'Having civilized them', he wondered, 'and taught them the advantage of liberty and the use of European sciences, how are we to keep them under us, and to persuade them that it is for their good that we hold all the high offices of Government?' By the 1880s his enthusiasm for education had waned. The 1882 Education Commission, which sought to enlarge the scope and extent of education, and which Hunter chaired, Lyall derided as 'dressing up a subject artistically, trotting it out, and generally making the most of it, as of a horse for sale'. As for himself, he said, 'I have no belief in it in Indian politics except as likely to add to our eventual difficulties.' Nevertheless, he continued, 'as education is a thing that can't be refused, and that I would not if I could refuse, to the native, I don't mind its ultimate effects'.[41]

Stephen, steeped in James Mill's utilitarianism, dismissed as mere 'sentiment' all talk of India's eventual transformation. But he too, and the other opponents of the bill, had to fashion a firm basis of ideology in order to justify their position. In 1883 Stephen reiterated his insistence that India's variety of personal laws constituted an equivalent to the English demand for privileged treatment in the courts. The judges of the Calcutta High Court concurred. 'The entire structure of Indian society and the British administration', as they wrote, in a statement published in *The Times* of 1 August 1883, 'rests on personal laws, under which particular classes or individuals enjoy special rights apart from the general law applicable to the entire community.' The judges further argued that it was unwise to allow natives of India to exercise the powers of police and magisterial inquiry which were commonly combined with those of district magistrate. The present law, they said, unlike the proposed amendment, 'protects European British subjects from the exercise of this dangerous combination of duties by anyone but their own countrymen'. A European alone, in other words, could be trusted with the powers of a 'petty despot' in the countryside.

Though Stephen refused to acknowledge it, the concession of special privileges for Englishmen on the ground of personal law was more than a little disingenuous. After all, India's differing personal laws for the most part related to matters of substantive civil law such as inheritance and the like. Where the British sought uniformity, and where they prided themselves on securing an impartial 'rule of law' in

41 Durand, *Lyall*, pp. 89, 266.

India, was, as we have seen in chapter 2, in the area of procedure. Hence to create special exemptions for British subjects in the way the law was administered was to set them apart, not as one among several communities in India, each with its own body of laws, but as a privileged ruling race. Stephen's proud boast that the law was Britain's 'gospel', the 'sum and substance of what we have to teach' to India, was hardly compatible with an award, to the English alone, of the right of refusing trial in a properly constituted tribunal solely on the grounds of the racial origin of the presiding judge.

Only by reaching outside the framework of law could this special privilege find justification. As Stephen put it, provocatively, in his 1 March 1883 letter to *The Times*, legal distinctions between European and Indian were inherent in the nature of the Raj itself. The British Indian government, he wrote,

is essentially an absolute government, founded, not on consent, but on conquest. It does not represent the native principles of life or of government, and it can never do so until it represents heathenism and barbarism. It represents a belligerent civilization, and no anomaly can be so striking or so dangerous as its administration by men who, being at the head of a government founded upon conquest, implying at every point the superiority of the conquering race, of their ideas, their institutions, their opinions, and their principles, and having no justification for its existence except that superiority, shrink from the open, uncompromising, straightforward assertion of it, seek to apologize for their own position, and refuse, from whatever cause, to uphold and support it.

The Ilbert Bill, he concluded, was nothing less than a 'determination to try to govern India upon principles inconsistent with the foundations on which British power rests'.

Stephen thus repudiated the liberal position that Britain's superiority derived ultimately from its reputation for fairness, its 'superior moral worth' as lawgiver, in favour of an insistence upon the inherent superiority of a conquering people. This superiority had to be visibly represented for it to be effectual. As Ashmead-Bartlett argued in the House of Commons, 'It is not by force alone that British rule in India is maintained. The 60,000 British bayonets that garrison that vast country are but a drop among the teeming myriads by whom they are surrounded. It is the repute, the *prestige*, the innate sense of superiority that makes that little band of soldiers and administrators respected and obeyed by the masses around them.' If an Indian were to see an

Englishman tried and sentenced by one of his own race, he would soon 'lose the natural respect which at present is felt for an Englishman, and will begin a course of encroachment which can only end in trouble and mutiny'.[42]

Unlike the liberals, who were willing at least to contemplate that Indians would someday become like Englishmen, hence entitled to control their own government, the opponents of the Ilbert Bill recoiled from that now visible, even if still distant, prospect. The frankness, the 'belligerence' of their language, was an expression of an increasing fearfulness, linked to a newly perceived vulnerability. As the distinctions between colonized and colonizer were becoming blurred, it was necessary ever more insistently to proclaim India's inherent difference. Men like Stephen thus helped legitimate, and so gave voice to, a host of anxieties and insecurities widely spread among the British in India. As we have seen in our discussion of Kipling's stories, written in the years just after the Ilbert controversy, these fears ranged widely over the alleged inadequacies of Indian character, religion, and society, and extended even to the control of India's past. In the Ilbert struggle all the stereotypes that marked out India's inferiority were marshalled afresh and with a renewed intensity. Not surprisingly the non-official English in India, fearful of their loss of influence over a govenment they saw as their own, fought most tenaciously – through their newspapers, above all *The Englishman* of Calcutta, by petitions, and by monster protest meetings. In the end many officials, including the Viceroy Lord Ripon himself, acquiesced in the gutting of the bill in order to quell the fierce hostility of their own countrymen. Under its provisions as finally enacted in 1884, accused Europeans secured the right to claim a trial by jury, at least half of whose members were to be themselves European.

Throughout these debates no aspect of the 'difference' between Indian and Briton obtained greater prominence than that relating to gender. For many, indeed, the bill was pre-eminently about the treatment of women. As Kipling wrote in his autobiography, describing his own initial perception of the proposal, 'Just then, it was a matter of principle that Native judges should try white women. Native in this case meant overwhelmingly Hindu; and the Hindu's idea of women is not lofty.' The enduring opposition of the 'sensual' Indian male and the 'sacralized' white woman, given powerful form by the

[42] *Hansard's Parliamentary Debates*, 22 August 1883, col. 1684.

rape tales of the Mutiny, now focused upon images of 'pure and passionless' white women placed at the mercy of lascivious native male judges. Even though the Ilbert Bill said nothing about women, and the educated Indian elite were at no time implicated in any of the occasional assaults which did take place, the defeat of this measure, so the British convinced themselves, could alone protect the 'defenceless' white woman, and so secure the superiority of the ruling race.

On this occasion, however, the British women residents of India did not simply rely upon the 'chivalric' sentiments of their male protectors. Instead, they participated actively in the campaign against the Ilbert Bill, and even took the lead in linking the 'unmanly' sensuality of the Indian male with judicial unfitness. Those who degraded their own women, so these English women claimed, disqualified themselves from sitting in judgement on a more 'civilized' race. Most outspoken perhaps was Annette Akroyd Beveridge, wife of Henry Beveridge, one of the most liberal members of the Indian civil service and himself a supporter of Indian political advance. In a controversial letter to the *Englishman*, Annette Beveridge condemned the bill as a 'proposal to subject civilized women to the jurisdiction of men who have done little or nothing to redeem the women of their race, and whose social ideas are still on the outer verge of civilization'. Pressed by liberal friends to justify her position, she insisted that, 'speaking as an English woman', she could not but 'call uncivilised a people which cares about stone idols, enjoys child marriage and secludes its women, and where at every point the fact of sex is present to the mind'. Ironically, in presuming, on the grounds of the 'pride of womanhood', to defend Indian women, Annette Beveridge only set herself apart from them. As Mrinalini Sinha has pointed out, 'the native female's own experience of the gender and racial hierarchies of colonial society ... found no place in Akroyd's woman-centred outrage against the bill'. By celebrating 'difference', Annette Beveridge, despite her protestations to the contrary, inevitably made gender subservient to race, and so to empire.[43]

Anger at the Indian claims to equality expressed in the Ilbert Bill controversy informed even British scholarship on India's ancient past.

[43] Lord Beveridge, *India Called Them* (London, 1947), pp. 227–28, 248; Mrinalini Sinha, 'Chathams, Pitts, and Gladstones in Petticoats: The Politics of Race and Gender in the Ilbert Bill Controversy, 1883–84', in Nupur Chaudhuri and Margaret Strobel (eds.), *Western Women and Imperialism* (Indiana, 1992), pp. 98–116.

Though not a member of the Indian civil service, Babu Rajendralal Mitra was a distinguished Indian scholar; during the 1870s he had, with the support of the Indian government, undertaken the first detailed archaeological survey of Orissa. Such pretension threatened those like James Fergusson, who in such works as the *History of Indian and Eastern Architecture* (1876) had long claimed the right authoritatively to define the nature of India's past. Hence Fergusson set out to put the upstart Mitra in his proper place. He did so not simply by a scholarly critique of Mitra's evidence and interpretations, but by disparaging his ability, as an Indian, to undertake such a study at all. The British, he argued, by their policies had weakened the influences of caste and religion, which had given stability to Indian society. In its place 'we have tried to substitute an education, which they [the Indian people] cannot assimilate, and which in consequence remains, in almost all instances, a useless and empty platitude'. For Fergusson, Mitra was a 'typical specimen' of that educated class whom the Ilbert Bill sought to empower as 'governors' of the country. The 'real interest' of his scholarly work, therefore, Fergusson continued, 'in these days of discussions of Ilbert Bills', lay in the evidence it supplied 'as to whether the natives of India are to be treated as equals to Europeans in all respects'. The answer was decisively negative. 'If, after reading the following pages', Fergusson wrote, with a bold leap, in the introduction to his critique of Mitra's scholarship, 'any European feels that he would like to be subjected to his [Mitra's] jurisdiction, in criminal cases, he must have a courage possessed by few.'[44]

The insistent assertion of British privilege at the time of the Ilbert controversy, then, caught up not only such obvious arenas of contention as the preferential treatment of Europeans in the courts, but the control of India's past and the distinctions of gender which portrayed Indian men as sensual and unmanly. The claims alike of Annette Beveridge and James Fergusson announced that neither scholarship nor the 'pride of womanhood' were exempt from the demands of empire. Above all, this controversy revealed how the hierarchies of race and gender conspired together to sustain the dominant ideology of 'difference'. For women like Annette Beveridge, despite a commitment to English feminism, the Raj involved not the rule of men over women, or even of 'masculine' men over 'effeminate' men, but rather

---

[44] James Fergusson, *Archeology in India, with Especial Reference to the Works of Babu Rajendralal Mitra* (London, 1884), pp. vi-vii, 4.

an avowal of inherent superiority on the part of English men and women together. By the last years of the nineteenth century, however, such claims required a vigorous denial to keep the opposing claims of equality at bay.

EPILOGUE: RAJ, EMPIRE, NATION

THE RAJ AND THE EMPIRE

The British Raj in India did not of course exist by itself, or solely in its relationship to Great Britain as the metropolitan power. It participated as well in a larger network of relationships that defined the entire British Empire. Ideas and people flowed outward from India, above all to East and South Africa and to Southeast Asia, while the administrators of the Raj had in turn to take into account events that occurred in Africa, and even in Canada and Australia. Participation in this larger arena opened up fresh territories in which the ideologies of the Raj were to find expression. Such notions as 'indirect rule' through compliant princes, and the demarcation of communities on the basis of ethnicity and religion, shaped the working of the British Empire from South Africa to Malaya. In addition, the ties to the larger empire both reinforced India's 'distinctiveness' as a land set apart, above all from white settler dominated colonies, and yet made possible an assertion of India's membership in a community which secured all of its members equal rights of movement and citizenship. The existence of the British Empire thus forced the British to confront once again the tensions between the two enduring ideals that shaped their rule of India. Was the ideology that sustained the Raj meant to link India as an equal with Britain's other colonial territories, including those of British settlement, or to reaffirm its 'difference'?

This controversy found expression most prominently in the movement of Indian traders and indentured labourers to an array of British colonial territories around the globe. Throughout the nineteenth century, as the extension of empire provided security and opened trade routes, especially between India and Africa, Indian traders and businessmen followed behind the British flag. In addition, the British saw in India a source of labour, initially to replace that of slaves on the plantations of such colonies as Mauritius, and then, more generally, to develop the resources of the tropical empire. These 'warmer' British possessions, as Lord Salisbury put it in 1875, only 'want population by an intelligent and industrious race to whom the climate of those countries is well suited, and to whom the culture of the staples suited to the soil, and the modes of labour and settlement, are adapted'. The result was the adoption from the 1840s onward of a system of indentured labour recruitment in India that ultimately brought Indians to colonies as widely spread as Trinidad, Natal, and Fiji. Although the various colonial governments through agents in India carried out the recruitment of potential labourers, the Government of India appointed Protectors of Emigrants at the ports to supervise their activities, while protectors in the colonies were charged with overseeing the conditions of labour for indentured workers on the plantations.

Although the Indian labourers were often harshly treated – indeed, one author has described the indenture system as 'A New System of Slavery' – the Indian government still believed that through the appointment of the protectors it had discharged its responsibilities to its subjects in a way consistent with the paternal vision of empire. The British conceived further that emigration offered an opportunity for India's 'surplus' population to obtain more 'lucrative employment', and hence a better life, than they could at home. Although free passages back to India were made available to indentured labourers, few took advantage of them, as they preferred instead to remain in their new homes after the expiry of their period of indenture. For many years few objections were voiced, either in India or the colonies, to the working of the indenture system. With the award of self-government to colonies such as Natal, where an Indian and a white settler population uneasily coexisted, the British were, however, brought face to face with the question of India's, and the Indians', proper position within the larger empire.[1]

As we have seen in chapter 2, mid-Victorian liberal imperialism set off the white settler colonies, on the path to becoming self-governing dominions, from an autocratically ruled India and the tropical dependencies. One of the smaller settler colonies, Natal received responsible government only in 1893, with a franchise restricted to whites. Its white and Indian populations nearly equal, at 50,000 each, set amidst some half-million Africans, Natal immediately set out to check the growth in the number of its Indian residents, seen as rivals in trade,

[1] See Hugh Tinker, *A New System of Slavery: The Export of Indian Labour Overseas, 1830–1920* (London, 1974).

and to confine the Indian to what they considered his proper role, that of plantation labourer. To secure this objective, stringent literacy requirements for admission to the colony were imposed, trading licences were restricted, and an annual £3 tax was placed upon free Indian residents.

Confronted with this series of restrictive measures, the British, at once in India and in London, insisted that Indians in Natal, like British subjects anywhere within the empire, were entitled, as the Indian Secretary Lord George Hamilton put it, to 'fair and equitable treatment, involving complete equality before the law'. Such notions accorded with those ideals of the rule of law upon which the Indian Empire was itself grounded, and expressed the larger concept of an imperial system bound together by common principles. Even race could be used to support a system of equal rights for Indians. As the retired Indian civil servant Lepel Griffin observed, the Indian 'is, like the Englishman, of an ancient Aryan stock, a fellow subject of the Queen, and an industrious and law abiding citizen'. Indeed, he urged, the white and brown inhabitants of Natal ought to make common cause against the 'rapidly increasing and dangerous Kaffir population'. Indians should not in any case, so Curzon's government insisted, be included in the same category with the black African, for the African stood 'far below them' in the 'grades of humanity'. The ideology of Indian 'difference' was never the same as that which defined the distinctions between European and African.

A deep ambivalence nevertheless remained. Some repudiated the whole attempt to enforce an equality between the Indian and European. In a manner reminiscent of Stephen's attack on the Ilbert Bill, J. Westland, the finance member of the Indian government in 1897, insisted that he could not 'see any reasonable foundation for the doctrine that when we conquer a race or a nation by the force of our arms, the people of that nation acquire rights as against members of the conquering race who happen to have cast their lot in tropical or subtropical colonies'. More pragmatically, Indian officials such as Sir John Woodburn acknowledged their sympathy with the British working-class emigrant, who sought, as he said, to 'exclude Indians and Chinese, accustomed to a lower standard of living', from those few places, Natal among them in their view, where he could 'work with his hands'. 'We must', Woodburn said, 'recognise this and allow for it. It is selfish; it isn't magnificent and it isn't magnanimous but it is human nature.' We say India for the Indians, he went on; 'It is just and right and our bounden duty. It is their country. But just in the same way there are certain tracts, for which the Britisher can as fairly claim the colonies for the colonist.'[2]

Much of the enthusiasm for the Indian cause in South Africa reflected calculations of political advantage within India. As Curzon delicately phrased it, the educated classes in India, who most resented the treatment of Indians in Africa, attached great value to 'those principles of freedom and equality which they have learnt to regard as the right of a British subject; and though not without its inconveniences, which are indeed daily becoming more obvious, it constitutes almost the only basis upon which an active loyalty to the rule of an alien conqueror is likely to be developed'. Support of Indian rights overseas, in this view, marked out less an enduring commitment to equality than a device to contain, and safely channel onto less contentious ground, the challenge these ideals posed to British supremacy in India.

Curzon, even so, took care to limit his claims on behalf of his Indian fellow subjects. 'We do not for one moment suggest', he told the Indian secretary, 'nor do we regard it as possible, that Indians should enjoy in an African colony an absolute equality of rights with the white colonists, for such equality does not exist even in India. We do not, for instance, claim for them admission to the franchise, or inclusion on the general jury roll, for these institutions are foreign to their ideas.' Similarly, Curzon was not prepared to accept the view that 'all citizens of the Empire, independently of colour or origin, ought to be at liberty to live and labour in all parts of it on the same footing, unhampered by any racial disabilities or social and economic restrictions'. Britain's Indian subjects might be for Curzon 'our people', whose rights he stood ready to defend, but such rights remained always hedged round by an insistence on difference.[3]

Only in England itself, where several Indians won election to parliament during the 1890s, were Indians able to make good a claim to full political rights, and to secure unfettered rights of immigration. Yet even there, as Sir Arthur Lawley, the Transvaal lieutenant governor, presciently pointed out, ideals of equality flourished only because

---

[2] Notes of 15 March 1897 and 26 October 1897 in NAI Emigration Proceedings, November 1897, no. 17–20; also Emigration Proceedings, July 1898, no. 1–4.
[3] For Curzon's views, see NAI Emigration Proceedings, May 1903, no. 36–39.

Indian migration posed no threat to the livelihood of the English people. 'As India is protected by her climate against Europeans', he wrote, 'so England is protected by the same agency against the invasion of the Asiatic, to which this country [South Africa] is subject. But if it were not so, would the faith of those pledges [of equal treatment] be held to entitle the Indian shop-keeper to eliminate from English society the small shop-keeper and farmer?' Fifty years later British race riots and immigration restrictions made evident the accuracy of this observation.

The Indian government, responding in large part to the protests of educated Indian opinion, ended indentured migration to Natal in 1911. By that time, however, the vision of an empire in which all of its members shared equally in its rights and privileges was no more. In the previous year South Africa's Indian residents were abandoned to their fate, when the country was handed over to the defeated Boers, who were left free to implement whatever restrictive legislation they chose. An act presented to the British public as the triumph of a generous liberal imperialism, the creation of the self-governing Union of South Africa in fact concealed an acknowledgement that Indians and Africans alike had no claim within the empire upon a 'complete equality before the law'. Where Indians were after 1910 not denied residence altogether, as for the most part in Australia and Canada, their racial 'difference' consigned them only to the status of subject peoples. Imperial federation as an ideal could not contend successfully with a colonial nationalism determined to secure the right of the fledgling dominions to control their own immigration as well as fiscal and, after 1920, defence policies.

Other institutions linking India with the larger empire also forced the British to confront the contradictions in their imperial ideology. One small but telling instance was that of Baden-Powell's Boy Scouts. Shaped by the experience of the Boer War, the scout movement, founded in 1908, was meant to nourish discipline and self-reliance among boys in a Britain which was seen as increasingly weak and vulnerable. Suffused with patriotic and imperial sentiment, especially in the years before the First World War, the movement sought to insure that its young members would 'be prepared', above all, to serve their country, and its empire, in its time of need. Yet at the same time, the scout movement set forth an ideal of comradeship founded upon universal values of brotherhood and mutual understanding. As scouting spread to India, this tension between the notion of an 'imperial race', with its implied contempt for 'natives', and the liberal ideals of multi-racial harmony, placed the government, and Baden-Powell himself, in an awkward dilemma. Unable to decide what to do, the Indian government at first discouraged scouting on the ground that it would expose Indian boys to potentially seditious 'evil influences', only to change in 1921 to a policy of patronizing the movement as a way of checking the growth of rival organizations under the control of Indian nationalists.

The issue throughout was that of 'Character'. For Baden-Powell, Indian boys were 'singularly without character by nature'. Nor was there in their training, he insisted, in keeping with the enduring British deprecation of Indian masculinity, 'as yet any discipline or any attempt to inculcate in [them] a sense of honour, of fair play, of honesty, truth, and self-discipline and other attributes which go to make a reliable man of character'. They were 'merely crammed up with knowledge and visionary ideas till their heads become too big for their hats'. How far such people – 'not possessed of the same ideas and minds as white men' – could be transformed by scouting remained for Baden-Powell, as for the British more generally, an uncertain prospect. Though scouting flourished in India during the 1920s and 1930s, Baden-Powell insisted to the end that Indians possessed no notion of 'honour', the 'keystone to character', for in his view no equivalent word expressive of this concept existed in the Hindustani language. Hence Indians could not fully appreciate the ideals of the Boy Scout movement. In 1938 a discouraged Indian scout movement severed its ties with imperial headquarters.[4]

As the British in the early twentieth century struggled to construct a vision of an empire united by a shared attachment among its diverse peoples, they did so in part by devising new symbolic centres. One was the celebration of Empire Day. Invented by the imperial enthusiast Lord Meath in 1904, Empire Day was meant to evoke a spirit of patriotism and devotion, and so to create an imperial race 'worthy of responsibility, alive to duty, filled with sympathy towards mankind and not afraid of self-sacrifice in the promotion of lofty ideals'. The

---

[4] Michael Rosenthal, *The Character Factory* (New York, 1984), chapter 9; and Allen Warren, 'Citizens of the Empire: Baden-Powell, Scouts and Guides, and an Imperial Ideal', in John MacKenzie (ed.), *Imperialism and Popular Culture* (Manchester, 1986), pp. 232–56.

holiday was celebrated on Queen Victoria's birthday, 24 May, with the ritual observance primarily focussed on lectures and parades for schoolchildren. Canada and Australia almost at once adopted this holiday, as a way of showing their enthusiastic participation in the larger imperial system. The British themselves, oddly, in part because of Liberal and socialist opposition, and in part too perhaps because many took the empire for granted, did not officially recognize the holiday until 1916, when the war provoked a fresh appreciation of the value of the empire.

In India the celebration of Empire Day had to contend with the contradictions that bedevilled the underlying ideology of empire, for it was difficult for the British to conceive of Indians as patriotic members of an 'imperial race'. Hence the Indian government sought to sidestep the issue by cultivating instead a feeling of 'personal loyalty' to the sovereign. As the director of public instruction in Bengal wrote, 'I think that the keynote of all the Empire Day addresses should be the personality of the King-Emperor as the centre of the British Empire and not an insistence on the benefits of British rule in India or the vast resources of the British Empire.' The British had imagined, going back to the award of the title of Empress of India to Queen Victoria, that Indians as 'Orientals' were especially susceptible to 'sentiment' and with it to personal distinctions of rank and honour. Hence a focus on the monarch was 'the only way', as one secretariat official argued, in which an Empire Day could be made 'to appeal to the sentiments of the Indian race'. Practical political concerns intruded as well, for the government wished to avoid 'misrepresentation and attacks' by a resurgent Indian nationalism not easily able to accommodate itself to the sentiments underlying Empire Day.[5]

As a result, Indian celebrations carefully avoided the date of 24 May, which in any case fell in the height of the hot weather during school vacations, and with it the term 'Empire Day'. Instead the government strove whenever possible to turn to advantage the undoubted prestige of the king-emperor. The most prominent such occasion was the Delhi durbar of 1911, when King George V came to India to celebrate his own coronation, and at the same time, conceding the new found power of Indian public opinion, to announce the reversal of Curzon's

---

[5] For the discussion, see NAI Home Public, August 1907, no. 45; for the larger issues, see J.A. Mangan, 'The Grit of our Forefathers: Invented Traditions, Propaganda and Imperialism', in MacKenzie, *Imperialism and Popular Culture*, pp. 113–39.

bitterly opposed partition of Bengal. Pictures of the monarch, with the durbar proclamation printed on the back, were distributed to every village in the UP, and the headmen were instructed to read out the text to the assembled villagers. In subsequent years, although the king-emperor's birthday was observed as a formal public holiday throughout India, for the average schoolchild, as Prakash Tandon remembers it, that day, and similar events such as the visits of high British dignitaries, meant little more than an occasion for the distribution of sweets.[6] Increasingly, as time went on, Indians insisted upon defining for themselves their links to an empire that made little provision for their inclusion as equal members with full rights of citizenship.

CONFRONTING NATIONALISM

With the coming of the twentieth century, the British in India had to confront an increasingly powerful and well-organized nationalist movement. Even before the rise of Gandhi, Indian nationalists, in the streets as well as the legislative arena, had forcefully challenged British predominance – from Tilak's 'swaraj' campaign, to the struggle against the 1905 Bengal partition, to Annie Besant's Home Rule movement. Nevertheless, only in 1917, with the Montagu Declaration, and the Montagu–Chelmsford Reforms two years later, were the set of assumptions that underlay the Raj called into question. Even then constitutional change came linked with the explosive upheaval of the 1919 Amritsar massacre and lingering doubts, especially among British conservatives, that persisted through the 1920s and 1930s. The Indian independence portended in August 1917 eventually took place only thirty years later, in August 1947.

As we have seen in the previous chapter, the Ilbert controversy forced the British for the first time seriously to consider how they should accommodate the demands of India's educated for a share of political power. Previously such questions, outside the realm of practical politics, could be ignored in discussions of the nature of the Raj. During 1883, by contrast, as they debated the Ilbert Bill, the British found themselves unable any longer to evade the issue of India's political advance. The strategies hammered out on that occasion, whether by supporters or opponents of the bill, defined the nature of

[6] Prakash Tandon, *Punjabi Century* (California, 1968), pp. 119–20.

the British response to Indian nationalism in the years that followed. Each crisis in turn was met by a reiteration of the opposed ideologies that had emerged from the debates of 1883. Furthermore, despite the triumph of the bill's opponents in gutting the reform, the Ilbert debates did not put an end to anxiety and ambivalence. Indeed, as the political conflict intensified, so too did the contradictions underlying Britain's vision of the Raj become harder to contain. Insistence upon India's 'difference' uneasily coexisted with measures whose only justification was to be found in the presumption of 'similarity'.

The tension was most evident in the so-called Morley–Minto reforms of 1909. These reforms, in large part a response to the intense agitation triggered by the Bengal partition, vastly extended the range of Indian participation in the governance of their country. The various legislative councils were dramatically increased in size, with non-official members predominating in the provincial councils and only a small official majority retained at the centre. Election, although often by special constituencies, was made the usual method of selecting members, and the powers of the councils were enhanced by award of the right of interpellation of ministers and approval of the budget. All of these changes, in line with British procedure and parallel with those adopted in the white settler colonies just before the award to them of responsible government under the Durham reforms, anticipated a transition in time to full parliamentary self-government for India as well. As Edwin Montagu, the Indian secretary a decade later put it, these reforms constituted 'a decided step forward on a road leading at no distant period' to a consideration of responsible government for India. Such an expectation was further enhanced by the fact that one of the authors of the reforms, John Morley, the Indian secretary in London, was a Liberal schooled under Gladstone.

Yet at the same time, Morley, now aged and cautious, and with him the viceroy, Lord Minto, insisted that these reforms involved no change in the fundamental assumptions on which the Raj had been established during the preceding half-century. Minto had come to India in 1906 convinced of the 'hard fact' that Western forms of government were 'unsuited' to India, and that 'we must be physically strong or go to the wall'. He developed the same ideas more fully in sending the reform scheme home to London for approval. Representative government, he argued, 'could never be akin to the instincts of the many races composing the population of the Indian Empire'. 'A

Western importation unnatural to Eastern tastes', it was wholly opposed to Asian styles of government, which 'from time immemorial' had 'rested in the hands of absolute rulers'. Hence the sovereignty of India had to remain in British hands. In Minto's view, what India required was a 'constitutional autocracy which binds itself to govern by rule', and which invites to its councils 'representatives of all the interests which are capable of being represented'. None of this was, of course, at all original. Rather, it expressed enduring British views of Indian 'difference', and of the nature of the Raj itself. Consultative constituencies ranged around an autocratic centre was a logical extension of ideas that had long informed British policy.[7]

The Morley–Minto reforms did, however, embed deeply in Indian life the idea that its society consisted of groups set apart from each other. Most portentous was Minto's conception of India's Muslims as a distinct community who deserved representation on their own. By Minto's time, community based electorates had become ever more visibly a device to secure a base of support for the Raj in the face of an increasing nationalist challenge. Minto's 1906 creation of special Muslim constituencies was hailed as 'nothing less than the pulling back of sixty-two millions of people from joining the ranks of the seditious opposition'. Yet such electorates could still be justified as a necessary accommodation to India's inherent diversity. As Minto put it, 'any electoral representation in India would be doomed to mischievous failure which aimed at granting a personal enfranchisement, regardless of the beliefs and traditions of the communities composing the population of this continent. The great mass of the people of India have no knowledge of representative institutions.'[8]

The creation of special Muslim electorates implied no enthusiasm for Islam as a religion, nor for a populist Muslim politics. Indeed the British endeavoured to keep religion out of politics by defining as an unfair electoral practice appeals to voters based on threats of 'divine displeasure' or 'spiritual censure'. As David Gilmartin has written, within the structure of the colonial political system, religion was defined as a form of 'ethnic identity', fixed, identifiable, and unconnected with the assertion of any principles of belief or political action. Such restrictions were of course in practice impossible to enforce. By

---

[7] Mary, Countess of Minto, *India Minto and Morley, 1905–1910* (London, 1934), pp. 29–30, 110–11.
[8] Ibid., pp. 45–48.

marking off a Muslim community and instituting elections within it, the British inevitably created arenas for ritual competition in which over time personal commitment to Islam melded with public assertions of religious solidarity to create a newly politicized vision of community. The result was the flowering of a new communal rhetoric, and, ultimately, of the Pakistan movement.[9]

Reconsideration of the fundamental nature and objectives of the Raj emerged ultimately from the dislocation, and discontent, of the First World War. By late 1916 a newly revitalized nationalist movement had brought together the Muslim League and the Congress in support of a joint demand for Home Rule for India. In response, the new liberal Indian secretary, Edwin Montagu, on 20 August 1917 issued the famous declaration that the British government's objective was to bring about the 'increasing association of Indians in every branch of the administration, and the gradual development of self-governing institutions, with a view to the progressive realization of responsible government in India as an integral part of the Empire'. This 'momentous utterance', as Montagu subsequently described it, marked out, in his view, 'the end of one epoch and the beginning of a new one'. To be sure, the Conservatives in the British wartime coalition government sought to contain the declaration within the framework of the old policy. Balfour spoke of parliamentary government as a peculiarly British system, which could not be adapted to Indian conditions, while Curzon insisted that never 'in the wildest of dreams' could India become a self-governing dominion like Canada or Australia. He envisaged instead a 'closer and more responsible co-operation' between Indian and Briton, with self-government put off to a distant future in which India's political unity might have disintegrated into new and different shapes.[10]

The contradictions within the old ideology had, however, been stretched beyond the breaking point. In their report of March 1918 Montagu, joining with the Indian viceroy, Lord Chelmsford, openly expressed, for the first time at the highest levels of government, the notion that India could be reshaped in the image of England, that responsible government, as 'the best form of government that they

[9] David Gilmartin, 'Divine Displeasure and Muslim Elections: The Shaping of Community in Twentieth-Century Punjab', in D.A. Low (ed.), *The Political Inheritance of Pakistan* (New York, 1991), especially pp. 107–11.
[10] Carl Bridge, *Holding India to the Empire* (New York, 1986), chapter 1.

[the English] know', should be extended to India. Developing and extending the implications of the Ilbert Bill, Montagu and Chelmsford systematically set out to demolish the barriers that the theory of 'difference' had for so long placed in the way of India's political advance. Despite its divisions of caste and sect, they insisted, India's sense of unity was growing; its 'inarticulate' peasant voters could over time learn to shoulder their political responsibilities; and, more generally, the 'helplessness' of India's peoples could be transformed into self-reliance by the exercise of responsibility, which would 'call forth the capacity for it'. Above all, they argued insistently, India's educated were not an irritant whom a strong government must push aside, but 'intellectually our children', who have 'imbibed ideas which we ourselves have set before them'. As the 'inevitable result of education in the history and thought of Europe' was the 'desire for self-determination', the present Indian unrest was therefore 'no reproach but rather a tribute to our work'. The task of the British government was to provide 'opportunities for the satisfaction of the desires which it creates'. With the Montagu–Chelmsford Report, liberal idealism – the 'faith that is in us' – had gained a place at the heart of Britain's Indian Empire.[11]

This new ideal was not of course meant to be implemented overnight, nor could the sheer force of rhetoric by itself overwhelm the doubts of those who clung to a belief in India's enduring 'difference'. Montagu and Chelmsford had themselves acknowledged the strength of religious contention, especially that between Hindu and Muslim, and argued that the government had to reserve to itself power to deal with it. In subsequent years an insistence that the British could alone protect the rights of 'minorities', and hence had to remain the rulers of India, was to anchor the faith of those who were reluctant to move down the path Montagu and Chelmsford had outlined. Distrust of the educated too, and a disdain for India's politicians, could not easily be laid to rest, especially as Indian nationalism under Gandhi's leadership grew at once more threatening and more difficult to contain. Indeed, the prospect of sharing power with Indian politicians only exacerbated the growing anxiety and fearfulness among the British in India. Montagu's 'faith' commanded a whole-hearted enthusiasm among few of

---

[11] Government of India, *Report on Indian Constitutional Reforms* (Calcutta, 1918), especially pp. 1, 84–95, 117–18.

those who had committed their lives, and careers, to the running of India's government.

The views of Malcolm Hailey, member of the viceroy's council and governor of both Punjab and the United Provinces during the 1920s, are in this respect perhaps typical. Nurtured in the paternalism of the Punjab school, accustomed to giving orders and to being obeyed, Hailey brought to his long years in the Indian central government that combination, as one visitor to the Punjab wrote, of 'deep sympathy and equable justice wherein lay the strength of the great Anglo-Indian administrators in the past'. By 1915, in Delhi, he had come to realize that it was 'no longer possible to represent the "intelligenzia" as a class which represents nobody but itself and voices no views but its own'. The political ferment now involved larger numbers and was part of 'a growing belief in the possibility of a social, moral and political "resorgimento" of the East'. Hence Britain ought to take 'every reasonable opportunity to meet this growing feeling of responsibility and independence'. Yet even then his conversion was only partial. Although, as John Cell has cogently observed, 'his mind might belong to the Liberals', his 'heart' remained in Shahpur, the rural Punjab district where he had begun his Indian career. This ambivalence bedevilled Hailey throughout his life. Even as late as his governorship of the UP in the mid-1930s, Hailey's intellectual recognition that Indian nationalism must succeed was yoked to an abiding antagonism toward the Congress, a willingness to play Muslim off against Hindu, and a reluctance to contemplate bringing the Raj to an end. This 'fundamental ambiguity', as Cell argues, was not Hailey's alone, but personified 'the contradictory nature of the empire he served'.[12]

History could be enlisted to contest change, as well as, in Montagu's vision, to support it. The standard histories of India had long laid out a pattern of recurrent anarchy whenever the strong hand of central authority was withdrawn. At once a renowned historian and a retired member of the Indian civil service, Vincent Smith endeavoured, in a 100 page tract on 'Constitutional Reform', written in December 1918, to bring 'the light of history', as he saw it, to bear on the recommendations of the Montagu–Chelmsford Report. He insisted that 'diversity' remained, in the present as in the past, fundamental in shaping the character of India's society. The 'old sores' of ancient feuds, he wrote,

---

[12] John W. Cell, *Hailey: A Study in British Imperialism, 1872–1969* (Cambridge, 1992), especially pp. 30–31, 54–55, 213.

still 'fester', and would not go away by parading a superficial appearance of unity. The institution of caste, above all, to which he attributed 3,000 years of history, 'suits Hindus and has become part of their nature'. Hence 'in all probability it will still endure for untold centuries'. A land so divided, and whose people craved personal rule, had to remain under British protection. It could not be made over in the image of England, nor could the 'purely foreign invention' of responsible government ever take root there. To think otherwise was to give way to 'vain visions'.

In 1919 the Amritsar massacre brought to a tragic climax the opposition to what Sir Michael O'Dwyer, the Punjab governor, called the subordination of 'honest administration' to 'dishonest politics'. It was not wholly by accident that this tragedy, in which some 400 unarmed demonstrators were shot dead in an enclosed garden, took place in the Punjab. The Punjab School ideology, as we have seen, had always emphasized firm, paternal rule by an elite of self-confident administrators, who conceived their duty as that of bringing order and prosperity to a contented peasant society. Unlike their colleagues elsewhere in India, they had had to confront few challenges to their authority before 1919. Hence they were perhaps more likely to break under stress, as had already been the case with the Kuka uprising of 1872, and to resort to a forceful assertion of their authority. Still, the cast of mind which led to the massacre in the Jallianwalla Bagh was by no means exceptional to the Punjab. The firing met with widespread support throughout the services, and, more generally, in England, where General Reginald Dyer, who ordered the shooting, was acclaimed by the House of Lords and made the beneficiary of a fund drive which raised some £26,000.

At no time was Dyer at all apologetic for his actions. He insisted always that he had simply done his duty in endeavouring to put down what O'Dwyer called the 'Punjab Rebellion of 1919'. As O'Dwyer later wrote, defending Dyer, 'he had the rebel army before him, he was practically isolated in the middle of a great city seething with rebellion, and hesitation would have been fatal'. Dyer himself insisted that the firing was not 'a question of merely dispersing the crowd, but one of producing a sufficient moral effect, from a military point of view, not only on those who were present but more specially throughout the Punjab. There could be no question of undue severity.' The firing in Jallianwalla Bagh cannot thus be viewed as an unfortunate mistake, marked with regrets on the part of its participants, but rather as expressing enduring assumptions about the nature of the Raj, and of Indian society. India, Dyer was saying, was different from England, and the British had responsibilities there that could not be shirked.[13]

Most telling perhaps was Dyer's use of the language of the schoolmaster in describing the events of Jallianwalla Bagh. Indians, in his view, were children who when 'naughty' needed to be punished. His actions, presented as those of the stern but watchful father, as he told the inquiry committee, though horrible, were 'merciful'. As with a good paddling at school, the Indians 'ought to be thankful to me for doing it'. I thought, he continued, 'it would be doing a jolly lot of good and they would realize that they were not to be wicked'. As children, Indians were for Dyer simply not capable of governing themselves. Hence any defiance of British authority was by definition rebellion against a properly constituted moral order. Like Governor Eyre in Jamaica in 1865, Dyer conceived of himself as standing between order and chaos.

The use of unrestrained force was, however, hardly compatible with the proud commitment of the British in India to the rule of law. Hence immediately after the shooting in Jallianwalla Bagh the government proclaimed martial law throughout the central Punjab. This placed civil government in the hands of military officers and permitted the meting out of summary punishments on the spot without recourse to the courts. Martial law, with its exercise of exemplary powers, had long been regarded as a legitimate device to contain threatening disorder, and a way as well to throw a cloak of legality over the actions of men such as Dyer. Yet it also widened the distance between India and England. In England, although the military were from time to time called out in support of the civil authorities, disturbances were met by the reading of the 'riot act'. Since the early nineteenth century, however, despite its roots in English common law, martial law had been employed only in the colonial empire and Ireland. Its use thus signified not just the existence of riotous behaviour, but a fearfulness, and a presumption, clearly visible in O'Dwyer's account of the 'Punjab Rebellion', of a people conspiring to overthrow constituted authority. In the colonial world the 'rule of law' had to bend to secure

13 Michael O'Dwyer, *India as I Knew It, 1885–1925* (London, 1925), chapter 17, especially p. 285; Derek Sayer, 'British Reaction to the Amritsar Massacre, 1919–1920', *Past & Present*, no. 131 (May 1991), pp. 130–64.

its own supremacy. The violence of martial law, in this view, could alone restore a challenged imperial governance.

Many of Dyer's critics, including among them senior officials of the Indian government, who secured his censure, described his actions as simply the excessive zeal of a misguided individual, and so sought, by making him a convenient scapegoat, to distance themselves from any responsibility. Montagu, however, disdained the Jallianwalla Bagh firing because he saw embodied in it a larger concept of empire that marked India out as a place apart, where such practices as 'terrorism' and 'racial humiliation' were to be allowed to flourish. The inhabitants of India, Montagu insisted, had a right to demand of those set in authority over them that they adhere to the 'standards of propriety and humanity' of 'the civilised world in general'. No more so in India than elsewhere, in this view, could massacre be justified on the ground that it had a valuable 'moral effect'. In place of coercion, Montagu put forward the idea of dyarchy, in which the British, while retaining ultimate authority, would slowly devolve power to elected Indian ministries, at first in the provinces and over a limited range of 'nation-building' activities such as education and agriculture, and then finally at the centre. Rather than wicked children who required punishment, the Indians in this liberal vision were more like adolescents who needed 'trust' and 'goodwill' as they approached maturity.

The Montagu–Chelmsford reforms passed through parliament with little opposition in December 1919. This legislation, which vastly enhanced the Indian electorate and the powers alike of Indian legislatures and ministers, envisaged an India consisting of a set of provinces, self-governing in local matters, under a central government 'increasingly representative of and responsible to the people of all of them'. There was to be no turning back. India's evolution to the status of a fully self-governing dominion within the Commonwealth, implicit in the 1919 legislation, was explicitly avowed as the goal of British policy by Lord Irwin in 1929. The transfer of power on 15 August 1947 was thus the only outcome that could be anticipated from the ideals that sustained the Montagu–Chelmsford scheme. There was, however, to be a great deal of foot-dragging, above all by those for whom the ideology of 'difference', and the consequent need for the continuance of the Raj, remained appealing.

This 'diehard' resistance, in which many senior, largely Conservative, British political figures participated, took various forms. All were directed to the objective, as Carl Bridge put it, of 'holding India to the Empire'. The resulting political manoeuvres have been described in detail in the writings of numerous scholars, among them R. J. Moore, John Darwin, and Carl Bridge. At the heart of the enterprise was what Bridge calls a 'grand design' for holding on to 'the commanding heights of the Raj while gaining important kudos for giving away inessentials'. This meant that Congress politicians should be diverted away from the centre to the provinces, and constitutional change should always aim, as the Conservative Indian secretary Samuel Hoare put it, at giving 'a semblance of responsible government' while keeping 'for ourselves the threads that really direct the system of government'. These various delaying strategies informed the 1935 Government of India Act. This legislation at once laid out a blueprint for India's subsequent independence, and yet signalled Britain's determination to thwart Congress control of the centre by proposing a federation dominated by princes, Muslims and minorities. An Indian dominion so constituted, the act's authors were convinced, would assure continued subordination of the country's foreign and defence policies to those of an imperial Britain.[14]

The most outspoken 'diehard' was Winston Churchill. In a manner reminiscent of Dyer after Amritsar, or Fitzjames Stephen during the Ilbert controversy, Churchill stripped away the evasive rhetoric to reveal underneath the enduring ideology that had sustained the Raj for so long. There was, he told the House of Commons in the debates on the 1935 Act, 'no real practical unity in India apart from British rule'. Hence 'liberty for India only means liberty for one set of Indians to exploit another'. The British may have been only 'the latest of many conquerors', but they alone had 'made the well-being of the Indian masses their supreme satisfaction'. As they had taken upon themselves this 'mission in the East', the British could not simply 'abdicate' it, and so 'withdraw our guardianship from this teeming myriad population of Indian toilers'. Gandhi, as Churchill put it in a memorable phrase at the time of the 1931 Gandhi–Irwin Pact, was no more than a 'half-naked fakir'; India's politicians, as he said on the eve of independence, were only 'men of straw' who represented no one and would be swept away in the coming storm. Of course, for Churchill the Raj secured as

---

[14] See Bridge, *Holding India*; R.J. Moore, *Endgames of Empire* (Delhi, 1988); and John Darwin, 'Imperialism in Decline? Tendencies in British Imperial Policy Between the Wars', *Historical Journal*, vol. 23 (1980), pp. 657–79.

well Britain's own position as a great power. Without India, 'the most truly bright and precious jewel in the crown of the King', the British Empire, he correctly discerned, would soon cease to exist.[15]

Neither the manoeuvrings of the Conservative party leaders, nor Churchill's empassioned defence of the Raj, could destroy the Congress, which held power in the majority of India's provinces from 1937 to 1939, or even halt the steady, if slow, march toward independence. Nevertheless, only in the 1940s, as Britain fought desperately for its own survival, was the ideal of empire in India, with the ideology that upheld it, decisively repudiated. In early 1942, moved by the liberal vision of an India transformed into an equal member of the British Commonwealth, the Labour leader Clement Attlee called for 'a man to do in India what Durham did in Canada'. Stafford Cripps's subsequent mission to India, though sabotaged by Churchill's unyielding refusal to allow Indian participation in a reconstituted war government, still made it clear that after the war a constituent assembly would be convened, and a constitution drafted to bring into existence a self-governing Indian dominion.

In July 1945, with Britain exhausted from the war, a Labour government under Attlee's leadership took office. Though long sympathetic to Indian nationalism, Labour had never devised a vision of Britain's role in India distinct from that of liberals such as Montagu. Indeed, the Labour Party had among its members many who believed in the value of empire. When briefly in office during the interwar period – in 1924 and again in 1929–31 – Labour had worked closely with its Liberal allies; while in 1940–5, as a participant in the wartime coalition government, the Labour Party had acquiesced in Churchill's suppression of all constitutional change in India. Hence, once in office after 1945, the Attlee government offered no new vision of the Raj, but they moved quickly to implement the ideals that had shaped British policy since the Montagu declaration of 1917. A Britain in debt even to India itself, and dependent on the United States for its postwar prosperity, had few enduring economic or strategic interests to stand in the way of what Churchill, defiant to the end, called the 'scuttle' of 1947. The Muslims were awarded the Pakistan they had demanded, but the princes were abandoned, and the Congress under Nehru left to claim power in a free India.

[15] Rhodes James (ed.), *Winston Churchill, Complete Speeches, 1897–1963*, vol. 5 (New York, 1974), especially pp. 5450–68.

After 1947, although a few Conservatives still spluttered about the loss of India, most Britons endeavoured to put the best possible face on the events of 15 August by taking credit for the award of Indian independence. In the process the liberal vision of India's transformation that had shaped Montagu's 1917 declaration was read back into the earlier history of the Raj, and the ideology that had for so many decades sustained the 'illusion of permanence', as Francis Hutchins described it, was either willed out of existence or attributed to a few isolated 'diehards'. Once men like Dyer and Churchill had been portrayed as exceptional, the 1947 transfer of power could then become the triumph of a spirit that had continuously informed Britain's purpose in India for over a hundred years. Macaulay and Mountbatten, the last viceroy, were thus linked indissolubly together as the beginning and the end of a chain forged of liberal idealism. During the 1950s, in the hands of liberal scholars, this version of the history of the Raj took on an authoritative shape, and sustained a quiet pride in Britain's achievements in India. Not only, as Percival Spear wrote in the 1958 reprint of the *Oxford History of India*, did India break 'her British fetters with Western hammers', but 'the fetters began to be removed by one side as soon as they began to be rattled by the other'. Macaulay's 'dream' had found fulfilment in the 'radical transformation' British rule had brought to India.[16]

Much in the ideology of 'difference' nevertheless lived on. Within India it left its mark above all in the conception of India as a society informed by a passionate commitment to community, and of the public arena as a site where communities contested for power. To be sure, after independence separate electorates were abolished and caste outlawed; and the 1950 Constitution enshrined the values of secular democracy. Yet underneath the liberal rhetoric of the Nehru era the structures constituted by the Raj, and affirmed during the course of the nationalist struggle, remained compelling. By far the most powerful were those of religious identity – as Hindu, Muslim, and Sikh. As time went on, and the central government itself, together with the leaders of religiously based organizations, began openly to manipulate these communal loyalties for partisan advantage, such ties became ever more deeply embedded in Indian society. Forty years after independence, as Gyan Pandey has written, 'questions of the defence of custom, of established religious institutions (including buildings), of

[16] Percival Spear, *The Oxford History of Modern India* (Oxford, 1965), p. 389.

the rights of (religious) communities have again assumed an over-whelming importance in the politics of India'. The 'colonial construction of the Indian past' lives on today not only in the halls of New Delhi but on the streets and byways of Amritsar, and Ayodhya, and Ahmedabad.[17]

Ideas of India's 'difference' also made their way to Britain. Indeed, by 1960 the British found that they had abandoned their empire overseas only to find it on their doorstep. Immigration from India and Pakistan during the early postwar years created a sizable South Asian community within Great Britain. Towns such as Southall and Bradford had such large populations, with mosques, halal meat shops, and turbaned men and sari-clad women on the streets, that they could almost be conceived of as extensions of Pakistan or India. In accommodating this immigrant community the British brought into play racial sentiments, and ideas of Indian inferiority, shaped during the long years of the Raj. From the late 1950s, despite Indian membership in a now multi-racial Commonwealth, the British government tightly restricted immigration from South Asia, while the country's South Asian residents met with often virulent harassment and hostility. Britain's South Asians, above all its Muslims at the time of the controversy over Salman Rushdie's *Satanic Verses*, were at once stigmatized for refusing to submerge their identity within the secular liberalism of British society, and denied the opportunity to do so. The enduring contradictions between the ideologies of liberalism, and of 'difference', have come back home as Britain copes with the multiculturalism of the 1990s.[18]

---

[17] Gyanendra Pandey, *The Construction of Communalism in Colonial North India* (Delhi, 1990), especially chapters 2 and 7.

[18] Talal Asad, 'Multiculturalism and British Identity in the Wake of the Rushdie Affair', *Politics and Society*, vol. 18 (1990), pp. 455–80.

BIBLIOGRAPHICAL ESSAY

GENERAL STUDIES

A variety of works assess British attitudes toward India, and the ways India was fitted into the larger set of ideas that sustained the Raj. Some of these works are idiosyncratic, even contentious in their approach, but all are lively and suggestive. Francis Hutchins, *The Illusion of Permanence: British Imperialism in India* (Princeton, 1967), though now somewhat dated, remains a stimulating account of how the British sought to assure their superiority over their Indian subjects. More philosophical, with a discussion of German as well as British scholarship, though tendentious in its argument, is Ronald Inden, *Imagining India* (Basil Blackwell, Oxford, 1990). Two stimulating works from a psychological perspective, the latter of which includes Indian as well as British responses to the colonial encounter, are Lewis Wurgaft, *The Imperial Imagination: Magic and Myth in Kipling's India* (Wesleyan University Press, Middletown, CT, 1983), and Ashis Nandy, *The Intimate Enemy: Loss and Recovery of Self Under Colonialism* (Oxford University Press, Delhi, 1983). Kipling's own writings of course, especially the enduringly powerful *Kim* (1901), are central to any understanding of the Raj.

Among a number of works based largely on the critical evaluation of literary texts the most informative are Sara Suleri, *The Rhetoric of English India* (Chicago, 1992) and Benita Parry, *Delusions and Discoveries: Studies on India in the British Imagination 1880–1930* (California, 1972). Though less accessible to the general reader, the writings of the literary critics Gayatri Spivak and Homi Bhabha contain much that is important for understanding the Raj. Specially useful are the essays in Francis Barker et al., eds., *Europe and its Others*, vol. 1 (University of Essex, Colchester, 1985). Of more general interest are the special number on race of *Critical Inquiry*, vol. 12 (autumn 1985), and Patrick Brantlinger, *Rule of Darkness: British Literature and Imperialism, 1830–1914* (Ithaca NY, 1988). Though it does not include India in its account, Edward Said's *Orientalism* (London, 1978) has shaped all subsequent discussion of the ideas that informed European views of the 'Orient'. For assessments of Said's argument as applied to India see Ronald Inden, 'Orientalist Constructions of India', *Modern Asian Studies*, vol. 20 (1986), pp. 401–46; and Carol A. Breckinridge and Peter van der Veer, eds., *Orientalism and the Postcolonial Predicament: Perspectives on South Asia* (Pennsylvania, 1993). The latter brings together a wide-ranging and stimulating set of case studies of law, language, mensuration, and other subjects.

Several works examine the shaping assumptions of the Raj through study of visual materials. Pathbreaking in its scholarship, though best on the early centuries before the British conquest, is Partha Mitter, *Much Maligned Monsters: History of European Reactions to Indian Art* (Clarendon Press, Oxford, 1977). The richly illustrated exhibition catalogue, *The Raj: India and the British 1600–1947*, C.A. Bayly, ed. (National Portrait Gallery, London, 1990) is exceptional for its interweaving of political narrative and visual representation. For a view of the Raj from the perspective of architecture see Thomas R. Metcalf, *An Imperial Vision: Indian Architecture and Britain's Raj* (California, 1989); for a stimulating discussion from the point of view of urban planning see Anthony D. King, *Colonial Urban Development* (London, 1976). An account which minimizes the political significance of colonial architecture in favour of the aesthetic is G.H. R. Tillotson, *The Tradition of Indian Architecture: Continuity, Controversy and Change Since 1850* (New Haven CT, 1989).

THE YEARS OF COMPANY RULE

The late eighteenth century era of conquest and discovery can be explored in the various writings of P.J. Marshall, including two edited volumes of original documents, *The British Discovery of Hinduism in the Eighteenth Century* (Cambridge, 1970), and *The Writings and Speeches of Edmund Burke*, vols. 5 (*India: 1774–1785*) and 6 (*India 1786–1788*) (Oxford, 1981, 1991). For the early British study of Indian languages and culture see Bernard S. Cohn, 'The Command of Language and the Language of Command', in Ranajit Guha, ed., *Subaltern Studies IV* (Delhi, 1985), pp. 276–329; O.P. Kejariwal, *The Asiatic Society of Bengal and the Discovery of India's Past, 1784–1838* (Delhi, 1988); and David Kopf, *British Orientalism and the Indian Renaissance 1773–1835* (California, 1969). For the early debates on property and land Ranajit Guha, *A Rule of Property for Bengal* (Mouton, Paris, 1963) remains authoritative, while Burton Stein, *Thomas Munro: the Origins of the Colonial State and his Vision of Empire* (Oxford University Press, Delhi, 1986) provides a useful study not only of Munro's life but of his challenge to the Whig theorists of the Bengal settlement. General accounts of the growing British conception of themselves as an imperial people during the eighteenth century can be found in Richard Koebner, *Empire* (Cambridge, 1961) and Linda Colley, *Britons: Forging the Nation* (New Haven CT, 1992).

Eric Stokes, *The English Utilitarians and India* (Oxford, 1959), though some of its arguments about the pervasiveness of theory in shaping policy have given way to subsequent research, remains the classic account of the formative role of liberal ideology in nineteenth-century British conceptions of their mission in India. Gauri Viswanathan, *Masks of Conquest: Literary Study and British Rule in India* (New York, 1989) offers a fresh look at the ideas behind British Indian education policy in the 1830s. The work of Lata Mani, especially her 'Contentious Traditions: the Debate on Sati in Colonial India', in Kumkum Sangari and Sudesh Vaid, eds., *Recasting Women: Essays in Colonial History* (New Delhi, 1989), has reshaped our understanding of the debates over sati and British social reform legislation. Two older but still important biographies are Ainslee Embree, *Charles Grant and British Rule in India* (New York, 1962), and John Rosselli, *Lord William Bentinck: the Making of a Liberal Imperialist 1774–1839* (California, 1974). Though badly dated, George D. Bearce, *British Attitudes Toward India 1784–1858* (Oxford, 1961) provides a convenient summary of ideas and opinion during this period. James Mill's classic *History of British India*, first published in 1818, is available in an abridged form from the University of Chicago Press (1975), while John Stuart Mill's writings are collected in Martin Moir, ed., *John Stuart Mill: Writings on India* (Toronto, 1990).

INDIA UNDER THE CROWN

The transformation of liberalism after the 1857 uprising is assessed in Thomas R. Metcalf, *The Aftermath of Revolt: India 1857–1870* (Princeton, 1964). For a suggestive, but long neglected view of the events of 1857, see F. W. Buckler, 'The Political Theory of the Indian Mutiny', in M. N. Pearson, ed., *Legitimacy and Symbols: The South Asian Writings of F. W. Buckler* (Michigan Papers on South and Southeast Asia, no. 26, Ann Arbor, 1985). For the larger mid-century crisis of liberalism Bernard Semmel, *The Governor Eyre Controversy* (London, 1962); and John Roach, 'Liberalism and the Victorian Intelligentsia', *The Cambridge Historical Journal*, vol. 13 (1957), pp. 58–81 remain valuable. For the revival of conservatism, and its connection to empire, see C. C. Eldridge, *England's Mission: The Imperial Idea in the Age of Gladstone and Disraeli* (Chapel Hill NC, 1973); and R. Koebner, 'The Emergence of the Concept of Imperialism', *The Cambridge Journal*, vol. 5 (1952), pp. 726–41. Exceptionally useful in assessing late Victorian conservatism are the essays in Eric Hobsbawm and Terence Ranger, eds., *The Invention of Tradition* (Cambridge, 1983), especially Bernard Cohn, 'Representing Authority in Victorian India' (pp. 165–209), which analyses the symbolic meaning of British durbar ritual by examining the 1877 Imperial Assemblage. The rise of popular enthusiasm for empire is explored in the richly textured essays collected in John M. Mackenzie, ed., *Imperialism and Popular Culture* (Manchester, 1986).

It is essential to consult the seminal works that shaped British understanding of India in the late nineteenth century. Most important are Henry S. Maine, *Village Communities in the East and West* (London, 1871), with his subsequent lecture *The Effects of Observation of India on Modern European Thought* (London, 1875; reprint Folcroft, Pa., 1974); James Fitzjames Stephen, *Liberty, Equality, Fraternity* (London, 1873); Alfred C. Lyall, *Asiatic Studies, Religious and Social* (London, 1884; revised ed. 1904); and his *The Rise and Expansion of British Dominion in India* (London, 1894; reprint New York, 1968). The classic study of India's historic architecture, informed by the assumptions of Victorian scholarship, is James Fergusson, *History of Indian and Eastern Architecture* (London, 1876; revised ed. 1910). British historical writing on India generally is assessed in C. H. Philips, ed., *Historians of India, Pakistan and Ceylon* (Oxford, 1961).

The memoirs of Indian officials provide unique insights into the ideas that sustained the Raj, as well as revealing its internal conflicts. Some of the most important are George Campbell, *Memoirs of my Indian Career* (London, 1893); Richard Temple, *Men and Events of My Time in India* (London, 1882); John Beames, *Memoirs of a Bengal Civilian* (London, 1961); and Michael O'Dwyer, *India As I Knew It, 1885–1925* (London, 1925). For a sympathetic account of the Indian civil service, and the ideals that motivated it, see Philip Woodruff [pseud. for Mason], *The Founders* and *The Guardians* (London, 1953–54).

CASTE, GENDER, AND COMMUNITY

Useful studies of British attitudes toward caste, seen as a central ordering feature of Indian society, include Nicholas Dirks, 'Castes of Mind', *Representations*, no. 37 (Winter 1992), pp. 56–78; Bernard Cohn, 'Notes on the History of the Study of Indian Society and Culture', in M. Singer and B. S. Cohn, eds., *Structure and Change in Indian Society* (Chicago, 1968), pp. 3–25; and Christopher Pinney, 'Classification and Fantasy in the Photographic Construction of Caste and Tribe', *Visual Anthropology*, vol. 3 (1990), pp. 259–88. British Victorian scholarship on the Indian village is assessed in Louis Dumont, 'The "Village Community" From Munro to Maine', *Contributions to Indian Sociology*, vol. 9 (1966), pp. 68–89; and Clive Dewey, 'Images of the Village Community: a Study in Anglo-Indian Ideology', *Modern Asian Studies*, vol. 6 (1972), pp. 291–328. Joan Leopold examines 'British Applications of the Aryan Theory of Race to India, 1850–1870', in the *English Historical Review*, vol. 89 (1974), pp. 578–603. For the official British view at the time the most authoritative account is Herbert Hope Risley, *The People of India* (1915; reprint Delhi, 1969).

Issues of gender, sexuality, and women's role under the Raj are examined in Kenneth Ballhatchet, *Race, Sex, and Class Under the Raj* (London, 1980); Mrinalini Sinha, '"Chathams, Pitts, and Gladstones in Petticoats": the Politics of Gender and Race in the Ilbert Bill Controversy, 1883–84', in M. Strobel and N. Chaudhuri, eds., *Western Women and Imperialism* (Bloomington Ind., 1992), pp. 98–116; and Sinha, 'Gender and Imperialism: Colonial Policy and the Ideology of Moral Imperialism in late 19th Century Bengal', in Michael S. Kimmel, ed., *Changing Men* (Newbury Park Calif., 1987), pp. 217–31. Literary representations of British sexual anxieties are assessed in Nancy Paxton, 'Mobilizing Chivalry: Rape in British Indian Novels about the Indian Uprising of 1857', *Victorian Studies*, vol. 36 (Fall 1992), pp. 5–30; and Jenny Sharpe, *Allegories of Empire: the Figure of Woman in the Colonial Text* (Minneapolis, 1993). Several of Rudyard Kipling's short stories, especially 'Without Benefit of Clergy' and 'Beyond the Pale', offer insights into the interplay of sex and race among the British in India. Although lengthy, Flora Annie Steel, *On the Face of the Waters* (London, 1896; reprint, New Delhi, 1985) provides a perceptive woman's account in fictional terms of the trauma of the 1857 revolt, especially as it affected the position of English women. For the later Raj E. M. Forster, *A Passage to India* (1924) is of course indispensable.

British notions of community, class, and the construction of an Indian 'public' sphere are examined in Sandria Freitag, *Collective Action and Community: Public Arenas and the Emergence of Communalism in North India* (California, 1989); in the special number of *South Asia*, ns vol. 14 (June 1991), on the 'public' in British India; and in Gyanendra Pandey, *The Construction of Communalism in Colonial North India* (Delhi, 1990). For the distinctive character of the Punjab in British ideology see Richard G. Fox, *Lions of the Punjab* (California, 1985); and David Gilmartin, *Empire and Islam: Punjab and the Making of Pakistan* (California, 1988), especially chapter 1. The role of the census in demarcating castes and communities is discussed in the essays by Frank Conlon and Kenneth W. Jones in N. Gerald Barrier, ed., *The Census in British India* (Delhi, 1981); and in Bernard Cohn, 'The Census, Social Structure and Objectification in South Asia', *Folk*, vol. 26 (1984), pp. 25–49. W. W. Hunter, *The Indian Mussalmans* (London, 1871; reprint Lahore, 1964) is central to understanding British attitudes to Muslims. A suggestive account of British conceptions of India's princes is to be found in Nicholas Dirks, *The Hollow Crown: Ethnohistory of an Indian Kingdom* (Cambridge, 1987), a case study of Pudukkottai in Madras.

The role of ideas about disease in shaping the Raj is discussed in the writings of David Arnold, especially his 'Cholera and Colonialism in British India', *Past and Present*, no. 113 (1986), pp. 118–51; and his *Colonizing the Body* (California, 1993). J. B. Harrison, 'Allahabad: a Sanitary History', in K. Ballhatchet and J. Harrison, eds., *The City in South Asia* (London, 1980); Veena Oldenburg, *The Making of Colonial Lucknow* (Princeton, 1984); and Marriam Dossal, *Imperial Designs and Indian Realities: the Planning of Bombay City, 1845–1875* (Delhi, 1991) discuss the connection of sanitation and urban settlement patterns. John W. Cell, 'Anglo-Indian Medical Theory and the Origins of Segregation in West Africa', *American Historical Review*, vol. 91 (1986), pp. 307–35 provides a comparative perspective. For the creation of a distinctive housing form for the British in India see Anthony King, *The Bungalow* (London, 1984). The hill station is the subject of Dane Kennedy's *The Magic Mountain* (California, 1995).

THE RAJ ON THE DEFENSIVE

Numerous works detail the contest between the Raj and Indian nationalism in the first half of the twentieth century. Most useful perhaps in exploring the larger issues at stake from the British side are the writings of John Darwin, John Gallagher, R. J. Moore, especially his *Endgames of Empire* (Delhi, 1988), and Carl Bridge, *Holding India to the Empire* (Delhi, 1986). John W. Cell, *Hailey: a Study in British Imperialism* (Cambridge, 1992) provides a careful biographical study of one of the main participants. Anil Seal, 'Imperialism and Nationalism in India', and the other essays in J. Gallagher, G. Johnson, and A. Seal, eds., *Locality, Province, and Nation: Essays on*

Indian Politics, 1870–1940 (Cambridge, 1973) provide a useful summary of the so-called 'Cambridge School' position. Douglas Haynes, *Rhetoric and Ritual in Colonial India* (California, 1991) suggestively assesses the relationship of the British with the English-educated nationalist elite by an examination of one town, that of Surat. Talal Asad, 'Multiculturalism and British Identity in the Wake of the Rushdie Affair', *Politics and Society*, vol. 18 (1990), pp. 455–80, offers a thoughtful perspective on the clash of imperial and liberal ideologies in contemporary Britain.

INDEX

THE NEW CAMBRIDGE HISTORY OF INDIA

I The Mughals and their contemporaries

II Indian states and the transition to colonialism

III The Indian empire and the beginnings of modern society

IV The evolution of contemporary South Asia

*Already published
†Available in paperback